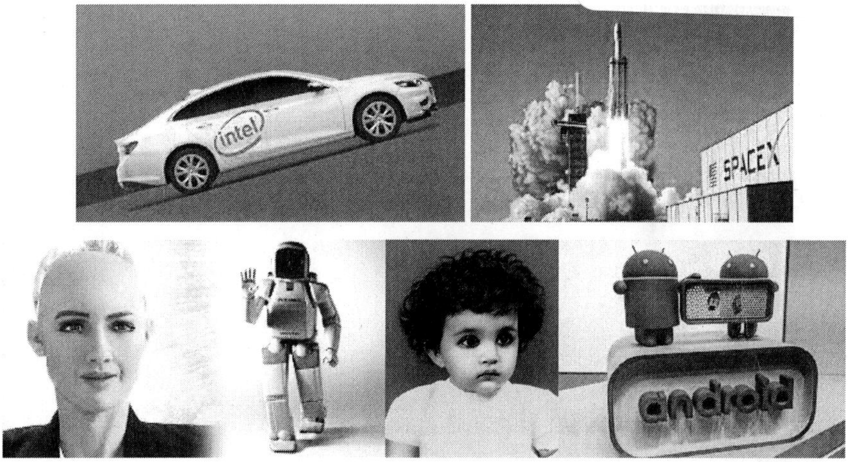

I' m a Google baby

INNOVISION

The Grand Challenges of 21st Century

Shifting from a Knowledge Economy to What we call an "Imagination Economy".

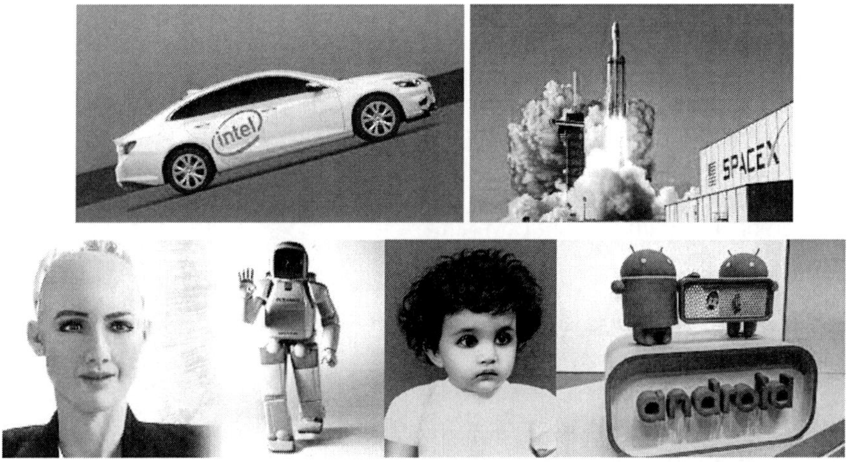

I' m a Google baby

INNOVISION

The Grand Challenges of 21st Century

Shifting from a Knowledge Economy to What we call an "Imagination Economy".

Chelat
Bhuvanachandran

KHANNA BOOK PUBLISHING CO. (P) LTD.
PUBLISHER OF ENGINEERING AND COMPUTER BOOKS
4C/4344, Ansari Road, Darya Ganj, New Delhi-110002
Phone : 011-23244447-48 Mobile: +91-99109 09320
E-mail : contact@khannabooks.com; Website : www.khannabooks.com

Dear Readers,

To prevent the piracy, this book is secured with HIGH SECURITY HOLOGRAM on the front title cover. In case you don't find the hologram on the front cover title, please write us to at contact@khannabooks.com or whatsapp us at +91-99109 09320 and avail special gift voucher for yourself.

Specimen of Hologram on front Cover title:

Moreover, there is a SPECIAL DISCOUNT COUPON for you with EVERY HOLOGRAM.

How to avail this SPECIAL DISCOUNT:

Step 1: Scratch the hologram
Step 2: Under the scratch area, your "coupon code" is available
Step 3: Logon to www.khannabooks.com
Step 4: Use your "coupon code" in the shopping cart and get your copy at a special discount
Step 5: Enjoy your reading!

Price : ₹ 395.00

ISBN: 978-93-5538-114-9

InnoVision

by Chelat Bhuvanachandran

First Edition: 2022

Published by:

Khanna Book Publishing Co. (P) Ltd.
Visit us at: **www.khannabooks.com**
Write us at: **contact@khannabooks.com**
CIN: U22110DL1998PTC095547

To view complete list of books, Please scan the QR Code: KPH

Printed in India.

To my parents

SHRI. M.K.K. MENON & SMT. CHELAT LEELAMMA

Who live in my pleasant memories

To Nirmala Pulapre, my wife

who adjusted so well to my deep obsession with this work.

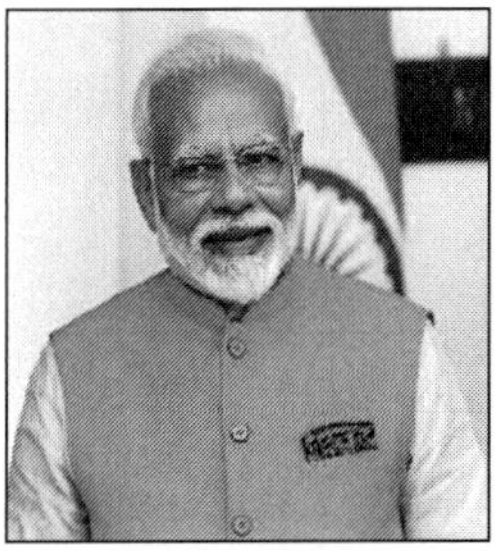

"Start-up Innovations to drive India's GDP in next two decades"

(A Start-up Vision by Shri. Narendra Modi, Hon' Prime Minister**)**

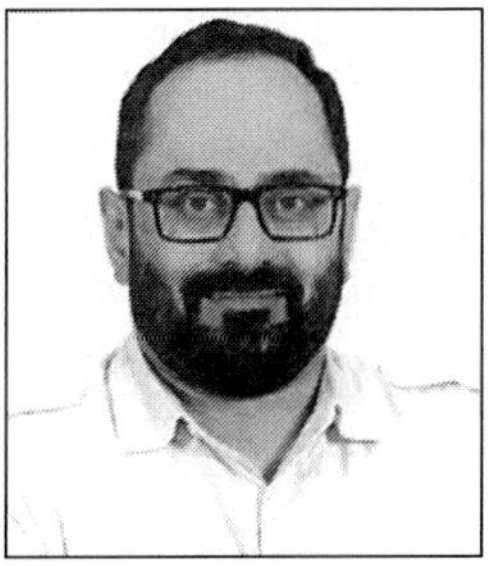

"India will conquer the world in next two decades"

(-Rajeev Chandrasekhar while swearing as MoS-EIT & Skills)

We have syllabus books on technology subjects,
with hardly any tool for Entrepreneurs.
This brings an Insight that could foster
'**Start-up Entrepreneurship**'.

Dedicated to :

MoE-AICTE Innovation Mission,
Affiliated Institutions and
Our Aspiring Future Innovation Brains.

It's the Passion; also the Nerve!

The last three decades, India's GDP surged on IT and Software exports. Recently our Prime Minister envisioned that Start-up Innovations will drive our GDP during the next two decades. How this could be made possible? Dawn of July this year, Sri Rajeev Chandara Sekhar reigned in as our new MoS-EIT and Skill Development, was so optimistic that India will conquer the world in next two decades. How we make this happen?

'InnoVision' is the confluence of Innovation with Vision. As most successful scripts are written around a theme, I would say that this book is built around a theme of "Passion and Nerve", which are the two most critical attributes of Start-up Entrepreneurship. Not a technical degree alone and not any seed funding or manpower, it is "The Passion and The Nerve" the most vital factors that drive any successful start-up enterprise. After closely tracking many of those successful innovators and entrepreneurs like Henry Ford, Gordon Moore, Bill Gates, Steve Wosniak and Steve Jobs, Sergey and Larry, Zuckerberg and Elon Musk, the most important two attributes which had driven their fortune were the relentless Passion and Nerve followed by other traits like idea, technology, R&D, finance and marketing.

My childhood to remember is full of disobedience at home, problematic to teachers, questioning rule, follow what is not instructed, not sensitive to other's opinion, later I started getting into conflicts with what I believed to be right. Such a nature gradually got a Nerve into me, throughout my life and work. As a result I did not make any true friends, also not much enemies. Doing different than others, striving to reach beyond my merit and being dissatisfied of own achievements, winning audacious goals and breaking own records, my most winning attributes were 'The Passion and The Nerve' that made me different from those around me.

Great results are won with a humble beginning. Unless we start, we do not progress forward. Here the prime minister's vision for next two decades was my inspiration. The same Passion and Nerve acted as the fuel to start this book. No matter if it becomes a failed exercise, what is common with the visionary and the script writer is that both hardly knew much about start-up innovation. At this stage, I opened my MS Word with an idea to begin on the subject. About the new technologies, we have scholars and academicians who authored several books on technology and science, mostly syllabus tools. Kindly not be misguided that I am a master in technology subjects, hence do not expect a similar content related to technology, hence I worked on Entrepreneurship.

We heard so many such ‘moon-shots’ in the past, where our primary economic sectors remained weak, from farming, industry, power sector, infrastructure, healthcare and education, human-nature conflict, child nutrition, drinking water to housing, etc. Did our GDP growth in the past three decades ever help to solve these setbacks? To become a welfare state, we have a too long and turbulent a road to travel. It requires first an audacious dream, determination and leadership drive to achieve such challenging goals. Despite whatever negative aspects conferred upon, our Prime Minister has a strong willpower and determination. He makes sure that his team follows what he envisions. His leadership is admirable than ever before where goals are more audacious than ever in the past.

Like our Prime Minister, John F. Kennedy proclaimed to put a man on the moon but he did not know how to do it. Now it remains as the responsibility on the nation to achieve his vision, where every idea and vision coming from highest to the lowest of citizens shall not be ignored. In contrast, I do not have an education in engineering, science or maths, but it comes from a college drop-out without patience to complete his PG in economics, and with a satisfactory career in selling. When we have a series of texts in engineering and technology, what suits me best is the subject of what could probably help a visionary to become a successful start-up entrepreneur.

Most of the change leaders of the future are obviously those disobedient, problematic and rule-breakers during their childhood. We know our past and present, but now it is too late to change them; we do not know our future but the right time we can change it. Unlike in the past where our near future was an extension of our recent past, from now on the near future will be a cut-off from our recent past and it will be totally different, where our intuition of whatever we believed to be right has no relevance for this future. In life, our past is becoming longer and longer and our future is becoming shorter and shorter and to conquer it, we have to work so alerted as if we will not live tomorrow, with the change cycles are getting shorter and shorter. To tame this unknown and uncertain future, our intuition earned from our past knowledge and experience is mostly unlikely to help, except but an imagination and future vision.

To drive this vision of Start-up Innovation, we start with no syllabus, teachers or schools to teach this subject. This means do we know how to start, where to start, and what to start? More we depend on academics and scholars with their rich knowledge and experience, the problem is that many of them are too past-focussed and every decision and solution derives from their intuition summed up from their past glory. This is in conflict with a future vision, which is nothing but the unknown and uncertain future. Probably what is workable is the brain of people with less of past but more of future, ie those in their late twenties or early thirties. If passion exceeds knowledge, failing is tolerable, audacity and agility can supersede norms and rules, a relentless drive caused by a creative dissatisfaction, these are the traits required, never any complementing lessons from conventional projects before. To capture an unknown future, is extremely risky hence any fear for risk is likely to be in conflict with encountering the future.

Unlike established firms, start-ups start from zero, with no money, no office, no employees, no advisors and bank account but with a dream, determination and drive to achieve something non-existing and unknown, working from a garage, but with risks everywhere around. I jumped into the fray knowing that it is too hot to touch. One needs courage to enter such fray despite knowing that you will fall, courage is to fight Mike Tyson knowing that you get your jaws broken, courage is also to jump into the deep see without knowing swimming. Dreaming has no barriers, strength comes not from success, but from struggles, failing again and again. That is what the reality of a start-up mindset.

Internet enables even an ordinary person to aspire and execute extra-ordinary dreams. Nothing wrong if a carpenter dreams to become an astronaut, a farm worker dreams to become a scientist, or a school drop-out dreams to script a book. These are all today possible with the help of Internet. Internet re-writes the rule of any field of expertise being reserved for specialists which is today open for anyone from anywhere. When mostly everything we believed we knew is wrong, this is the best time so far in history to be alive. In absence of a syllabus, we start with this learning tool, then correct, improve and empower and perfect it in such a relentless and ruthless way until a recognized document on "Start-up Innovation". For every Start-up, starting somewhere is most important that takes you forward to achieve what you dreamed or something close by.

We have every reason to make possible of what our PM envisioned about the next two decades. If ancient India had contributed more than modern India, today we are blessed with access and application of every advanced technology than many developed nations. I was most convinced by two reasons that if big problems are big opportunities, which no other country has more problems than India has, and if creativity thrives when constrained, we have more constrains than any other region. Hence we are blessed with enough of problems and constrains which have the potential to make India the fertile soil for opportunities and creativity, empowering the world's largest domicile of Start-ups and Innovations to the benefit of billions. Besides the rest of South Asia, Middle East and CIS look upon India as a potential force towards transforming the region. Among the seventeen Sustainable Development Goals set by UN for 2030 like poverty, hunger, healthcare, education, clean water and energy, carbon footprint, banking, transport, etc the South Asia region lags behind 100 ranks. These goals open to huge innovation and enterprise opportunities, with a significant impact on our economy.

We have one of the most motivating and determined government leaderships, a healthy competition among states to become innovation hubs and a racing spirit among private sector and universities, where our only limit is our own ambition. If it is in the extreme situation, we witness the best and worst of humanity so that the country is left with only an optimistic future. As the wealthy ones are contented with prosperity hence nothing much left for them to dream, the promises are with the middle class with a fire in the belly, and still more with a burning flame among the underprivileged. That is India, where there is too much to dream the future that leads a determination to invent and discover.

People were mostly linear and local, who wished the near future to be an extension of our recent past. Now we will be a total cut-off from present and recent past, and will be totally aligning to a new future. As we were habituated with the rules of the present and past, we cannot look for that easy and adjustable to cope with the new future unless we adapt to the forces of technology which dictate the future- a very optimistic, peaceful and most liveable than ever in the past. "We are going to transform the world in the next ten years more than we did the entire past hundred years!" – Said Ray Kurzweil, a US Computer Scientist on humanity's merger with the technology it created.

CONTENTS

1 Imaginative Economy & Lessons from US Tech Firms

The largest five technology companies in US have a combined Market Value of $.8.96 Tril in 2020-21, which contributes to 39.44% to the world's largest economy of $.22.72 Tril and together they make almost 60.87% of Chinese GDP-$14.72 Tril ($18 Tril in 2021). The combined value of these five companies makes to 166% of Japan's GDP-$.5.38 Trilliion, 213% of Germany's GDP($.4.2 Tril) 294% of India's $.3.05. This shows the might of today's Start-ups in shaping the future economy of any nation.

Some of these five technology titans are valued closely behind the GDP of India, Germany or UK. It will be interesting to note their valuation as on 2021, as given below:

Microsoft	:	US$.2.28 Trl
Apple	:	$. 2.08 Tril
Google	:	$.1.68 Tril
Amazon	:	$.1.71 Tril
Facebook	:	$.1.21 Tril.
Total for Five	**:**	**US$.8.96 Tril**

These companies had a humble beginning as Start-ups, where they innovated new technologies that did not exist before. These companies, Apple, Amazon, Microsoft, Google and Facebook, which were founded by people who were not smarter than many of us, but touched and improved almost every human life and business.

Established companies grow incrementally, whereas these technology start-ups grow in multiple folds, hence they are named as "Exponential Companies". Today US has the largest number of Start-ups in the world attracting the highest amount of VC and angel investors than elsewhere. Out of an estimated 600 Unicorns (is scaled up to $.1

Bil market value), the U.S. leads the globe with 242 unicorns, followed by China with 119, with a market value of $250 Bil. The U.K. and India both have 24 each (2020). On the other side, a tiny country in the Middle East, Israel has the highest per-capita start-ups and VC funding in the world, where technology goods and services achieved an all-time record of 45.8 billion dollars, about 46% of the combined Israeli exports in 2019.

US is an example how Start-ups will drive the economy in future. None of the manufacturing, energy, retail or banking companies could imagine achieving this level of market valuation in the history. Those top four India's technology firms make up to $.267.56 Bil/FY 2019-20 (9.32% of GDP). America's GDP is 24.5% of the world's total GDP of 87.55 Tril and the valuation of these five technology companies in US contributes to 10.23% of global GDP. An amazing indication of the reality of our future!

If the Industrial revolution created capitalists and workers, it did not address any solutions to the world's biggest problems like poverty, hunger, literacy and healthcare. IT revolution resulted the beginning of a shared economy where it generated a lot of well paid jobs to middle and lower middle classes. But Digital revolution addresses to an all-inclusive development, which not only did create a burgeoning mass middle class, but also improved the livelihood of billions even the poorest from Africa and South Asia. Surprisingly the new technologies like Internet, AI, IoT, ML, Automation, Sensors, Advanced Robotics, 3-D Printing and Genomics have a solution to every big problem remaining unsolved before the humanity. This will change our future which looks very optimistic.

Prime Minister recently addressed the nation explaining the importance of nurturing Start-ups to drive the country's economy at a faster pace to catch up with rest of the world. If India has the largest pool of Technology graduates in the world that too educated in English language, it creates a solid base for nurturing and incubating Innovation start-ups than any other country in the world. It is also to be noted that, such a daring vision certainly requires a strategy under a ministry for AI and Innovations. See the US, where NY is the financial and stock market capital, LA is the global capital for entertainment, so Houston-Texas for energy, Boston for education and Silicon Valley for technology and high-tech start-ups. With this new race, Detroit lost as automobile capital and Texas for oil. In Silicon Valley, 36% of population is made of foreign born residents. This foreign talent has provided diverse and critical engineering skills to the Silicon Valley. On the other side, Frankfurt once known to be a financial hub along with London and Zurich, today shelters over five thousand software firms including SAP and Symantec is the Internet capital of Europe. Most of these corporate have their headquarters in vast campuses, away from the cities.

With Hong Kong losing down its past glory, Singapore captured the opportunity; today has the highest density of regional APAC head offices relative to its GDP in the world. Nearly half of all the large foreign subsidiaries in emerging Asia outside China are located in this city. In 2012, P&G moved its beauty and baby care divisions from Cincinnati to Singapore. Unilever opened its first training centre there in 2013. Rolls-Royce relocated its marine division from London to Singapore, recognizing Asia's emergence as the world's centre for shipping. No wonder if Singapore becomes the Asian Financial hub in the near future with Hong Kong gradually losing its glory. In China, Guangdong is for industry, Wuhan is for higher education, as Shanghai for shipping and Beijing for financial services. Even Dubai has emerged as the largest hotspot for trade, tourism and finance.

In India, Bangalore retains its position as capital of IT and Software for three decades. The quad axis of Bangalore, Chennai, Hyderabad and Pune for information technology has also complemented to attract the automobile industry in its corridors, as both complement each other. Mumbai is the country's financial centre, which is too late to relocate considering the ageing and decaying of the city. Such a vast developing country with fifth rank in global GDP, India does not have its equivalent sea port to rival Colombo, Dubai or HK, and an airport hub like Dubai, Doha or Singapore. We have high-growth potential cities like Aurangabad, Coimbatore, Surat or Kakinada/Vizag for manufacturing and shipping which could be developed to Tianjin, Guangzhu and Jalan-Selangur. We enjoyed the real fruits of Software & IT which charged our GDP in the last three decades, where the next normal is to come from Digital Technology, hence India may require a special vehicle to create and develop Free-Zones in such tier-2 cities. The entire east coast shoring Bay of Bengal has no major business or technology hubs except Chennai.

To achieve this GDP growth during the next two decades, one of the most critical opportunities at our door step is to collaborate with the newly established technology venture between UAE and Israel, which was endorsed by the UAE Minister of AI with the CEO of SNC (Start-up Nation Central) of Israel, which will combine the strengths of Israeli innovation and UAE's venture capital. As this project requires large number of high skilled labour at affordable cost, there is no other country like India with such resources. Once it begins to reach its second phase, it will attract more countries like CIS and GCC to form a giant regional co-operation like RECP in the east. This makes us living in an era of universal collaboration.

Next the world's largest manufacturing country, China has most of its factory facilities based on manufacturing and assembling, where 3-D Printing will grow to create a $.3-4 Tril business of the present $12 Tril global manufacturing sector by 2025. With the rapid decline in its working class population due to its one-child policy three decades ago, China faces a severe threat of relocation of manufacturing to any other countries with low-wages and high skills, where manufacturing process itself is undergoing a major change with automation, robotics and 3-D printing. Then an economically distressed China will be compelled to call back its huge debt funds. This lost opportunity of China could possibly relocate to Vietnam, Indonesia, India, Taiwan and Thailand.

In India, we had seen the growth of Middle Class consumption during the last two decades, and the next phase of growth will be accelerated by those born after 1985. It will be a prototype model of what we had seen in China in the last two decades. This imposes an immense pressure and responsibility on our ministry of education as well as Ministry of New Skills and Digital Technology.

Perhaps no one would have dared to think and script such an elaborate and detailed report on this subject ever in the past. Interestingly this has come from an ordinary citizen who has all the disadvantages of academics, past knowledge and subject specialisation, but with the audacity, eagerness, nerve and daring with a childhood chutzpah at his seventies. This submission shares a lot of ideas that could help our government to formulate a successful strategy to nurture and incubate a large number of innovation start-ups which could drive our GDP to the glory of pre-colonial rule.

We are largely comfortable to talk and think from memories, because memories are what we know. We are also comfortable in talking to those who mostly agree with our views and decisions, because we know them. This is so common with most of the scholars, academicians, bureaucrats and every other decision makers. As a result, every crazy idea is questioned and discouraged by finding a way how it cannot move forward. More aged they are, the more filled with the knowledge that existed, they are left with little space for future. On the other side, we hardly talk and think from imagination and ideas, because we do not know much about it. We have very limited and few minds who can talk new ideas, what do not exist and not easy to accomplish. A strong purpose, necessity and deep passion are essential for driving and fulfilling such dreams.

First we need to reset our intuition where our future vision is limited within our visibility curve and from our past knowledge and experience; as there is a powerful human tendency to want the future to look much like our recent past. A year later in 2021, Apple became the first company in the world to cross a market value of $3Tril and Microsoft is closely behind to cross this benchmark in 2022, which is equal to India's GDP in 2021.

To solve the challenges of today and tomorrow, we can no longer use the techniques, thinking and processes of yesterday. We need to embrace the opportunities from the fastest technological and most innovative period in history. Technology is disrupting almost every industry, and the pace of change had never been more rapid, with a positive impact on a billion lives.

Future is more important and we should be all seriously concerned about it because we will have to spend the rest of our lives there, which we do not know much about. Therefore what went right in the past is unlikely to go right for our future. As a HSE student has endless dreams of an unknown and uncertain future, an experienced and educated man at his sixties endlessly dives deep into his past glories. Therefore, there is a pressing demand to reset our intuition, which we gained from our past knowledge and experience therefore, we need young people whose minds are less filled about past, but with more space to think and imagine about future.

We have several works on each technology subjects, of which many are recognized text books in technical universities. On the other side, what seeds a start-up innovation is the Idea intertwined with Entrepreneurship, where technology education complements or can be outsourced. The fact remains that Entrepreneurship is not taught in universities.

Whatever can go wrong, will go wrong! "InnoVision" fosters insights into developing this entrepreneurship required for success in start-up innovations.

Lessons from US Tech Firms

Knowledge is what already exists, with too much of its specialisation means narrowing the subject and makes one to think in its narrow and specialised perspective. We are all comfortable of talking about what we knew, and also to people whom we knew; but we talk and think very less of what we do not know and to whom we do not know. With too much of past knowledge filled in our mind, it is left with less space for new knowledge. We hardly engage in talking and thinking about future which we do not know and as a result, we have very less thinkers, where creative thinkers are so high in demand. Hence, knowledge and experience have to be replaced with a future vision!

We generally arrive to an 'Intuition', from our past knowledge and experience and it has a strong influence on our decisions and imaginations. As stated here, if past knowledge and experience are to be replaced with a future vision, what we call such intuition enabled decision and imagination are unlikely to shape a realistic instinct about an unknown future. This rules-out the scope for engaging scholars, academicians, management thinkers, bureaucrats and Venture Capitalists in any result-oriented Start-up Innovation bodies. Then where we find the 'future brains' to drive and discover innovations? This is an attempt to disrupt what we believed right, and show directions to a right strategy.

If intuition is considered to be a successful resource in every field of decisions from management, finance & administration, HR, marketing, investment, bureaucracy to governance, why the same intuition cannot be successfully used in Start-up Innovations? This is enough a reason for restricting their engagement into running start-up innovations as they are largely risk-averse.

Every country badly needs people of thinking about future, visualising what we do not know and imagining what does not exist. Where we can find them? Most of them are in the back benches of our IITs and NITs, especially those with a classroom conflict and clash with their teachers. In a beginner's mind there are more possibilities, but an expert's mind has few.

"No Ordinary Disruption; The four forces breaking the trends", a book authored by Richard Dobbs is an analysis of how we need to reset our intuition in the advent of four forces colliding and transforming the global economy:

The Rise of Emerging Markets

The Accelerating Impact of Technology on the Natural Forces of Competition.

An Ageing Population

Increasing Inflow of Trade, Capital and People.

Our intuitions formed during relatively a comfortable and happy period of the global economy, often termed as Global Moderation. Asset prices were rising, cost of capital was dropping, people resources plenty and generation after generation was growing up more prosperous than their parents. With the Global Moderation disappeared, the cost of capital may rise with more volatility in prices of grains and steel. World's labour force may shrink, and people with weak job skills are at risk of growing poorer than their parents.

Many of us cannot spot those 400 new cities which will scale to half of the global economy by 2025, where a single less known Chinese city called Tianjin with a GDP of $130Bil in 2010, almost equal to Stockholm, will rise to around$625 billion, equal to all that of Sweden. Such relocation economy indexes will demand for shifting their present corporate offices of several Fortune-500s to such unknown geographies. In this gripping and insightful roadmap to our near-future, how wave after wave of exponentially accelerating technologies will impact both our daily lives and community as a whole. What would happen with AI, Robotics, VR, Digital Biology, and sensors crash into 3D printing, block-chain and global gigabite networks? How will these convergences transform our present industries? What will happen to the way we raise our kids, govern our nations and care our planet? How will the science of technological convergence will reinvent every part of our lives-from transportation, advertising, retail, education, health, food and finance, taking humanity into uncharted frontiers and reimagining the world as we know it?

The "Next Big Things" or Twelve Emerging Technologies-including Mobile Internet, Big Data, 3-D Printing, Robotics, Autonomous Vehicles, Energy Storage and Advanced Genomics are to reshape the world, where government and business should not only know what on the horizon but also start preparing for its impact. These twelve "Next Big Things" are estimated to add another $.14-33 Tril to the global economy by 2025.

Most of the life's smart things we have around, and most of the innovations that touched and improved our lives, are brought to us by those people who were less smarter than many of us. Most of them were college drop-outs who had severe classroom disobedience, and were problematic to their teachers. Their minds were dreaming around something invisible and non-existing beyond any career aspiration. Once slipped out, they can turn to become negative and sinful citizens therefore institutions shall not miss them from getting integrated to disruptions and innovations. Unlike frontbenchers, they are fit to work in tough and adverse situations with far superior soft skills like relationship, teamwork, collaboration, resilience and consistency.

India has 23 IITs, 31 NITs, one IISc, 2 BITs, besides a number of Grade-1 technical colleges. We shall narrow down to just ten of those high-ranking campuses in the first year. Shortlist 40 brain students from Physics, Maths and Comp. Science and filter the list to five in a college who form the core innovation team. Like how we have Faculty Chairs sponsored by corporate, these students shall be directly placed with Military, Military contractors, Corporate in auto, metal, IT & software, Banking & Finance, etc who will pay for their internship, hostel, food, etc and absorb them into their research and innovation department on completion of the course. If the nation is in the race to become one of the top three in start-up innovations, what we can learn from US and Israel is that the ownership has to be essentially controlled by local VCs and angel investors, otherwise they will remain successful unicorns of foreign ownership, especially Chinese Off-shores.

During their course, they will adhere to a three months of tough military training which instils patriotism, values and purpose, besides stretching mentally and physically that train them to withstand any adversaries and failures and turn them fearless and daring. Apart from the course syllabus, they are to spend weekends and holidays on experimenting and innovating new things, either better alternatives to existing ones, and inventing new products and technologies. They will undergo frequent workshops and classes by visiting guest lecturers.

After the program, they are conferred with dual certificates, each from university and the sponsor. They are drafted to respective research laboratories with adequate materials, equipments and assistance that help them to discover alternatives and improvements to every existing method and product, besides innovating and developing new things, with superior features and strike rate, technology, automation, etc. New materials like plasticisers, elastomers, polymers, resins, graphite, titanium, crystal, ceramic, acrylic, carbon etc have proven to be superior, light-weight, durable and low-cost alternatives to depleting and non-replenishable materials like steel, copper, aluminium and hydrocarbon with massive applications in aircrafts, ships, artillery, infantry, automobiles, battery, appliances, television, cell phone and computers.

To achieve this, things are to be viewed not from conventional and academic perspective, but mostly an audacious, restless, disobedient and disruptive outlook which challenges every algorithm and norm which we believed to be right. Year after year, we shall increase the number of students and campuses, besides corporate partners, otherwise we miss many innovators.

This is the best time to be alive; when almost everything we thought we knew is proving wrong. This signals that our past knowledge and intuition are due to replace with a future vision.

2 India's Glory-Discoveries & Inventions

Discoveries and inventions in Ancient India

If we explore the history, we can see that ancient India made more contributions to the world than modern India. Ancient India was the cradle of most of the discoveries and inventions than rest of the world put-together.

India invented the number system. Aryabhata born in 476-AD, invented Zero and its application in Arithmetic.

The place value system, the decimal system was first invented in India in 100-BC.

Examples: soonya = void, akasha = space, kha = sky, bindu = dot.

The method of graduated calculation was documented in Pancha-siddhantika, the five principles in the 5th century. But the technique is said to be dating from Vedic times circa 2000-BC.

The value of pie is calculated by Budhayana, and he explained the concept of what is today known as Pythagorean theory.

British scholars have officially published in 1999 that Buddhayan's works date back to 6th century, which is long before the European Mathematicians.

Algebra, Trigonometry and Calculus were originated in India

Quadratic equations were also founded by Sridharacharya in 11th Century.

The largest numbers that used by Greeks and Romans were 10 to 6 (6 to the power of 10) whereas Hindus used numbers as big as 10 to 53 (10 to the power of 53) with specific names as early as 5000-BCE during Vedic period. Even today the largest used number is Tera 10 to 12 (10 to the power of 12).

Sanskrit is the mother of all European languages. "Sanskrit is the most suitable language for computer software", reported in the Forbes magazine, July 1987.

Bhaskarcharya calculated the time taken by the earth to orbit the Sun hundred years before the astronomer Smart. Time taken by earth to orbit the Sun was arrived during 5th century at 365.258756484 days.

The origins of Ayurveda have been traced to around 6,000 BCE when they originated as an oral tradition. Some of the concepts of Ayurveda have existed since the times of Indus Valley Civilization. The first recorded forms of Ayurveda as medical texts evolved from the Vedas.

The art of navigation was born in the river Sindh 6000 years ago. The very word of navigation is derived from the Sanskrit word 'Navgatih'. The word navy is also derived from Sanskrit "Nou".

Pranayama teaches how one can float over the water steadily for long, but it is hardly being taught to sailors.

In Ramayana, Pushpaka aircraft was controlled by remote, a central point of the palm.

According to the Gemological Institute of America, up until 1896 India was the only source for diamonds to the world.

Chess (Shataranja or Ashta Pada) was invented in India

Sushruta is the father of surgery, where he and health scientists of his time, conducted complicated surgeries like caesareans, cataract, artificial limbs, fractures, urinary stones and even plastic surgery and brain surgery 2000 years ago. Usage of anaesthesia was well known in ancient India, where over 125 surgical equipments were in use. Deep knowledge of anatomy, physiology, digestion, metabolism, genetics and immunity is also found in many texts.

The earliest reservoir and dam for irrigation were built in Saurashtra.

When many cultures were only nomadic forest dwellers over 5000 years ago, Indians established Harappan civilization in Sindhu valley (Indus Valley civilization).

India's contribution to Production Technology and Mechanical Engineering.

In ancient times, commodities like sugar, palm oil, coconut oil, cotton cloth, clarified butter, cast iron, ten sheets, copper vessels, dyes and pigments like Ochre/cinnabar, indigo and lacs, perfumes from Sandalwood oil, musk, costus, macir, camphor and even crude glass crockery were exported from India..

The earliest recorded use of copperware in India has been around 3000-BC as per the findings at Mohen-jo-Daro and Harappa. The earliest documented observation of something of metals in India is by Greek historians in 400-BC.

India's contribution to Astronomy and Astrology

"In India I found a race of mortals living upon the earth, but not adhering to it. Inhabiting cities, but not being fixed to hem, possessing everything but possessed by nothing". Apollonius Tyanaeus, a Greek thinker and traveller of 100-AD.

In India the first reference to astronomy are to be found in the Rig Veda which is dated back to 2000-BC. The calculation of Eclipses and the earth's circumference, known as the Heliocentric Theory of Gravitation. This facsimile or reproduction is from the Panchasiddhantika (five principles) dated around the 5th century. The text graphically shows how eclipses are calculated. Thus this text foreshadows what Western astronomers propounded nearly one thousand years later.

Astrology is the science of future telling. It starts with the birthday and time of an individual and calculate his present status based on positions of the solar planets, making it more an arithmetic calculation linked to logical assumptions in order to foretell one's good and bad possibilities in his future.

India's contribution to Physics and Chemistry

"Ancient theories lacked an empirical base but they were brilliant and imaginative explanations of the physical structure of the world and to a large measure agreed with the discoveries of modern Physics". A.L.Basham, an Australian Indologist.

The Five Basic Physical Elements:

'Anu and Paramanu' are Indian ideas of Atomic Physics.

Contributions to Medical Science

"In the great teaching of the Vedas, there is no touch of sectarianism. It is of all ages, climes and nationalities and is the royal road for attainment of great knowledge" Thoreau, an American thinker.

Shastrakarma is the art of surgery and Ayurveda is the science of life longevity. Yoga is the health of body and mind.

India's contribution to Fine Arts

"If I am asked which nation had been advanced in the ancient world in respect of education and culture, then I would say it was India" Max Mueller, a German Indologist. Music, Painting, Linguistics, Dance Theatre, Sports and Games in Ancient India like, Chess, Snake & Ladder, Playing Cards, Polo, martial arts like Kalari, Judo and Panchagusti were practiced in India.

Contribution to Philosophy

"In religion, India is the only millionaire; the only one land that all men desire to see and having seen once, by eye of a glimpse would not give that glimpse for all the shows of all the rest of the world combined". Said Marc Twain American American Author 1835-1910.

India was the First Democracy to Elect a Woman Prime Minister

According to recent data, USA has as many as 3.6 Mil Indians living there. 38% of doctors in USA are Indians, 12% of scientists, 36% of employment at NASA, 34% in Microsoft, 28% in IBM, 17% in Intel and 13% at Xerox.

India was the first democracy to elect a woman Prime minister. India is the 7th nuclear power and 5th largest economy in the world. The largest democracy in the world, India has the second largest population. It is the fourth nation in the world to develop a nuclear submarine. India is the 4th nation in the world, to be able to develop cruise missiles to be launched from land and sea.

During 1990s, India was the first and only country in the world to have a minority Muslim as elected President, another minority Sikh elected as Prime minister, and a lady of foreign origin as the most powerful political leader, despite being a nation of over 80% Hindu majority. This can never happen anywhere else! That is her religious tolerance and respect for pluralism and democracy.

SUMMING UP

Human excellence is related to development of culture! World's first ever culture (ref: Yajurveda 7/14: Sa Prathama Sanskriti Vishwara): Many small civilizations were formed but were confined to small region. Only Indian culture can be called as first world culture. Indian culture is Human culture that focuses on inculcating human values in a man!

Unique features of Indian Culture

Freedom of thought- Every thought is allowed to develop internally and freely without limits. Theist and Atheist- Vedanta speak of soul as image of the Supreme- Everyone is free to imagine and accept God's form according to his own faith and belief. Every thought school is inclusive in Indian culture, that is unity in diversity, a garden with variety of flowers and plants. This diversity increases the beauty of the garden.

THEORY OF KARMAPAL-REBIRTH

Warfare- Technology of Destroyers and Interceptors

The present day of warfare, see how AI-supported I-Dome shields our land with Interceptor missiles which sense the inward enemy missile and rocket attacks? This has to read back to our Kurukshetra war where Agneyastra (Fire arrow) was intercepted with Varunastra (Rain arrow)? Did the technology of AI and sensors existed in Sanskrit and known to us way back 4000 years?

Idealistic Joint families

Abundance of saints and reformers.

Division of societal order based on personal choice, interest and capabilities, besides personal life for self-development and for development of society.

India is the only country where a crown prince abandoned his palatial fortunes and came out in searching for eternal bliss of life and soul.

What great thinkers said?

It is already becoming clearer that a chapter which has a western beginning will have an Indian ending if for mankind is the Indian way.

"it is not to end in the self-destruction of human r... dangerous moment in history the only way of salvatio... Toynbee, the British historian 1889-1975.

"India is the cradle of human race, the birthplace of human... the mother of history and grandmother of tradition. Our most valua... and most constructive materials in the history of man are treasured up in India only" Mark Twain.

Will Durrant, American Historian 1885-1981: India was the motherland of our race and Sanskrit is the mother of Europe's languages. India was the mother of our philosophy of much of our mathematics, of the ideals embodied in Christianity... of self-government and democracy. In many ways, Mother India is the mother of us all.

"If there is one place on the face of this earth where all dreams of living men have found a home from the very earliest days when man began the dream of existence, it was India" Romain Rolland- French philosopher 1886-1944.

Albert Einstein: We owe a lot to the Indians, who taught us how to count, without which no worthwhile scientific discovery could have been made.

"India conquered and dominated China culturally for twenty centuries without ever having to send a single soldier across her border". Hu Shih, former Chinese Ambassador to US.

"Why we see saints only in India? Why all great legends take rebirth in India?" Mao Tse Dong asked historian K.C.S.Panicker the Indian Ambassador to China.

Grant Duff, British historian of India, "Many of the advances in sciences that we consider today to have been made in Europe were in fact made in India centuries ago".

Sanskrit as the Mother Language

Sanskrit is the oldest integrated language in the world, where other known dialects existed in ancient Egypt without a script, and a Chinese script without a dialect, but did not make a complete language in absence of both dialect and script. Ancient Sanskrit is known to have used Devanagari script, a divine language which traces back to thousands of years.

...is a classical language which flourished in India ... of years ago. Pali is also an ancient language that has ...idely used in the Buddhist scriptures. The Sanskrit language is ... older than Pali. Sanskrit had been the language in use from the ...dic period.

Sanskrit is one of the oldest known languages. It is also called "Dev Vani" (the language of gods) as it is said that Brahma introduced this language to the Sages of celestial bodies. It is believed that the Sanskrit language came from Indo-European language family of Indian subcontinent. Deutsche, the official language of Germany has closer similarity and adaptation to Sanskrit than English or French.

Pre-historic period of discoveries and inventions

As detailed in the beginning of this text, a large number of discoveries and inventions were achieved during a time writing instruments or writing media were not available. The most widely used media for writing was leaf of Palm tree and instrument was a sharp nail tipped tool. Sanskrit was so refined language with most of its words were with multiple meanings hence, a short write-up contained a wide variety of messages, so powerful that it could remain long in memory.

Sanskrit was the mother language on which all those ancient India's discoveries and inventions were drafted and improved. Its glory and majesty lasted until 9th century when Ghazni dynasty invaded India, followed by Ghori, Mongols, Lodhi and Moghals which ruled the country until the British East India Co and became a British colony until its independence in 1947.

During the foreign rule, the invaders destroyed and set fire of the world famous knowledge and research centres of Takshashila and Nalanda and smuggled out most of the invaluable scripts in Sanskrit. Most of the Sanskrit knowledge centres were paralysed without funds for development. From our history, one can see that all research, discoveries and inventions came to a halt under the foreign rule. As British rulers brought western media education, our glorious tradition of research, discoveries and inventions was replaced with creating workers of astute obedience to masters in their offices and factories.

Independent India

If foreign rule had destroyed Sanskrit, the tradition of discoveries and invention, independent India made more damages to the language. The new rulers were with western education in English, with their close slavery mindset towards their old masters and followed an education system just an extension of the British system where education becomes the merit for securing an employment.

Later on the linguistic division of states, rising importance of minority vote bank, Sanskrit could not secure its prominence than a language just for teaching, as compared to the high importance given to regional languages and Arabic. As a result, once so majestic and rich language Sanskrit remained limited to priests and munshis and India did not make any single worth discovery and invention for more than 800 years until now.

Ancient model of Educations

Sanskrit had a unique method of learning, which first recognizes God in the form of teacher who shares a status that equals to father and mother.

Education is the Gurukul model, where children live with the teacher throughout the course of learning, enjoying an equal status irrespective of family origin, eating the same food, taking bath, playing and praying together. It is so important to win the recognition and blessing of the teacher. The course of education contained not only in areas of knowledge, but also in games, sports and war games, besides living in hardships like a life in the forest, stretching one's limits to withstand adverse and difficult situations. It is altogether a testing ground for ones physical and mental potential.

Tharkashastra is a logical mode of learning through asking questions. It is a Sanskrit term for the philosophy of dialects, logic and reasoning and the art of debate that analyses the nature and source of knowledge and its validity. Tharka means a debate or an argument, which in other words is an intellectual wrestling. It has two sects, purva paksha and apara paksha. When one group raises a point, the apara paksha group opposes it. Then the debate starts and each side tries to support its point of view by getting various references. The debate continues until supporting argument defeats the opposing argument or vice-versa.

Anyonyam is a very well known annual debate between two Rig Veda schools in Kerala, which goes on for days with scholars divided between supporting and opposing perspectives. It is an intellectual wrestling which results much higher level of knowledge acquisition.

Tharka is a basic form of raising logical questions to arrive an answer. This is believed to be the platform that encouraged human thinking extended to achieve discoveries and inventions in ancient India. Surprisingly many of the discoveries listed at the beginning, stand uncontested and valid even today, though some had gone through improvements.

Astrology or Jyotisha in Sanskrit is an interpretation of future prediction. As most people enjoy talking and thinking of the past or about what they already knew, we can see hardly anyone talking about the future because we do not know it. Knowledge is what already existed but future is what we do not know and not taught in schools. Here it is very important that knowledge and experience should be replaced with Vision in order to be successful in the future. Astrology is a science, an arithmetical calculation to forecast the future based on the positions of solar planets. Its predictions are mostly on how the planetary positions influence one's future. This shows how Astrology as a science is connected with Astronomy, the science of universe and planets. Bhaskaracharya discovered the year as 365.258756484 days in 5th century AD based on earth's 360 degree turn and the movement on the orbit encircling the sun.

The traditional wisdom and knowledge as we see in Sanskrit, had ignited curiosity and eagerness among the scholars to new discoveries. We had to see that such new inventions were achieved despite having no access to paper and print, transport, communication, references and technology.

3 Chutzpah! The Second Oldest Religion and the Second Oldest Language

When the oldest religion and oldest language on earth were losing their glory in their home turf, on the other side of the planet, the second oldest religion Judaism and its language Hebrew recovered from a twenty century old darkest period of slavery, holocaust, extinction and forceful evacuation from its homeland to become one of the most recognized countries to drive its economy through discoveries and inventions. The most winning factor behind this achievement was the willpower of the founding fathers of the nation, who closely adhered to the historic tradition of their religion and language.

Chutzpah is a word in Hebrew, which does not have a right translation to English. In Hebrew, it means the quality of audacity, a creative discomfort even when nothing to worry, challenge even best accomplishments, not to celebrate success and whatever achieved today is not enough for tomorrow. It is supreme self-confidence, an eagerness and curiosity, burning appetite, firmness, daring, defiance and a nerve! It is surprising to note that our Marwari Banias are successful entrepreneurs who are equally difficult community as Jews to negotiate and convince, because they still hold deep to their traditional religious faiths, lifestyle and language than others.

Chutzpah gives the courage to break away from conventional thinking to be determined, courageous and optimistic that anything can be achieved. It is a daring mindset, audacity to challenge the normal rules, an ability to laugh at oneself when others feel an eccentricity and madness. Even fallen on the floor, kicked out by others, rejected as misfit, you raze and wreck the obstacles and rise up from thrash and attempt again with double the strength; then you achieve your goals, if not something nearest to that once looked impossible. If it looks impossible, most people give-up. The root of Chutzpah is a determined approach to life to win what looks impossible for others.

Israelis are too open that question almost everything, hence most difficult to convince. The right answers are the outcome of audacious questions. A subordinate questions what is the merit of his boss to be his superior? A student questions the teacher, so the children at home or a soldier to the officer. In today's management or leadership practice, when a subordinate comes with a problem to the boss for a solution, the boss asks the same subordinate what he thinks the right solution? Mostly the subordinate has the right answer for the solution. It is one's right to question. Chutzpah combines the maturity of experience with the eagerness of childhood, that can help an aged person to live young. You grow younger with learning and get aged once you stop learning. All the experts are experts on what was; then we need experts on what will be the reality of future? To achieve this, vision must replace experience.

This is widely accepted as a social culture which is considered to be disrespect and disobedience in other countries or societies. When something is questioned, it brings the answer or as throwing a stone to fall a mango. Why a crow is created in Black? Why a cherry is always in red? No answer yet, but raise questions audaciously. When a tool is made, it is questioned how it can be made with less material, by saving cost, at higher speed and better finish. When they cultivate potato, next they think how the harvest cycle can be shortened and yield can be improved per Sq,mtr. Chutzpah questions everything that existed and explores how to improve quality, speed and numbers at lower cost and time. Israel has enjoyed tremendous advantages and benefits by practicing this widely in all fields. This approach opens up equal or more opposing reasons for every supporting reason before any final decision.

Waiting for two hours is too long for a child, but too short for an adult. Chutzpah is deeply inherent and impregnated to children but loses its fire and burst while growing up. Recent study showed that ninety six percent of Children at early learning schools are more confident that they can become what they aspire in life, but it comes down to hardly four percent at their eighteens. Education shall not destroy this confidence and aspiration. If their confidence and optimism can be nurtured towards a grown-up stage, it becomes an astute form of disruption which makes the seed of innovation. Most of the Chutzpah-inspired adults behave like wilful children.

"Many children branded as problematic by their teachers are in fact Chutzpah kids who are gusty, extrovert, resilient, audacious, sociable and brazen; the same adjective we use to describe our maverick entrepreneurs" said Steve Mariotti, a NY consultant in school counselling. When we behave with Chutzpah, we are reverting to the daring and cheeky children we once were. Why do most of us lose our Chutzpah as we exit our childhood? Through our different stages of schooling, the education model encourages kids to grow out of their childhood Chutzpah.

Dov Maron was rated by his teacher below average in his primary school. An adult with a degree in Engineering from Technion Uni, he became the commander in microprocessor section of Israel Navy. Today his name features with forty patents raising few billion dollars as capital.

So stretch your imagination until you get your door of Chutzpah opened. "Imagination is the beginning of creativity. You imagine what you desire, you will what you imagine and finally you create what you will", said George Bernard Shaw. So if you want to do things different, try Chutzpah. To make an unexpected and unconventional response to a situation, try Chutzpah. "Shall I start preparing to write a symphony?" a child asked Mozart. The answer was a blunt "No." Child asked again, "But didn't you write a symphony when you were at my age?" Mozart replied, "Yes, but I didn't ask anyone".

Chutzpah ignites children how to think and not what to think, is the fire and the power that can differentiate their future. The more Chutzpah one displays, the higher his tolerance for being criticized and laughed up. It is defying conventional wisdom and conventional logic. Children catch up easily with the mechanisms and apps offered by a computer and mobile phone and explore the devise's maximum options as well as stretching limits than the adults. In Israel, HSE offers cyber-security as an optional curriculum.

Chutzpah means listening to your own inner sense, instinct and intuition no matter what others think, and act accordingly.

Parental education and financial security are those key factors in entrepreneurial success. Nurturing a openness to criticism, tolerance, resilience, experimentation and resting limits to failure can mould children to become flexible, agile, resourceful and collaborative as adults. With the technological cycles changing faster at an unprecedented rate, nearly 50% syllabus knowledge acquired during the first years of a four years technical degree gets outdated and irrelevant by the time a student graduates. Thus a general assumption that excellence in education translates into scientific innovation and business competence is proving incorrect.

When the world is thinking of development of skills in car service, construction and appliances and MEP services, Israel's Secondary schools are exploring to creating soft skills as well as new skills required for an unknown future; not what to create but how to create? Doctors are supported by digital technology invented by college drop-outs to make the surgery simplified and less painful. Teachers are not the ultimate source of learning, where learning is made easier by Apps invented by technical students. Diagnostic tests are supported with AI and satellite imaging. Not alone measuring a student's success, but measuring their failure is an indication of their learning rate. Alternative education methods in schools nurture creativity, maturity, social skills and independent thinking. Schooling motivates children to fail and fall, so they get back and fall again. Those who not fall, pay a price as adult.

Every successful innovator from Wright Brothers, Kalashnikov, Edison to Henry Ford and Steve Jobs, contained a variant of this eccentric and experimental syndrome, which dragged them into a world of eagerness and adventure to disrupt the norms and innovate. If we believe that techno-preneurs have to be reasonably good at maths, science or finance, it is surprising that none of the successful start-up countries score well in these subjects, where most of the best known innovators had a childhood clash in their maths and science classrooms. This culture supports creative thinking, challenging and risk taking, a tradition of curiosity, eagerness and questioning as part of education and grooming. It encourages the required skills and ability to withstand the unpredictability in life and work. World Economic Forum-WEF has recognized this tradition as the 'Skills for the Future'. That is Chutzpah which has no real meaning in English dictionary! It is time to redefine how a child should be brought up and groomed without losing his childhood chutzpah?

The Chutzpah dynamics

Audacity, daring, courage, self-confidence, boldness, bravery, fearlessness, conviction of objective and a never give-up attitude are the Chutzpah attributes.

Nerve- a mental stubbornness, so target focused, winning despite a merciless or rude approach, upkeep honesty and character.

Eagerness and curiosity to know anything new and what does not exist.

Tough and strong- a military type of training to make one so tough and tenacious, physically and mentally during adverse situations.

- Temptation to break rules, and go beyond what is instructed.
- To defy norms, to follow own instinct and intuition.
- A conflicting mind of supporting and opposing ideas.
- Zig-zag around when doors that won't open.
- A nerve so focused on dreams and the guts to leave your comfort zone.
- Waling boldly where other fear to tread.
- Charging ahead when reason indicates otherwise.
- Attempt things that no one had tried before.
- Ability to conclude on equal number of supporting ideas with opposing ideas.
- Stretching the boundaries of own creative imagination.

Most start-up founders and innovators behave as wilful children, where they have not exited their childhood chutzpah even as adults. Success is a lousy teacher. It seduces smart people to thinking they can't lose.

Right but not correct judgments

There is a general reasoning that academic subjects like science and maths create a distinct advantage for disruption and innovation. But the nations considered to be most successful in innovation start-ups do not score high ranking in these subjects.

There is a misjudged conclusion that any start-up struggles due to shortage of money, but it is well established that it is the start-ups that attracts money at its stages of expansion and valuation.

Adults think that children are to be taught discipline and to follow instructions, but it destroys the power of Chutzpah with an early destruction of their creativity.

Most of the established firms fail in absence of speed, technology, guts and leanness, where most of the start-ups fail in absence of a future vision, HR, values and governance.

An extremely successful technical education results in successful innovation, but most of the founders of successful start-ups were back benchers or drop-outs from colleges who were highly problematic to their teachers.

Many children so laggards in the classes and disliked by their teachers, were found gusty, extrovert, resilient, audacious, sociable and brazen, the same adjectives we use to describe our maverick entrepreneurs.

As adults, when we behave with Chutzpah, we are reverting to the daring and cheeky children we once were.

The conventional belief that those brilliant brains are from the front bench is proven wrong, as the best brains were found on the last bench of the classrooms.

A child so eager to feel the rain, so curious to jump and play in water, crawling on the floor in full force to reach-out a toy or ball, expressing his full resistance once rejecting him a chocolate, a child tearing away his animal book in resistance to instruction, we miss all these during schooling, and more when we enter higher colleges, resulting a total exit from this childhood Chutzpah.

Children are to be raised in high-risk situation than in insulated and protective environments. Israel ranks third among the best countries to raise a family, far ahead with France at twenty, US at forty and Brazil as the last, despite children living in a high situation of close proximity to cross-border terrorism and war mongers across borders. It is just few hundred feet close to Syria, Lebanon and Hezbollah. Around Gaza strip is exposed to missile attacks and walking in the streets around Jerusalem, one has to fear for suicide bombers. A series of terror attacks in Paris, locals were asked to stay home with the entire city was dark and empty. A similar situation in Brussels, city was shut for four days without offices, schools and transports. In Israel, surrounded by hostile neighbours with close proximity to terror outfits, rocket and mortar sprays are not strange, schools and offices still work as usual except when sirens blare. In schools, children address teachers by their first name so that it narrows down the distance between and teacher to student that clears all barriers to ask anything about everything.

As a result children are raised without fear and childhoods are purposely shaped with challenges and risks, in a culture that encourages and rewards Chutzpah. Innovation is a result of combining eagerness, curiosity and disruptive mindset of childhood with maturity, creativity, imagination and vision of an adult. It is important to preserve these childhood attributes across the campus and workplace. Henry Ford said, one has to get out of any fear because the one who fears the future, fears failure hence limits his efforts. Failure is the only opportunity more intelligently to begin again. No disgrace to honest failure, but it is disgrace to fearing to fail. This demands students in professional colleges and universities to carry forward their childhood's disruptive mindset to fostering innovation.

Schooling has to motivate children to fail and fall, so they quickly get back and fail again. One cannot rise up unless once knocked down. Those who not fail, pay a price as adults. It helps to withstand the unpredictability and unforeseen crisis in future life and work. Hence it is important not to destroy, but to sail forward without losing the childhood chutzpah.

Elon Musk said, 'If things are not failing, you are not innovating enough'. In the words of Confucius, 'our greatest glory is not in never falling, but rising every time we fall'. Chutzpah is recognized as the most suitable and challenging behaviour and skills for the future by WEF-2019 in Davos.

Military Training

Most of those start-up founders and innovators carry a strong attribute of Military elite forces, especially in areas like the nerve, daring, courage, self-confidence and offending and assaulting spirit. Examples are US Marine Seals, IDF Elite forces. In Israel, Elite military forces like Talpiot and Unit 8200 are best training grounds for university students who go through tough training partly in Military operations and rest in innovations, especially in areas like upgrading arms, strike efficiency, new technologies like cyber security, surveillance, missile shield, satellite mapping, AI supported sensors and drones, network communication, robotics etc. After three years of service, the cadets are free to either continue with military service or to leave for private sector. Today an internship term with Unit 8200 merits a cadet to secure a private job than any university or technical degrees. As a result of the military's influence on the founders, every such new start-up is founded with a spirit of business patriotism and intangible objectives of jobs creation, compliance to regulations and to improve livelihoods which no doubt ensures the tangible goal of profit.

The military training at Talpiot or Unit 8200 transforms a cadet to stretch his willpower to face adverse situations, also to rise up from defeats and failures to make repeated efforts until he achieves something impossible goal or nearest to that. It also gives practical lessons of to be ready with his backpack and tools within short notice and get ready for hours long walking through deserts and forests carrying limited food and water. Perhaps the next test could be pushing him to deep water to learn swimming. Towards the final pass-out, the cadet becomes a true crisis-tested individual capable of fighting and winning any difficult surrounding, which shapes up an unyielding and relentless individual who cannot accept nothing but success. They are trained to encounter the challenges and risks that do not exist, but a probability of future.

The recruits are instructed to invent new weapons and military technology for which the cadets have to ask for help and materials to begin his work, but without external help. It gives a message that during helpless situations and difficulties, we are alone with nobody to help. They have to develop tools that minimise the casualty to fellow soldiers, but maximum destruction to the enemies. It could be a medical invention which can mobilise injured soldiers the fastest way to the base camps. Talpiot and Unit 8200 deploys the advanced technologies like AI, Machine learning, Avionics and Satellite mapping to training the cadets. It is surprising to note that most of the founders, both men and women of successful technology start-up were once trained at IDF Elite forces. This has gained Israel a reputation for first-choice for US technology giants either in acquisition of start-ups or employment in Innovation labs. Working with military commanders, helps to develop confidence and courage without any fear to approach and communicate with high level tough individuals. Education combined with military training garners a rare but unique perspective that helps one to achieve a balanced maturity at a young age. There is a common thread between a commander and innovator; a mix of fearlessness, consistency, nerve and 'a never give-up' behaviour.

Israel is a country that did not exist before, is independent since the last seven decades, which has the highest per-capita start-ups than any other country in the world. In Israel, start-up technologies accounted to

27% of its total exports in 2018, the single largest contributor to GDP. The country boasts the second largest number of unicorns $.1 Bil valuation in the world after United States.

Gordon Moore and Robert Noyce, the founders of Intel and Andrew Grove, Intel's legendary CEO were Jews. Intel remains without worth any competition since its founding in July 1968. Its core business is Semi-conductor chips and Microprocessors, the most inevitable component in a Personal computer.

After HP and Lenovo, Dell is the world's third largest selling computer, with a turnover of $.92 Bil revenue in 2020, was founded by Michael Dell, an American Jew in 1984 with a seed capital of $1000, when he was a student at Uni of Texas. Was it not a disruptive, audacious and daring attribute of an adult chutzpah?

Marc Zuckerberg was a college drop-out when he founded Facebook in 2004 while at Harvard College. Sergey Brin and Larry Page were Stanford batch mates when they dropped out to start Google in 1998. All of them Marc, Sergey and Larry were Jews who shared a similar classroom conflict with an equal impatience and audacity, a sign of an adult chutzpah.

No wonder Jews make 29 percent of Nobel winners, despite a miniscule of 0.2 percent of world's population.

4 What Drives an Innovation Culture?

A mindset not so organized and disciplined, an attitude of hurry and impatience, a behaviour of questioning everything that existed, a temptation to break the rules and norms, challenging own assumptions and beliefs, what ignites disruption and innovation is the below attributes, which can be noticed in most of the reckless adults during their childhood.

- Ignoring negativity of friends and family.
- Zig-zaging around when doors that won't open.
- A nerve to fulfil our dreams and the guts to leave your comfort zone.
- Walking boldly where others fear to tread.
- Charging ahead when reason indicates otherwise.
- Attempt things no one has ever tried before.
- Shamelessly seeking out anyone and anything that helps us to achieve our goal.
- Stretching the boundaries of creative imagination.
- Break the established norms.
- Most difficult to change and convince.
- A habit of talking abrupt and tough, with no sugar-coated dialogues.
- Impatient, eager and curious, same time very resilient.
- Ability to stick and hold back, also jumpstart to new ideas.
- Eccentric, highly imaginative and embraced to dreamful wishes.

- Ability to stand frequent falls and defeats, more vigorous in rising from failures.
- Takes strength not from success, but from struggles, falls and hardships.

Most start-up innovators are from technical education, with many of them either drop-outs or backbenchers, and surprisingly their motivation and development were attained not from classrooms and teachers, but what they learnt outside the classrooms.

Though science and mathematics are the basic foundation of a technical education, it conflicts with the reality that most innovators had a classroom crisis with these subjects and also with their related faculties.

When most successful students were dreaming deep into making a career with their most passionate subjects, these drop-outs and backbenchers were dreaming of unknown fortunes that demanded by an uncertain future. On the other side, the latter possessed high level of optimism and courage than those first benchers.

It is a reality as we see that those reasonable and outstanding students adapt to the world's existing opportunities obediently and the unreasonable and backward students persist in trying the world to adapt to themselves in conflict with available opportunities, then all the progress depends on those unreasonable and backwards. See those successful start-up innovators, it is surprising to see that they were not those brilliant students in their classroom or who settled with an available opportunity.

Success in classroom does not guarantee any success in future life. A study reveals that those successful students made average or next level success in future life, it was those backbenchers who made far more successful future, with a more impact to the society.

Henry Ford attended a one-room school for eight years and completed an apprenticeship for 2-3 years but his deep thirst for motor car made him a great inventor of Model-T20 and reducing its cost as affordable to common man through assembly line automation and by eliminating excess weight and parts. Bill Gates did not have a college degree. He was enrolled at Harvard to study law but changed to graduate computer course and dropped off before completion. Sergy Brin and Larry Page were together at Stanford to study Computer Engineering but left the campus halfway to start the search engine-Google. Steve Jobs attended Reed college in 1972 but left halfway to travel to India and got enlightened to Zen Buddhism before joining Apple at its founding stage. Robert Iger, the legendary Chairman of Walt Disney Co had just a college degree. Marc Zuckerberg, the founder and chairman of Facebook, did not complete his degree at Harvard, which was honoured afterwards to him.

Vision Brains of Backbenchers and Drop-outs

What we believed right from our past experience that people either enter inherited business or start new ones which they were familiar and knew before, is proven wrong. Start-up founders did never know about their new business before, neither qualified nor with any academic brilliance.

Present owners of Walmart had a deep upbringing and mentoring in their retail companies, but not true with Jeff Bezos of the e-commerce retail giant Amazon. Unlike the founder Henry Ford, Edsel and Henry Ford-II had already acquired good knowledge of cars from their early age, but Windows O/S was unknown to Bill Gates until he discovered it. The present family owners of JP Morgan were born with a Banking DNA, whereas Sergy Brin and Larry Page did not know about Search engines and Android until they invented them. DuPont had an inheritance of successors who knew about Chemicals and life sciences from birth, where the any past knowledge was not the rule of law for an orphan up-bring like Steve Jobs of Apple and Pixar.

Best students have a fire in their belly, with deep eagerness, curiosity and impatience. Most of them are also so weird, daring, bold, cheeky, naughty, creative and audacious dreamers. They do not guarantee to be obedient and disciplined as students. Hence forcing them towards what to learn and what to think is unlikely to be practical and successful. By doing so, they push backwards in syllabus studies and disliked by teachers as problems that gradually cause to a classroom crisis leaving them an option between remaining as backbenchers or becoming drop-outs. As grown-ups they are not filled with too much of past academic knowledge, but in contrast their mind is too much engaged and occupied with dreams of an unknown and uncertain future. They are the right DNA to become future innovators.

Backbenchers are generally problematic to the faculties and written down by institutions, where they possess a hidden treasure of creativity and innovation than their frontbench colleagues. If an exemplary syllabus score is the merit to secure a job, it is the soft skills that qualify an employee to grow faster and be successful in new positions. In contrast, it is the backbenchers mostly possess better soft skills than frontbenchers. The discrimination between these two categories can be equalled when the education model changes from focusing syllabus towards focus on students.

These laggards in classrooms are generally rated to fail in campus recruitments, not because they were weak in academics but for lack of discipline and obedience. On the other side most of the successful businessmen were largely those backbenchers or dropouts, but they possessed extraordinary soft skills of being extrovert, audacious, resilient and smart in decisions and relationship. Same time, we have to see where those backbenchers and dropouts turn if they have no resources to start business? Failure in securing job or absence of capital to start a business, they naturally turn to internet abuses and frauds, becoming a sin for the society and nation. This segment carries an admirable mindset and spirit required for entrepreneurs, who can be very successful in innovation start-ups, where money is not an obstacle to begin with.

Those brilliant students in classrooms dream for a good employment after studies, but not true with those backbenchers and drop-outs. In contrast, employment was not any priority for those backbenchers and drop-outs, where not so with those frontbenchers.

Frontbenchers have short-term dream about a well known employer with high entry-level salary package, where it is not anything like big money but long-vision accomplishment that attracted those backbenchers.

Brilliant students are more obedient and disciplined at workplaces, where laggards get into questions and conflicts with bosses and procedures. The former group get along well with bosses but not with subordinates, where latter group get along well with subordinates but not so with bosses.

Brilliant students tend to follow short-cut methods by stealing good results of subordinates to raise themselves, but those backbenchers do not take credit at the cost of his fellow team. Frontbenchers strictly follow the company rules, but laggards use more common sense and compromise on rules to retain good employees and customers in long term. Brilliant students hesitate to stand by the mistakes of their subordinates, but not so with laggards if for a good cause.

Backbenchers create humour and adventure around their workplace, under whom subordinates enjoy and embrace even difficult and unassigned tasks, where money does not stand a factor of motivation. They spread courage and self-confidence, and make more winners by raising ordinary men to perform extra-ordinary tasks. This is not same with frontbenchers.

If brilliant students are dreaming for a coveted job, now more than half of the desired core skills considered so important for many of the jobs are not crucial for the same jobs in the wake of 2020. Today social skills like emotional intelligence, attitude, behaviour and mentoring are in higher demand than narrow technical skills such as programming, machine operation or assembling. As a result knowledge of maths and science or programming experience are not the core requirement for a technical job. it is not performing robotic jobs or repeating just same work, but skilled computing system that can perform multiple tasks.

Start-up founders do not have any profit-first objective like others entering businesses. For them profit is a long-term goal, where their core focus is to increase the enterprise value and scaling up the business. Gradually, they keep offloading ownership to anchor investors and VCs which in turn keep the enterprise value growing up and also higher valuation for their declining stake. As investors do not engage with the management, the founders enjoy an increasing rate of their trust and independence in running the business and to scale-up the growth and expansion. They had demonstrated a much long-term vision and business ethics than non-technology enterprises which follow an 'invest and take back' business policy. These founders, mostly written-off as problematic to teachers and with classroom conflicts turn to be business visionaries with high business ethics, good examples of teamwork, relation, resilience and employee motivation where profit does not come any first priority.

Drop-outs and backbenchers pool to become as large as 25% or more of the total frontbenchers. Still this 25% is not that a small number to be ignored. If half of them could be rehabilitated to our national mainstream, this group gets reduced by half which is in fact turning a reverse resource to become a national asset that makes a positive patriotic contribution to the country. If population was once a liability for the country, today it has become an asset; next opportunity for the country is to convert the backbenchers to an asset of the country. What looks impossible for frontbenchers, it remains not that difficult for backbenchers and dropouts. If anything looks difficult, it becomes more difficult to do and whatever looks possible to do, it becomes less difficult to do where the difference is one's attitude and perspective. Any survey on world's most successful innovators, what was most common among them was that they were not those brilliant students in their classrooms and whomever called to be brilliant were not any innovators.

Technical and Science universities shall list those students failing to secure campus recruitment and secure training under Military's Innovation cell which will mould their body and mind to that of a soldier with deep sense of patriotism. This will prevent them from turning to technology fraud and abuses and shape them to become new class of smart start-up entrepreneurs.

B-School academics were hardly any successful corporate leaders, where we can see several corporate leaders as outstanding guest speakers in B-Schools. Similarly Technology academics were hardly any start-up founders, also those brilliant students from technology campuses. If we see those successful start-up founders, they were backbenchers or drop-outs, who were not that obedient either to their parents or teachers, but with an eagerness to new experiments and trials, outside what is taught in classrooms. Parents get them admitted to ivy colleges dreaming an outstanding career, but they knit their dreams around entrepreneurship, which is today mostly of an unknown future. If the technology is rewriting every algorithm of education, workplace, business, and life, why it cannot rewrite the norms and rules that drive disruption and innovation? The backbenchers, drop-outs and laggards in the technical universities open a huge untapped resource for disruption and innovation.

Migration drives innovation

US is the most sought after destination for people to migrate and its most brilliant brain pool is made of immigrants. Israel is a country founded by migrant Jews who came from as many as sixty seven countries and as a result it has become a cradle of start-up innovations with highest per-capita start-ups and VCs in the world. It is a fact that people who migrated away from their home prospered than those remained around their birthplace. This acceleration is more deeper when they migrate outside their country. If the fear for losing restricts the conventional businesses from expansion, migrants have nothing to lose hence very aggressive in venturing out.

In our history, expeditors not only invaded other regions, but they also brought their knowledge, methods and skills in farming and tooling. This helped in exchange of culture, food habits, dress code, art and literature, language, technology and medicines. With large rate of migration happening to cities, the density also drives innovation. With more and more people getting liberated from extreme poverty, and were to earn better wages, with food, shelter, clothing, healthcare and education becoming more affordable, it is technology that enabled to this achievement more than anything else. For example, mobile phone penetration and connection alone has contributed to this achievement. Migration rolls out diversity in thinking and ideas, which once shared, pooled together accomplish audacious goals.

Immigrants pool a great asset for the country's group diversity which rolls-out creativity, Innovation and entrepreneurship. In US alone, second generation immigrants shore up to 40 percent of Fortune 500, not to mention about the founders of new start-up firms mostly of foreign born or children to them. They are open to take risk than those home-grown, as they have nothing to lose- a name or shame. They are adaptable fast to the new land, and willing to exit ny comfort zone with a burning aspiration in life. They are reaching a stage of close to running governments in US, UK and not a different story in Israel and Canada.

Digital Technology, the platform for start-ups

With an increase in knowledge which changed the world, today digital technology is changing is faster, where one can communicate anything from anywhere at no cost. With technology so widely applied in Banking, the future will require only banking but no banks. With so many learning apps in the education sector, the future will require only learning than any schools and campuses. With technology having conquered the vast retail sector, the future is for e-commerce and online shopping than retail stores. The advent of virtual and augmented reality in space, customers can choose a luxury car or furniture without visiting a showroom.

During the manufacturing age, products were launched after intensive customer surveys, where digital technology fosters a culture that products and features are introduced without having asked for. Cell phones were used to talk, but the data support has helped companies to come out with features required for the future without anyone having asking for. What's App, Twitter, Facebook or messaging were just invented and launched which customers embraced full heartedly. What's App and Zoom redefined the way business was conducted and the customers make more money than Apple, Samsung and the facilitators.

These technology companies like Apple, Amazon, Facebook and Google did not exist twenty five years back, and the same way we cannot foresee those companies which will dominate our planet after a decade or two. Technology cycles are short-lived than brand cycles, hence unless frequently upgraded or reinvented, it will perish and extinct. This opens up for a large possibility, space and opportunity for new technology start-ups in future with a high rate of mortality and this will increase in multiples on its way forward.

Food delivery is a whopping US.35 Bil/p.a. in US alone and it is one of the largest job creators in the world. Cloud kitchen will lead a new revolution and cost benefit in the online food delivery business. Uber offers a chauffer driven car for just half the cost of a taxi hire and without any risk of an own car. Vanguard, Softbank, Naspers, TPG and such venture capitals are knocking every closed door of a start-up lab. Indian origin American VC investor Vinod Khosla is a frequent traveller into the streets of Tel Aviv to grab those eccentric youths in Jeans and T'Shirts with backpack to shop their start-ups.

AI and Cloud enabled to do away with the conventional rule of large server rooms for data storage which is prone to internet viruses and hacking, and replaced with remote stored Cloud data storage with full internet security at a fractional cost and convenience. It also connects all stages of logistics status tracking to both seller and buyer. It can also track an individual's past purchase and payment behaviour, his personal data, medical and travelling pattern, diet preferences, income group, and many more.

US technology giants are shopping around the start-up hypermarket streets of Tel Aviv and Bangalore looking for acquisitions or investing.

5 The Might of AI and the Convergent Technologies

Internet is among the few things we have built that we don't truly understand. It began as a means of electronic information reporting has transformed to an important universal networking and data storage facility, supported by a computer which from a room-sized monster to a miniature from of palm-sized devise despite its memory and storage grown in a multiple pace. Internet helps us to buy anything online, plan our travel and stay, expand relationship, to find jobs, remote working, search information, order taxis, paying bills, online education and banking transactions without going out. It is the world's largest space without any regulation. Never before in our history, we have so many people, from so many locations, with so much power at their fingertips. It makes us many times more efficient, productive and creative. As a result, working has become more exciting, with relationship, sharing and collaborating between people without meeting each other.

Everything that internet touch will transform rapidly, as we had seen in e-commerce, car-hire, food delivery, education and autonomous cars. Being an unregulated universal platform, it is going to reduce the role of governments because we had seen that traditional political parties no longer fulfil the people's political and governance needs. Governments restrict freedom and rights, with increase in taxes and corruption, these technologies are coming to the citizens almost free and plenty and also in equality without discrimination of rich or poor.

AI-Artificial Intelligence; an Introduction

John McCarthy (1927-2011), was an American computer scientist and cognitive scientist. McCarthy was one of the founders of the discipline of artificial intelligence. He co-authored the document that coined the term "artificial intelligence" (AI), developed the Lisp programming language family, significantly influenced the design of the ALGOL programming language, popularized time-sharing, invented garbage collection, and was very influential in the early development of AI.

Artificial intelligence is intelligence demonstrated by machines, unlike the natural intelligence displayed by humans and animals, which involves consciousness and emotionality. *AI* is a wide-ranging branch of computer science concerned with building smart machines capable of performing tasks that typically require human *intelligence.* It is the endeavour to replicate or simulate human *intelligence* in machines.

AI is the future of how Humans, Industries, organizations will consume software and IT systems. It has started to transform how humans consume services, how industries operate, manufacture and market products. "AI is an area of computer science that emphasizes the creation of intelligent machines that works and reacts like humans." "It is the capability of a machine to imitate the intelligent human behaviour." One of the most popular AI Applications is the Google search engine. Artificial intelligence is widely used to provide personalised recommendations to people, based for example on their previous searches and purchases or other online behaviour. AI is hugely important in commerce: optimising products, planning inventory, logistics etc. A good example is how an Amazon delivery is tracked, how a food delivery company can track the past orders of a customer, his credit card details, eating habits, etc. AI can help Banks to track a client's other borrowings and default status when he applies for a fresh loan or credit card.

When AI surpasses humanity in general intelligence and becomes «super-intelligent», then it could become difficult or impossible for humans to control. An example is when an AI enabled robot disconnects from controls, it could turn destructive to other facilities around including lives, so perhaps the fate of humanity depend on the actions of a future machine super-intelligence. Imagine a Robotic controlled spacecraft or satellite go out of control and collapse over a civilian community, what it can cost to humanity? AI stretches its reach to as diverse areas from unemployment, safety of autonomous cars, life extension and encoding the genomic data.

AI- Seven Stages of Development

1. Reactive Machines

These are the oldest forms of AI systems that have extremely limited capability. They emulate the human mind's ability to respond to different kinds of stimuli. These machines do not have memory-based functionality. This means such machines cannot use previously gained experiences to inform their present actions, i.e., these machines do not have the ability to "learn." A popular example of a reactive AI machine is IBM's Deep Blue, a machine that beat chess Grandmaster Garry Kasparov in 1997.

2. Limited Memory

Limited memory machines are machines that, in addition to having the capabilities of purely reactive machines, are also capable of learning from historical data to make decisions. Nearly all existing applications that we know come under this category of AI. All present-day AI systems, such as those using deep learning, are trained by large volumes of training data that they store in their memory to form a reference model for solving future problems. For instance, an image recognition AI is trained using thousands of pictures and their labels to teach it to name objects it scans. When an image is scanned by such an AI, it uses the training images as references to understand the contents of the image presented to it, and based on its "learning experience" it labels new images with increasing accuracy.

Almost all present-day AI applications, from chatbots and virtual assistants to self-driving vehicles are all driven by limited memory AI.

3. Theory of Mind

While the previous two types of AI have been and are found in abundance, the next two types of AI exist, for now, either as a concept or a work in progress. Theory of mind AI is the next level of AI systems that researchers are currently engaged in innovating. A theory of mind level AI will be able to better understand the entities it is interacting with by discerning their needs, emotions, beliefs, and thought processes. While artificial emotional intelligence is already a budding industry and an area of interest for leading AI researchers, achieving Theory of mind level of AI will require development in other branches of AI as well. This is because to truly understand human needs, AI machines will have to perceive human as individual whose minds can be shaped by multiple factors, essentially "understanding" humans.

4. Self-aware

This is the final stage of AI development which currently exists only hypothetically. Self-aware AI, which, self explanatorily, is an AI that has evolved to be so akin to the human brain that it has developed self-awareness. Creating this type of Ai, which is decades, if not centuries away from materializing, is and will always be the ultimate objective of all AI research. This type of AI will not only be able to understand and evoke emotions in those it interacts with, but also have emotions, needs, beliefs, and potentially desires of its own. And this is the type of AI that doomsayers of the technology are wary of. Although the development of self-aware can potentially boost our progress as a civilization by leaps and bounds, it can also potentially lead to catastrophe. This is because once self-aware, the AI would be capable of having ideas like self-preservation which may directly or indirectly spell the end for humanity, as such an entity could easily outsmart the intellect of any human being and plot elaborate schemes to take over humanity.

The alternate system of classification that is more generally used in tech parlance is the classification of the technology into Artificial Narrow Intelligence (ANI), Artificial General Intelligence (AGI), and Artificial Super-intelligence (ASI).

5. Artificial Narrow Intelligence (ANI)

This type of artificial intelligence represents all the existing AI, including even the most complicated and capable AI that has ever been created to date. Artificial narrow intelligence refers to AI systems that can only perform a specific task autonomously using human-like capabilities. These machines can do nothing more than what they are programmed to do, and thus have a very limited or narrow range of competencies. According to the aforementioned system of classification, these systems correspond to all the reactive and limited memory AI. Even the most complex AI that uses machine learning and deep learning to teach itself falls under ANI.

6. Artificial General Intelligence (AGI)

Artificial General Intelligence is the ability of an AI agent to learn, perceive, understand, and function completely like a human being. These systems will be able to independently build multiple competencies and form connections and generalizations across domains, massively cutting down on time needed for training. This will make AI systems just as capable as humans by replicating our multi-functional capabilities.

7. Artificial Super-intelligence (ASI)

The development of Artificial Super-intelligence will probably mark the pinnacle of AI research, as AGI will become by far the most capable forms of intelligence on earth. ASI, in addition to replicating the multi-faceted intelligence of human beings, will be exceedingly better at everything they do because of overwhelmingly greater memory, faster data processing and analysis, and decision-making capabilities. The development of AGI and ASI will lead to a scenario most popularly referred to as the singularity. And while the potential of having such powerful machines at our disposal seems appealing, these machines may also threaten our existence or at the very least, our way of life.

At this point, it is hard to picture the state of our world when more advanced types of AI come into being. However, it is clear that there is a long way to get there as the current state of AI development compared to where it is projected to go is still in its rudimentary stage. For those holding a negative outlook for the future of AI, this means that now is a little too soon to be worrying about the singularity, and there's still time to ensure AI safety. And for those who are optimistic about the future of AI, the fact that we've merely scratched the surface of AI development makes the future even more exciting. It is amazing to note that if AI has grown to its seventh stage of ASI within a short span of the last three decades and still growing, and with much shorter cycle of continued innovation, where it will reach by the end of next decade and another two? Perhaps it could collaborate with our ancient transcend intelligence- the sixth sense; in other words an ability to rise above human senses towards an invisible future. That is what AI could play in our future lives.

Gradually with more data getting distributed across e-commerce, online banking, food delivery and other services, AI is creating a wide umbrella over people, which reminds us the trend in our past purchases, genomic test results, eating habits, preferred travel spots and clothing preferences with size details and many more which we hardly knew. This leads to a situation that as much as this technology is so helpful to make life easy, it is still our worst enemy, which destroys all privacies and discretions of oneself that an individual will like to keep.

AI is a shift from computers having only logical intelligence to that also have an emotional intelligence; ie, it is funny, loving and creative which can either equal or surpass the human abilities. The ever-increasing might of AI and its invisible presence in every sector and humans, those who adapt to it will prosper and those who do not will go bankrupt.

AI was once considered to be a distant future technology, which came early to our life in a human perspective. It was two researchers by name Geoff Hinton and Kai Yu who brought AI to the forefront of our daily lives and in the process, created billion worth of new businesses. One day soon, when computers and sensors are safely driving our roads, advanced robotics replace factory workers, elder care and drivers, 3-D Printing replaces assembling and supply chain, automation rules on e-commerce, banking and government services, AI will put still harder grips in our lives without privacy and discretion.

ML-Machine Learning

Machine learning is an application of artificial intelligence (AI) that provides systems the ability to automatically learn and improve from experience without being explicitly programmed. Machine learning focuses on the development of computer programs that can access data and use it to learn for themselves. The process of learning begins with observations or data, such as examples, direct experience, or instruction, in order to look for patterns in data and make better decisions in the future based on the examples that we provide. The primary aim is to allow the computers learn automatically without human intervention or assistance and adjust actions accordingly. It can reset the available scattered data from its memory to a sequence in order to reach future events.

Machine learning is the ability to accurately perform new, unseen tasks, built on known properties learnt from training of historic data, and based on prediction, which enables analysis of massive quantities of data. While it generally delivers faster, more accurate results in order to identify profitable opportunities or dangerous risks, it may also require additional time and resources to train it properly. Combining machine learning with AI and cognitive technologies can make it even more effective in processing large volumes of information including prediction of weather, natural calamities and future economic trends.

Deep learning is a sub-sect of ML based on neural net technology. It allows a machine to discover new patterns without being exposed to any historical or training data. Leading start-up in this space is Deep-Mind bought by Google in 2014 for $.500 Mil.

IoT-The Internet of things

IoT describes the network of physical objects, so known as, "things", that are embedded with sensors, software, and other technologies that is used for the purpose of connecting and exchanging data with other devices and systems over the internet. Towards automation, all the data in complicated order get collected by IoT and turns them to next process of sequence and actions without human intervention. This can sense and determine driver's behaviour data, health analysis, analyse smart grid for energy and water, and many things. IoT is often imagined as a self-configuring wireless network of sensors interconnecting everything to one. This nervous system is the backbone of IoT, which interconnects cars, electric switches, thermostats etc through Internet which can trace your car keys, stolen things, to replenish items in fridge, groceries, etc. It gives commands to companies on raw materials and supply chains, also helps to reduce waste. It will change how we manufacture, sustain environment, logistics, recycle, water consumption, etc all plugged to achieve efficiencies as never before. IoT is connected to a range of sensors embedded in our mostly used electronic devises like home automation and security, appliances, TV and cars interconnected through Bluetooth, Wi-Fi or smart phones, which track our every activity, habit, conversation and movements leaving nothing as discretion and privacy.

Things have evolved due to the convergence of multiple technologies, real-time analytics, Machine learning, ubiquitous computing, commodity sensors and embedded systems.

Traditional fields of embedded systems, wireless sensor networks, control systems, automation (including home and building automation), and others all contribute to enabling the Internet of things. In the consumer market, IoT technology is most synonymous with products pertaining to the concept of the "smart home", including devices and appliances (such as lighting fixtures, thermostats, home security systems and cameras, and other home appliances) that support one or more common ecosystems, and can be controlled via devices associated with that ecosystem, such as smart phones and smart speakers. The IoT can also be used in healthcare systems. Despite all its advantages, the areas of concern and risk are related to privacy and security.

VR- Virtual Reality

AI has empowered retail to go online, with automation in ordering, paying and tracking its delivery, which clears a lot of time wasted, inconvenience of transport and parking. Once AI is converged with VR-Virtual Reality, a customer gets a 360 degree visual experience as in a showroom. In case a customer visiting a showroom physically, and by scanning his mobile phone at the entrance help him directed by a robot to the right slot where his required item of his choice, size and colour is stored. Once he exit with the item, the exit point senses and debit the amount to his bank account, which is automatically replenished with an order with the supplier, with no salesman or cashier.

VR facilitates a real-view experience of any tourist destination or locations in anywhere in the world without visiting there, saving money on travel, visa, hotels, food and transport. It enables us to experience a virtual program of Elvis Presley, classroom experience with virtual view of other universities and labs.

Further, this convergence of AI with VR enabled with AR, the shopping experience becomes most realistic inclusive of jewellery and furniture. McKinsey estimates that autonomous check-out will save retailers $.150-$380 Bil by 2025. Alibaba's cashier-less Hema Stores were tested in China even two years ahead of Amazon.

VR converged with AI gives a real-life classroom experience in education sector, especially when it is supported with 5G network and AR-Augmented Reality eye wear, it gives a 360 degree view of learning, that can convert a classroom to a real world experience. This enables deep learning and an extended memory. As all these technologies are accessible and affordable practically at no cost, education reaches out to everyone, with an uninterrupted flow of renewable energy, almost free of cost. Like how AR and VR could help avoiding a physical visit to a car or furniture showroom, it can also enable anyone to enjoy a virtual view of any tourism spot in the world, which consequentially could disrupt the tourism, hotel and aviation sector.

Advanced Robotics

Robots are essentially hardware controlled by AI software. The more advanced the software, robots become stable and more sensitive of their tasks. Lethal robots are already drafted to militaries, especially IDF which patrols the borders, capable of firing at infiltrators and sending signals and pictures back to the base command. In 2007 Stuxnet computer virus destabilised critical centrifuges out of control at Natanz, a secret uranium enrichment facility in Iran, and in another couple of months US and Israeli forces were able to remotely hack 1000 out of 5000 centrifuges spinning uranium enrichment in Iran.

One side these future technologies demand very high skilled workforce while eliminating those low skilled jobs. Today the automobile sector had already employed a large number of robots in assembly lines; so with electronics like Apple, Samsung, LG and others with a huge advantage in cost and time. Robots are one-time capital of $.28000 which do not require wages, holidays, shifts, paid vacation and healthcare, besides end-service benefits as in the case of workers. They work 24X7 without washroom breaks.

Daimler Financial Services' Sarah handles customers in areas of financing, leasing and insuring a car. Such an AI to AI negotiation, no human required. Pepper was the name of a humanoid robot launched by Softbank in 2010, so cute in white plastic body, four feet tall with two black eyes and a mermaid-tailed base. Its concept was to help humans enjoy life, greeting clients at Pizza Hut in Singapore, serving ice cream in Japan and she can dance with customers in an electronic store in Palo Alto. Walmart employs robots for shelf-stocking, Best Buy uses a robo-cashier and Lowe's Home store LoweBots, a large iPad on wheels to help customers to locate the specific items of their choice. Starship Technologies, a start-up by Skype founders Janus Friis and Ahti Heinla has an AI powered general purpose home delivery robot with fifty thousand sold in hundred cities in twenty countries.

Robots were employed in assembling products, especially electronics and cars, which used to repeat same job as programmed. But today, the new generation AI-linked advanced robots can think, sense, and behave in a customized manner. Over the next decade, robots will enter into healthcare, replacing doctors in routine surgeries and supplementing nurses in eldercare where it can talk empathetically and sensitive to seniors living alone. Given the fact that global market for unskilled labour is worth several millions of dollars, that makes a huge opportunity for robots. McDonalds has successfully adopted automatic order taking at its counters, also robots to cook and cook burgers in ten seconds, besides pommes fries.

Today Robots are AI-driven, which sense what is required. In homecare, robots speak to elders with empathy and politeness giving great relief to the patients, besides the timing for prescribed medicine and food. It can open door, fold laundry, take out drink from fridge and clean the house. With a large part of our population turning aged, robots are becoming in greater demand. Very soon, robots will drive trucks, taxis to warehouse and retail helpers and adapt to high-skill jobs. BMW achieved an 85 percent increase in productivity when the replaced their low-skilled assembly line process with human/robot teams. More than robots taking away human jobs, human are likely to replace additional jobs with the help of robots, that usually few men to do multiple tasks with robotic assistance.

Autonomous cars are driverless, driven by robots which address to 50Mil auto accidents a year across the world, with over 1.2Mil deaths, where sensors connected to AI can break automatically with line discipline in full compliance to traffic rules. Accidents cots 50Bil hours spent on road and $.230Bil, almost 2-3% of GDP due to human driver error. Against human versus robot, autonomous drivers began to outperform best race car drivers. Drivers-driven cars looks more human-friendly and feel safe inside the cabin, where a driverless car looks a monster, a machine to which it is too risky to leave our destiny to a software with no human control. This will make sure that all of us will use cars, without owning them, not washing and insuring them. The present range of cars from entry level to luxury and high-performance ones which can be counted to hundreds will shrink to just ten models.

Industrial robots can increase the production many folds, with better speed, efficiency and costs. In 1950 world GDP was roughly 4Tril dollars, in 2008 it rose to 61 tril with automation replacing manual work. Toyota produces 500 cars a day with less than 400 workers with automation. Now automation is entering into every household which will result many times increase in global economy. People in skilled industries are less likely to be replaced by robots, and more likely to be assisted by them.

These convergent technologies reinforce and empower another one- the rise of Cloud computing and Quantum computing enable more capable and multi-present AI which in turn allows to progressive robots with all human gestures and far higher performance. From now, robots will look and behave human-like, and also do human-like jobs and with robots becoming more smarter than humans, can make us helpless victims in our own planet. As we cannot think of living without our smart phone, very soon it looks difficult to imagine without robots as our friends and companions. By next decade, machines will exceed humanity.

If computer on wheels can drive away the fuel-injected automobiles from our streets, the Computer on robots poses a grave challenge to the present genomic humans in our planet. Humanoid robots in coming decade will be better, sharper and smarter than, also less expensive and more obedient and collaborative than us.

3D Printing

If a computer can command a colour printer to print same as the image in its monitor, the printer senses and mixes the colours to match the image and get physically printed. It is the same case in photo printing. Earlier days, Paint manufacturers used to install computerised colour mixers at every retailer which adds a mix of strainers to base white to finally match the required colour. This helped companies and retailers to save in inventories to great economies. University of Southern California developed a large 3D-Printer which can extrude concrete for buildings at unbelievable costs with rapid speed. It is the newest form of digital manufacturing. Autodesk printed a motorcycle and aircraft engine. It can apply to anything from clothes, building panels to human organs.

Until two decades back, CNC routers, cutters and lasers were used to shape a piece of metal, plastic or wood in a subtractive process by slicing and dicing until the desired product is achieved. The 3D-Process is just opposite from subtractive method where every item is produced from a single material; to additive manufacturing which has a choice of using multiple materials without waste, saving in areas of logistics, vendor supplies and warehousing. This method has more options of experimenting, prototyping and alternatives which hardly cost anything, where computing is cheap, and getting almost free, besides scope for easy scaling up through cloud. With infinite computing coupled with 3D-Printing, a design made in China can be perfected in India and printed in Brazil and sold in Mexico, all the same day.

3-D Printing or additive manufacturing is a process which can change the conventional process of manufacturing- subtractive manufacturing which is cutting out / hollowing out a piece of metal or plastic with for instance a milling machine to a simplified format of making three dimensional solid objects from a digital file. It can print an accurate shape of object ranging from an automobile spare to aerospace component to as wide applications as human parts like knee ligament and elbow joint. It can substitute slaughtered meat with clone-cultured meat with great ecological, animal-friendly and health benefits. 3D printed units can assemble housing units that saves time and costs.

3D Printing can redefine the entire $.12 Tril global manufacturing sector, which results a substantial price benefit to the customer. The advantage is that shifting to 3D printing, it can eliminate production waste, avoid supply chain and no replacement of spare parts needed. 3D can customise a product once the mobile data is fed into it. Reebok and New Balance are examples of delivering customised products with speed and precision. GE had already adopted 3-D Printing into their production facilities. Other major companies which migrated to this technology are Boeing which made over 20,000 parts for its military and commercial planes, Nike, Ford- mostly spares, American Pearl (Jewels), DIY Rocket, Hasbro, Hersheys, etc. Adoption to 3D printing increases the productivity not by replacing human with machines, but rather by augmenting machines with humans.

Exponential technologies enable the small teams with the ability to tackle large problems. Same time, the world's biggest problems are also the world's biggest business opportunities. Online orders are changing to voice-driven commands like Amazon Echo, which is projected to leap from $.2.0Bil today to $.8Bil by 2025. A recent Zendest study reveals that a good customer service increases the possibility of a purchase by 42 percent, where a bad customer service translates to 52 percent of losing a sale.

3D Printing gives a great potential threat for China, the factory of the world. Despite all its advances for the last three decades, China's manufacturing sector is predominantly designed to produce largely cheap plastic goods from manufacturing and assembly lines, with a sizeable dependence on vendors, logistics and supply chain. 3D Printing eliminates these three areas of cost with a significant saving on manpower. This emerges an opportunity for another region like Vietnam, India, Indonesia, Philippines, Bangladesh and Thailand to replace their might. This has a ripple effect when an economically distressed China decides to call back its overseas debts.

Energy Storage

With Sun being the largest resource of energy for mankind, the last two decades saw a substantial growth in Solar power with its cost coming down as the cheapest source of energy, which could be almost free considering the government subsidies in order to preserve our planet from CO_2 emissions. Next as the poorest countries are located in high tropical regions, Solar power becomes the cheapest choice of energy which neither thermal, Hydro nor Nuclear sources could solve. With an accelerating speed in Solar Power and storage, the planet will have more renewable power than what we require, practically free of cost.

Like how oil and gas were major imports for developing world, Lithium is likely to replace as new imports. New innovations are very promising with cheaper and plentiful materials as sodium and water which are neither flammable nor lethal with a great potential to reduce the energy storage much lower levels. This together with the much lower costs and increasing production of PV cells and thinning down the silicon wafers will result a ten-fold cost reduction in solar power.

The automobile industry is moving fast to electric version with massive investments, where vehicles are adopting to driverless in equal pace. Modern material science changed the rules of energy storage with high capacity Lithium-ion batteries can power not only surface transport, but also railroads and aviation soon. It is growing to reach $.100 Bil by 2025. US, closely followed by China have highest investment in Lithium-ion batteries.

Ford alone has invested $.11Bil to electrify forty vehicles by 2022, Daimler invested little more on ten pure electric cars and forty hybrid models, with the largest being VW at $.40Bil to electrify forty vehicles by 2030. The total commitment in e-vehicles and hybrids is more than $.300Bil. This will rewrite the car as a combination of battery and software.

Next Gen Genomics

With extension of lifespan, developed countries are facing problems of managing the substantial funding required for the healthcare sector. The convergence of technologies like networks, AI and sensors overturn the medical diagnostics. 3D Printing and Robotics are re-writing the nature of medical procedures and AI, quantum computing and genomics are transforming the medicines by itself. With AI already into your mobile phone, very soon it is to become your doctor. Alphabet's healthcare division called Verily Life Science is developing sensors that can monitor our glucose to blood chemistry.

Synthetic biology is essentially the digital-enabled genetic engineering. Today it can manipulate DNA with computers, mix and match genetic code, spell and error check, shuffle pieces around and becoming drag-and-drop easy. DNA can be reprogrammed and Nature's original code can be swapped out for new, human written code. Anything we know manufacture industrially, we will eventually be able to assemble biologically to release custom-designed probiotics to balance our microbiome. Biotechnology is accelerating its speed in such a way that it doubles in power at half the price in every four months.

The way our technologies are transforming our planet, we will have everything we need in another two decades, no matter food, homes, clothes, water, energy, transport etc which are all becoming surplus and cheaper.

Data is the new Intel-Inside. Given that the 55000 trucks of UPS American fleet make 16 mil deliveries a day, there could be a threat of inefficient routing which can save up to eighty five million miles a year when applied with telematic, resulting a saving of $.2.55 Bil/year. Google is the most data driven than others right down to its hiring process.

Walmart launched its own satellite tracking inventory and supply chain transfers, which could crush the completion by consistently outperforming other chains like Sears and Kmart by 15% net gains.

Automation

Change brings challenges. But it's equally true that change brings opportunities. Automation has huge potential to change the nature of work, most obviously by freeing up workers from repetitive and tedious tasks. The challenge for enterprises and society at large is to ensure that automation is used to augment rather than replace the workforce, better jobs, not fewer. And, potentially, more jobs. As a recent analysis of artificial intelligence (AI) found, companies that use AI to support innovation rather than just cut costs are employment creators.

Accordingly, while many types of jobs will disappear, the need for employees will not. What is not as widely recognized as it could be is that for many jobs, the nature of the tasks required to perform them means that the human element will always be required. McKinsey estimate that by 2030, 375 million workers globally and more than 30 percent of the total workforce in the US will need to change jobs or upgrade their skills significantly. Assembly lines in factories, future vehicles, space research and traffic control are most potential fields for automation.

If automation can destroy about 85 Mil unskilled assembling jobs by 2025, Innovation can create 140Mil new smart jobs which demands heavily on re-skilling and up-skilling. This poses a big challenge to those talent-pool nations like India, China, Philippines and Vietnam to up-skill their vast manpower.

Global majors in AI- technologies

As the scope of artificial intelligence is growing, big tech organizations are investing a huge amount of money, towards the research and development of AI solutions. These organizations are in a race to achieve AI supremacy. In this article, we will explore the Top 5 companies with market share, leading the arena of AI.

01. **AWS:** The market Revenue of Amazon for the year 2019, accounted for US$2,130 million, with a market share of 7.1%. The company's cloud service remains the widely utilized cloud service and accounts for 35% of the company's revenue. With the record of cash flow, its parent e-Commerce business has the might of enough fund to support its AI and Cloud business than its rivals.
02. **Google** has a market revenue of US$2,450 million, with a market share of 8.2% in 2019. This is integrated in almost all its applications, be it Google Maps, YouTube, Google Search Engines or Google photos it provides customer experience. The company leverages technology such as Google Cloud, and Deep Learning for storing the user's data, and analysing the users' habits especially while recommending the videos. Deepmind, is an AI-company acquired

by Google which was formed in 2010, is leveraging machine learning for bringing new ideas in the field of healthcare, mathematics, and computing infrastructure. Google today has become the largest advertising earner followed by Facebook pushing back those print and visual media titans. It is working on "Next Big Things" technologies which are expected to change our life and habits in coming decades. When all auto majors are seriously working on E-cars, Google has far reached on a driverless car. Its Calico-California Life Co is researching in anti-ageing technologies.

No company like Google which had modified Internet to become an indispensible factor in our lives. It generates almost all its revenue from Internet advertising and with this cash cow, the company expands rapidly into other transformative projects like Space, Life extension, cloud, Youtube mostly at high speed and no cost. Google drives shifting of power from companies to consumers with the combined use of Internet, Mobile and Cloud computing.

03. **IBM:** With a market revenue of US$3,070 million and a market share of 10.3% in 2019, IBM is leading the artificial intelligence world. With its AI technology IBM Watson, it is utilized in all industries. IBM Watson is a data analytics processor that leverages natural language processing for analyzing human speech to understanding the meaning of human speech and syntax. With its data analytics capabilities, it enables for processing a large amount of data, human speech, and answering questions which were not possible earlier. With its machine learning capabilities to process the new data that is entered in the repository, IBM Watson delivers insightful outcomes to the users, especially in translation, transcription and voice detection. The main focus of IBM Watson is in its services for cyber-security and also to clear out unstructured data and documents by learning the subjects and pairing answers and questions.

04. **Microsoft:** From making series of Window processors for computers, to heavily investing in the research and development of AI, Microsoft's contribution is equated in both the evaluation of computers and that of Artificial Intelligence. For the year 2019, the market revenue of Microsoft accounted to be at US$2,279Mil, with a market share of 7.6%.

The company's Microsoft Cortana utilizes natural language processing to communicate with the users and Microsoft Bing utilizes image recognition techniques for recognizing images. The company's cloud platform Microsoft Azure deploys intelligent cloud services for seamless operations to the customers. The company's Microsoft 365 leverages data analytics for providing meaningful insights to the customer. In 2019, Microsoft funded the US$1 billion to the AI-research lab OpenAI, to research and explore the possibilities for amalgamation of GPT-3 and Microsoft Azure, for developing super-computing capabilities.

05. **Facebook:** Facebook has grown from a social network site to an organization whose prime focus remains on artificial intelligence. For the year 2019, Facebook, reported a market revenue of US$.1,979 million. It leverages AI technologies such as Facial Recognition, Language Translation, and machine learning algorithm, amongst others to improve the user's experience. It leverages AI for thwarting the cases of suicide, by scanning the posts and comments, and identifying which indicates depression and sadness.

    The company's research group Facebook AI Research (FAIR), is working in technologies such as conversational AI, Natural Language Processing, Computer vision, to provide breakthroughs in AI technology. The humanity is becoming cornered all around by AI and one handset phone is enough to leave you without personal discretion and privacy, which can track your eating habits, types of medicines, health reports, customized dimensions of clothes and shoes, bank account details, IT returns, besides all past purchases and ordering patterns.

The Changing algorithm of a Car

Car used to be an assembling of a number of hardware fitted together, until recently some disruptive new players from outside the automobile industry made it of software than hardware. They changed the rules from manufacturing, servicing to marketing to a new framework. The new E-cars are more of computers on four wheels with battery replacing the fuel tank.

Future car industry does not guarantee that it will remain with the present car manufacturers. More than existing manufacturers, it is changing fast as a product of specialisation under new innovators who are mostly from outside the car industry, where past experience and research do not weigh any head start.

The future car is likely to outsource the service and maintenance, recharge, repairs and spares which are not going to remain under the manufacturer any longer. Another decade, it will change the car ownership format to corporate which provides the car to the user as and when required, with or mostly without driver. Way-side oil-silt workshops will be an unknown business later.

Connectivity and the explosion of the Internet of Things mean that automakers can offer a more seamless, personalized ride. Although fully autonomous cars could be a decade or more away, advanced driver-assistance systems now use automated technology to make commutes easier. Through the use of sensors and cameras, safety features detect blind spots, help drivers maintain a safe distance from other cars, and automatically apply emergency braking that can avoid accidents and save lives.

The use of connected-car data also represents an important opportunity. Further enhancement has identified nearly 40 use cases that could represent up to $400 billion in value by 2030, including adding in-car entertainment options and using data to help fleet operators manage vehicle maintenance. Next is the world's first 3-D printed car with fewer than twenty parts. Caterpillar has a set up to develop autonomous heavy construction and mining equipment.

The market for surgical robots is growing by 11.4% a year and is expected to be worth $9.5 trillion by 2026, according to market research firm Mordor Intelligence. A tiny robot could locate and remove tumour and other masses from the brain while leaving healthy tissue alone, unlike the risk in conventional surgery. Advanced robotics have enhanced senses, dexterity, intelligence and precision which can benefit by making surgeries less painful and specific to the affected spot, without damaging surrounding cells.

Next Big Things

As stated earlier, those twelve emerging technologies or "Next Big Things" estimated to impact with an additional $.40 trillion to global economy by 2025 are as listed below:

Mobile Technology	:	11 Tril.
Automation of Knowledge Work	:	07
IoT	:	06
Cloud	:	06
Advanced Robotics	:	04
Autonomous & Near Autonomous vehicles	:	02
Next Generation Genomics	:	1.5
Energy Storage & Batteries	:	01
3D Printing	:	0.8
Advanced Materials	:	0.7
	=	**$.40 Tril.**

At present humanity uses thirty percent more of our planet's natural resources than we can replenish and it is getting shorter day by day. If everyone wanted to live in equality with Europe, the planet needs three times the present resources, and if in equality with North America, is five times.

World is getting hugely connected, full of challenges and benefits which can withstand the combat of such shortages, which no one could believe until recently. When our planet is getting ready to accept the reality of a 9Bil population in two decades, more than what we think the world can bear, where the additional food, clothing, housing, healthcare, education and transports come from and that also at what cost? These "Next Big Things" in collaboration with each other technology will multiply the agriculture and food production, increase the factory output by two fold, revolutionise the housing sector, simplify the healthcare services, bring quality education for all and a carbon-free mass transportation, all for a fraction of its present cost and speed.

Mobile phone penetration is growing rapidly, from two percent in 2000, to twenty eight percent in 2009 to seventy percent in 2013 and to an expected to cross 9Bil (hundred percent) by 2030 for absolutely free for services and connectivity. Internet, if combined with wireless communication and microfinance can uplift the livelihood of those poorest into an emerging market force.

Today the poorest American has a TV, Phone, electricity and flushed toilet which most Africans do not. A century back, wealthy Americans like Henry Ford or John Rockefeller enjoyed very few of these luxuries. From those days, our thinking had changed from 'local and linear" to "global and exponential", mostly for a single reason of Internet. As a result, if GE or Coke took decades to reach \$.iBil, You Tube took eighteen months to touch \$.1.6Bil and Groupon touched \$.6Bil in two years.

Democracy is the most preferred form of government for more than seventy percent of global population, which energises free and independent thinking that nurtures innovation. This liberated more high-middle class families in India which was struggling with world's largest number of poorest families, and also halved the number of people earning less than \$1 per day. Compared to five decade back, liberalization brought Chinese ten times richer, with one third fewer babies and 28 percent with longer lifespan.

Genomics: With our understanding of genomic structure of human body increases, it enables us to manipulate genes and improve health diagnostics and treatments. This will offer similar advances to our knowledge of animals and plants, which potentially invent new opportunities to improve farm yields and high value substances like bio-diesel and ethanol from biological orgasms such as bacteria and E-coli.

Energy Storage: With an objective of storing energy for future use, such as lithium-ion batteries and fuel cells are already being used to power electric and hybrid vehicles, besides millions of portable personal electronics. In future, new discoveries in energy storage technology could make electric vehicles more cost competitive, take electricity to remote areas and improve efficiency of power utility grid.

E-commerce: Retail is shifting to online at a greater pace. With migration to AI, VR and AR, the customers can visualise each item without visiting showroom, track every order including the day-to-day status of logistics, contactless delivery, at unbelievable lower prices as a result of savings on showroom rent and staff, expensive interiors and utilities, zero-inventory, and high-speed cash flow. This has changed the conventional method of food delivery and taxi ride.

The technology of linking the physical and digital worlds, generates up to \$.11.2 trillion a year globally. It captures new metrics more than any GDP effects.

From Start-up to Scale-up

It is an idea, developed on a technology platform which drives an innovation start-up. It is a founder or founders who begin with the technology platform and gets a couple of clients after relentless presentations and marketing until it wins a couple of investors, whose money is used for scaling up to next level. After the first few months of start-up, it is followed by a number of scaling up and leveraging process to the extent of more and more investment coming in.

When the start-up stage is fully controlled and managed by founders, the next phase of scaling up requires a different skill of management, which includes HR, Finance, Marketing, new and additional technology platforms, etc. Though the VCs invest and own the company in proportion to their investment against an enterprise valuation, they leave the management to the founders without getting involved. At this stage, founders without the right vision and leadership, tend to infuse known people at top than competent managers, which could lead to a stagnation or decline of the business.

Every successful start-up to become a successful scale-up requires a different talent and skill at the top and also across the organization which means a start-up is not the same a scale-up organization. How successful start-ups changed to successful scale-ups, we can see that the founders recruited professionals from established organizations. Successful Innovation Start-ups have a combination of speed, agility, eagerness and vision, largely contributed by the founders, where established organizations have HR, Business procedure, Governance, and Experience and a combination of both make the successful and sustainable, both in the case of start-up or established companies. One of the most successful start-up- 'Better Place' an Electric Car venture founded by Shai Agassi from Israel which pooled US$.900 Mil investments, failed in wrong hands at its next phase of scaling-up. Better Place opened hundreds of battery charge stations across US and Israel and all such audacious ventures went bankrupt without right talents, planned vision and management.

Up-gradation and innovation

The future of any futuristic nation is innovation start-ups. Start-ups at its scale-up stage, win much higher enterprise valuation than established capital-intensive companies. One reason is that the development cost of a technology or service by start-up is a fraction of its price to the customer, example a internet security system costs just 14-15% of what it costs to the user, making a net of 85% margin.

On the other side, technology has a shorter lifespan than brands. Every technology is short-lived or replaced by a competitor at a much reduced price, hence there is forced need to either upgrade or innovate even before any customer asking for. This demand for a greater role of the founders to concentrate on continuous improvement and innovation rather than getting into Scale-up functions like management of HR, Finance and Marketing which are core competence of hired executives. Hence founders have a lasting role in technology start-ups.

Today billion dollar enterprises are being created faster than ever, where trillion dollar companies are on their way forward.

Success v/s failure

Those whom we write off in classrooms, are more fearless and bold than the brilliant students. This compares how an audacious child is more fearless than adults? If one has to get out of fear because those who fears the future, fears failure hence limits his efforts. Failure is the only opportunity more intelligently to begin again. There is no disgrace in honest failure, there is disgrace in fearing to fail. Chutzpah calls the college students to carry forward the childhood's audacity and disruption towards fostering innovation. Basic quest to discover and invent begins with a childish disruption of breaking those existing norms. The rule of failure is not as same as before, but here failure is the basic motivation to rise up and fail again as quickly as possible.

It is an idea which turned into a dream fosters an innovation start-up, and then money follows by. Unlike other business, start-ups do not require capital to start with. Hence, no loans, no borrowings, no offices, no employment or wage, founder or banks do not lose money if it fails. If the fear for losing money is what makes a promoter more committed to his business, start-up can fail without loss of money and restart without money, hence the turnover of failure in start-up is higher. When a start-up fails, founders do not run away like in capital-intensive business, but they return back to next start-up taking lessons from their last failure. Such failure does not cost anything to the banks or nation.

Successful Start-up founders were so restless in a comfort zone of friends and relations. They were always hunting after dreams of unknown realities of the future. They come out from all sorts of comforts with people or wilful wishes, and dream of something others have not thought and attempted before. Knowing very well that success is very far away with failure waiting so close around, it is that eagerness, courage, nerve and conviction they achieve their dreams or something very close to it. If we closely look at all those successful start-up founders and innovators, we can see a great amount of audacity, eagerness, impatience and fearlessness, somewhere hiding inside them regardless of their education profile.

Unlike other traditional business, Start-ups do not require inventory, floor space, employees and other facilities that cost money. Any place from home or a single chair with a devise connected to Internet is enough to begin with. Every unicorn we see today, had its beginning this way. This gives a founder significant strength to work and manage without staff, office and facilities, resulting a mindset not to get attracted by position, status and social recognition. He spreads a spirit of motivation for those employees joining him.

Failure is a dreaded concept of most business people, where failure can actually be a powerful force of innovation. Most valuable extract emerges from so-called failures. When asked Thomas Edison how he felt like failing a thousand times, his answer was "I have not failed. I just found a thousand ways that don't work". No big-time success can be achieved without big-time failure.

Most of the changes that touched our lives in the past were invented by small groups of thoughtful and committed people, where bureaucracy did not exist to drag progress, they had very little to lose but great challenges to achieve, a passion to prove themselves, so they consistently outperform large organizations when it comes to innovation. They were not experts or specialists in any fields.

Most of them were less disciplined, not any experts. Dylan was bit tough, Martin Luther King Jr was a troublemaker, Edison did not respect any status-quo. Ford was against employing any experts, because no one considers himself an expert if he knew his job well. Thinking far ahead, trying to do more and make nothing impossible, those who go hunting for grand challenges, experts may not be the right companions. Those engineers behind the Apollo Mission were all in their late twenties who hardly knew that their mission was to do the impossible. It is necessary to get comfortable with failure. It guides you with an insight on your next step to innovation.

Those Four Disruptive Forces

A new force changed everything during the Industrial revolution of 18-19 century. Today we witness an even more dramatic transition with the four disruptive forces:

- The Rise of Emerging Markets
- The Accelerating Impact of Technology on the Natural Forces of Competition
- An Ageing Population
- Increasing Inflow of Trade, Capital and People.

In contrast to the Industrial revolution, this transition by these four forces leads a change by ten times, and 300 times the scale, or roughly 3000 times the impact. This will shift the centre of the world economy, as it is happening to Asia and more than half of those companies with an income of $.1 billion or more will move to new emerging cities. Global urban population has been increasing by an average 65 mil people annually during the past three decades, which is equal to six Chicagos a year, for every year where nearly half of global GDP in 2010-2025 will come from 450 unheard cities like Hsinchu in Taiwan, Santa Catarina in Brazil, Surat and Coimbatore in India besides Foshan and Tianjin in China. Each city could accelerate more to global growth between now and 2025 than Madrid, Milan, Hamburg or Zurich.

Beyond the Human Intuition

It took half a century for one telephone for every two Americans after its invention. It took 38 years for the radio to get 50 million listeners. But Facebook attracted 6 million users in its first year and this number multiplied 100 times for the next five years. WeChat has 300 million users, more than the entire adult population of US. Such an accelerated adoption invited an equally or more accelerated rate of innovation. In 2009, two years after i-Phone was launched, developers created around 150,000 apps, which rose to hit 1.2 million by 2014, where its end users had downloaded more than 75 billion total apps, more than average ten apps per person on the planet. Such a volatile speed is far beyond the power of human intuition to anticipate.

Mobile Internet

Technology offers the promise of economic progress for billions in the emerging economies at a speed that would have been unimaginable without mobile internet. Twenty years ago, less than three percent of the world's population had one, and twenty years later one third of world's population are able to communicate on the internet. Technology enables business such as What's-App to start and gain a communication scale sitting anywhere in the world with a stunning speed at no cost. This furious speed of technological adoption and innovation is shortening the life cycle of companies.

On February 19, 2014, Facebook acquired What's-App, a five-year old start-up, for a stunning $19 billion. The instant-messaging app, started in mid-2009 by two former Yahoo employees, had enlisted 450 million users — more than Twitter and more than the entire population of the US where many Wall Street bankers weren't familiar with the company. From zero in 2012, Facebook grew its mobile advertising to 66 percent of total advertising revenue in the third quarter of 2014. Among the four trillion-dollar start-ups, Facebook has been most successful for the inherent trust that the company has placed in its people especially its development team; as a result the company is rated for almost a zero-error encoding in its user data.

Internet Empowering a Democratic world

The twentieth century witnessed the ever biggest conversion of political ideology towards Compassionate Capitalism and Democracy, just caused by the global expansion of three US corporations- Coca-Cola, McDonald's and Philip Morris (Marlboro). The dawn of twenty-first century saw a similar mass influence caused by Internet, which alienated a large number of educated Muslim youths from religious extremism and radical violence to embrace democratic values, gender equality and human rights. When youths under thirty have access to Internet, they are mostly to shed radical extremism in Arab kingdoms, Iran and Pakistan and also under communist suppression as we see in China and North Korea. Once US spent billion dollars and lives to contain Soviet threats, which we saw how US giants like Coke, McD and Marlboro did in twentieth century and how it will be continued in a faster pace by Internet.

On the other hand, Arab Spring destabilised the Hosni Mubarak regime in Egypt where the most powerful weapon was Internet to spread commands and agitations against the government. Activists used Facebook to schedule protests, Twitter to coordinate and You Tube to tell the world. US spent $.800Bil to change the Saddam Hussein regime in Iraq, but it costs a fraction to lay Optic fibre cables in Iraq to network and empower the citizens to revolt. Internet is a powerful tool for Hezbollah, Hamas, Al Qaeda, and ISIS to recruit cadres.

With already over 1 Bil people connected to Internet, it is expected to cross 4.5Bil by 2022 and 7 Bil by 2030, resulting a diverse collaboration and networking and their voice being heard by governments and global corporations. They exchange new problems, ideas and solutions across the world. Such a diversity and networking can become so mighty and powerful tools to spread democratic values which no war or conflicts can result. If the monarchy system and autocratic governance had ever adapted to allowing more human rights and voting power, it is no doubt the achievement made by Internet. We are so close to seeing a democratic China and North Korea.

Accelerating impact of Technology

Technology and globalization have accelerated and intensified the natural forces of market competition. With the way that technology is disrupting things, employees will need to retrain in their lifetime. It's especially difficult when the news continually reminds you that everything you thought you knew about how the world works seems to be wrong, at least a little off. Dramatic changes come from nowhere, and then from everywhere. On December 1, 2014, Americans spent a record $2.65 billion online; in contrast on November 11, 2014, Alibaba, China's biggest e-tailer, recorded sales of more than $9.3 billion, a record for a single day anywhere in the world.

China's e-tail market, which has grown at a compounded annual rate of 110 percent since 2003, is already the world's second largest, after that of the United States. By 2020, China's e-tail market, led by Alibaba and the legions of Singles-Day shoppers, could be as big as today's markets in the United States, Japan, the United Kingdom, Germany, and France combined. The e-tail market is propelled to its present stage unless supported by AI, VR and Cloud.

On September 24, 2014, the jubilant scientists at a mission control centre celebrating a technical achievement, made a difference. This control centre was in southern India, not Houston in southern Texas, where many of the scientists wore brightly coloured saris. This ISRO team was celebrating its successful placement of a spacecraft into orbit around Mars. "We have gone beyond the boundaries of human enterprise and innovation," proclaimed Narendra Modi. "We have dared to reach into the unknown." The most astonishing feature that the entire venture costs: a mere $74 million, less than the science-fiction film Gravity in Hollywood. Nearly a year on, the Mangalyaan mission was the embodiment of India's culture of frugal innovation. Using lightweight instruments, employing components adapted from other uses, and applying engineering prowess to bring down costs, India managed to become just the fourth country whose space organization successfully placed a spacecraft in Mars's orbit—and the first country to do so on its first attempt.

This new normal, where a world in which China leads the globe in holiday consumption, the United States is the largest oil producer, a mobile messaging app is worth $19 billion, and India is a leader in space exploration. The same forces that lifted one billion people out of extreme poverty between 1990 and 2010 will help propel another three billion people into the global middle class in the next two decades. Whatever the forces which drive our global economy, creation of future wealth and livelihood in coming decades are all connected to technology and innovation.

Crossing Atlantic by an aircraft looked impossible until Charles A Lindberg did in 1927. Next eighteen months, the number of paid US passengers grew thirtyfold from 6000 to 180000, the number of pilots in US tripled, the number of airplanes quadrupled. Things look impossible until it is achieved.

As a result, the new world will be richer, more urbanized, more skilled, and healthier than the one it replaces. Its population will have access to powerful innovations that could address long-standing challenges, create new products and services for a growing consuming class, and present opportunities for a global entrepreneurial class. In many ways, those discoveries and technologies that existed in the past will become insufficient to fulfil the upcoming needs, hence the new drivers to fill this unknown future space will highly depend on digital technology and innovation.

Ageing population

We are getting older and greying with a falling fertility, where this demographic deficit which existed in US, Europe, Russia and Japan is spreading to China and Latin America, where the fertility rate needed to replenish each generation is 2.1 children per woman. In 2013, 60% of people lived in countries with fertility rates below its replacement rate. European Commission-EC estimates that by 2060, Germany will shrink by one-fifth with its working population will fall from 54 to 36 million less than of France. "Moody's, the credit-rating agency, in 2014 projected that the number of "super-aged" countries where more than one-fifth of the population is sixty-five or older would rise from 3 today (Germany, Italy, and Japan) to 13 in 2020 and to 34 in 2030." China's labour force peaked in 2012 due to its income-driven demographic trend where the fertility rate in Thailand had fallen from 5 in 1970 to 1.4 in 2015. The number of Chinese aged fifty-five and above is likely to rise to more than 43 percent of its population in 2030, from 26 percent today.

Worldwide, the share of older workers, above fifty-five years is expected to increase from 14 percent in 2010 to 22 percent by 2030. The greying of the workforce will be felt most acutely in advanced economies and in China, where the share of older workers will increase to 27 and 31 percent of the workforce, respectively. As a result, caring for a larger number of senior citizens puts severe pressure on government finances. This market is conquered by Robots, with patience and empathy, also sensitivity to seniors.

Between 1980 and 2010, 1.1 billion adults entered the twenty to sixty-four year old age bracket and joined the world's labour force and the global labour force growth will fall by nearly one-third by 2030. At the same time, technology is pushing for labour markets as never before. Computers, which historically replaced manual and clerical workers, such as stenographers and bank tellers, are now beginning to replace knowledge and skilled workers, like finance and stock analysts. By 2025, in fact, computers could do the work of 140 million knowledge workers, and robots could do the work of another 75 million people. And yet there will still be high demand for skilled positions in engineering, software development, and health care sectors. Four out of ten respondents in a McKinsey survey reported that they currently couldn't find the talent they need.

By 2020, on our current trajectory, businesses could be short of 85 million workers with college degrees or vocational training; at the same time, 95 million lower-skilled workers could be unemployed. As home-care for aged citizens in developed countries can employ many low-skilled workers, robotics will take away its remaining balance besides filling those low-skilled jobs in retail, assembling and building cleaning works.

By 2020, China will have 90Mil fewer people between the ages of 15-35 and 150Mil more people above 60 years. Running out of children, South Korean schools enrol illiterate grandmothers. Once the surplus talents migrated to those countries of talent shortage and by taking the advantage of remote working, global companies are migrating to countries where largest skilled talents are available.

Global connections of Trade, Finance, People and Data

The final disruptive force is the degree in which the world is increasingly connected; the Trade, Capital, People and Information Data. With Asia becoming the world's largest trading region with formation of RECP treaty, and China's trade with Africa so frightening from $9 billion in 2000 to $211 billion in 2012, global capital inflows expanded 25 times during 1980-2007. 5G connections will certainly increase the speed and once it converged to world's origins of capital, it can reach out to anywhere so faster, practically at no cost.

Resetting our Intuition

Those four disruptive forces as stated above gathered speed, scaled up to a new growth to a collective material impact on the global economy around the turn of 21st century. Today they are disrupting every long-established pattern in virtually every market and every sector of the world economy, and in every aspect of our lives. Everywhere we look, they are causing trends to break-down, to break-up, or simply to disrupt. The fact that these all four are happening at the same time which means that the world we live is changing radically from the one in which many of us grew up, prospered, and formed the intuitions that are so vital to our decision making. Also the same intuition is no more reliable to envision the unknown realities of the future already at our door step.

First we must be externally focused, so that we understand the changing world around us. These disruptions will create a lot of opportunities that an optimist will identify, whereas pessimists will only see the damage to their existing business model. To spot this opportunity, there needs to be more reliance on data and analysis, and less on intuition. As we think about how the world will change, there will be a need for a different set of skills. Two of the disruptive forces you identify are technology and great connectivity, which will continue to make the world a smaller place.

If we talk experts about any new technology to provide clean drinking water for the developing world, they will find it not worth a business or economic model because those four billion people earn less than two dollars a day. On the other side, already twenty five poorest countries spent twenty percent of their GDP on water. But four billion people spending thirty cents a day for water means $.1.2 Bil a day ie,$.400Bil a year. Almost 430Mil schooldays a year are lost due to water related deceases and about 2.3mil children die each year from drinking contaminated water. A normal rainfall makes Africa a conflict-less region which otherwise could lead to civil war between countries. Some two hundred rivers and three hundred lakes share international borders where neighbours are less friendly to share the water. When it comes to drinking water, we shall engage optimists, not experts.

This can play havoc with forecasts and pro-forma plans that were made simply by extrapolating recent experience into the near and distant future. Many of the assumptions, tendencies and habits that had long proved so reliable have suddenly lost much of their resonance. With i-Phone or Galaxy contains more information and processing power than the original supercomputers, we have never had more data and information at our fingertips as today. We work in a world in which even, perhaps especially professional forecasters are routinely caught unawares, partly because intuition still underpins much of our decision making. Between 1982 and 2013, the yield on the ten-year US government bond fell from 14.6 to 1.9 percent, a decline of 87 percent, which brings an end to easy money.

Globalisation benefited the well established and well connected, opening up new markets easily. With our intuition, so deeply founded from what we knew and experienced in the past, we could be well wrong in envisioning our future. Whatever worked successful in the past does not guarantee any success about future. We need to realize that much of what we think we know about how the world works is wrong; to get a realistic feel of how these four disruptive forces going to transform the global economy and to have the courage and foresight to prepare and respond.

If any country has the eagerness to take advantage of this new global disruption and gain its benefit that can add significant benefit to its economy, needs to adapt and adjust with these realities. There is a powerful human tendency to want the future to look much like the recent past, which caused collapse of many large corporate businesses. Therefore, we shall not look at and address these forces from our past perspective and thoughts, but from a new approach starting with these forces, backwards to where we have to begin and move forward.

With about 920mil people do not have enough to eat, we need to increase the food production, warehouse and delivery. Currently we farm about thirty-eight percent of the land. If not for adopting scientific and biotech farming, we would have required a land area of eighty-two percent, which is again an achievement of innovation. With the fruits of liberalisation, China's food consumption doubled during 1990 to 2005 with a demand to produce more. When Indian farmers changed to BT Cotton in 2002, the nation went from a cotton importer to exporter, from 17mil to 27mil bales, or an increase from $540Mil to $.1.7bil revenue for the growers. Dinner in LA includes beef from Chile (5585 miles), rice from Thailand (8263miles), mushrooms from NZ (6508 miles) where seventy percent of cost accounts to transportation and storage, which becomes a saving once countries begin to produce them locally. We shall wait for a day soon, when cultured meat grown from stem-cells will replace slaughtered meat without any added cost of butchering, transport, process, storage and any threat of infection.

With more and more people migrating to the digital experiences of banking, e-commerce and food deliveries, more data gets fed back to the AI that runs them. This heads to a future where AI will make most of our buying decisions, payment transactions of products or services that we did not know what we wanted. While it is full of opportunities, this era is deeply unsettling and there is a great deal of work to be done in resetting our collective intuition.

So far human beings were the most intelligent race on the planet, which is under threat today, where in twenty-first century machines will turn to exceed our intelligence with convergence of technologies like AI, IoT, ML and Cloud work hand-in-hand with each other.

The world what we know today, will be gone by 2030. World's cities occupying just one percent of the total land are fifty five percent of the population with eighty percent of total energy consumption and carbon emission. Today we have thousands of time-saving choices than our forefathers.

6 Start-ups-Business Patriotism, with a National Purpose

One of the main sources of India's robust GDP is her manpower, mostly under 35 years of age which contains the largest pool of technical graduates in English medium. They are mostly engaged in very respectable employments in the country as well as abroad, mostly those brilliant frontbenchers. Many of them had risen to very senior level positions including CEOs of global technology giants.

On the other side, the country does not have any data and statistics about those backbenchers and drop-outs in Technical universities, except few of them as successful and more as failed start-up founders and SME enterprises. The majority of them would have turned to technology abuses, digital fraud and crimes which we hardly know, though they are very large in number. At this stage, if they were provided with a 3 months military training, the advantage is that they attain a very good mental and physical strength to withstand failures and adversaries, besides a spirit of patriotism which will integrate them to live responsible citizens without offenses and crimes.

Imagine if we could liberate their resources towards disruption and innovation start-ups! As stated earlier, they are proactive, extrovert, with excellent soft skills of relationship, resilience, perseverant, empathetic, and team work than their frontbench counterparts. Though almost most of them had a classroom clash and were problematic to teachers, on the other side, their minds were roaming around something an unknown and uncertain future which does not exist today.

How to asset on these negative resources?

A 3 months Military training can integrate them to national mainstream than losing as offenders and law breakers. It can foster a discipline, patriotism and national purpose. The hectic military training can stretch their mental and physical limits to achieve what looked impossible for them till that time and withstand any setbacks and unknown failures in life and work. Dealing with tough seniors will boost their courage, self-confidence, ability to interface with difficult negotiations, problem-solving without help, resistance to hardships, willpower to stand non-existing and unknown crisis, long travel by any available means without booking and fuelling at way-side eateries. They are capable of withstanding adversaries and hurdle, also rise up very quickly from failure and make new attempts with a remarkable mental courage.

They behave in equality and compassion with team members and customers, empower others to perform higher levels and reward generously with respect for human element, thus upholding every success factor of business.

Technology cycle is short-lived

With the technological cycles changing faster at an unprecedented rate, nearly 50% syllabus knowledge acquired during the first year of a four years technical degree gets outdated and become irrelevant by the time a student graduates. Thus a general assumption that excellence in education translates into scientific innovation and business competence is proving incorrect.

Syllabus education remains relevant to secure a job as well as to remain there during the first two or three years of a career. Then it is the job related skills and more the soft skills support competence and career growth. Here even a very high academic score does not help after his first two-three years on job. It is self-education, what is not taught in classroom - the skill training and soft skills of attitude, behaviour, relation, resilience and compassion drive one's future success. Needless to mention again that such skills are more of personality traits that backbenchers score far better over brilliant students.

Innovation has created a large number of new organizations during the first two decades of 21st century, many of them surpassing the valuation of large manufacturing, engineering and technology companies. It is an idea that sparks innovation, it is surprising to see the true value that an idea can empower and change our world. As most of those innovation start-ups of the present Fortune-100 companies did not exist twenty years back, those to be in the list after twenty years remain unknown to us today.

India's Software and IT Business

India is the leading sourcing destination across the world, accounting for approximately 55% market share of the US$ 250-300 billion global services sourcing business in 2019-20. Indian IT & BPM-Business Process Management companies have set up over 1,000 global delivery centres in about 80 countries across the world. India has become the digital capability hub of the world with around 70% of global digital talent in the country.

Market Size

IT-BPM industry's revenue was estimated at around US$ 191 billion with 79% export revenue in FY20, growing at 7.7% y-o-y. It is estimated to reach US$ 350 billion by 2025. Moreover, revenue from the digital segment is expected to form 38% of the total industry revenue by 2025. Digital economy is estimated to reach Rs. 69,89,000 crore (US$ 1 trillion) by 2025. The domestic revenue of the IT industry was estimated at US$ 44 billion and export revenue was estimated at US$ 147 billion in FY20. The computer software and hardware sector in India attracted cumulative foreign direct investment (FDI) inflows worth US$ 62.47 billion between April 2000 and September 2020, as the second largest sector in ranking.

Government Initiatives

Some of the major initiatives taken by the Government and NASSCOM to promote IT and ITeS-IT enabled Service sector in India are as follows:

In 2020, the government released "Simplified Other Service Provider" (OSP) guidelines to improve the ease of doing business in the IT Industry, Business Process Outsourcing (BPO) and IT-enabled Services.

The Government has identified Information Technology as one of 12 champion service sectors for which an action plan is being developed. Also, the Government has set up a Rs. 5,000 crore (US$ 745.82 million) fund for realising the potential of these champion service sectors.

As part of Union Budget 2018-19, NITI Aayog was to set up a national level programme to enable efforts in AI and leverage AI technology for developing the country. In the Interim Budget 2019-20, the Government announced plans to launch a national programme on AI and setting up of a National AI portal. National Policy on Software Products-2019 was passed by the Union Cabinet to develop India as a software product nation.

Some of the major developments in the Indian IT and ITeS private sector are as follows:

In December 2020, Tata Consultancy Services (TCS) has expanded its business operations in Austin, Texas, with the construction of a new facility. By 2022, TCS plans to hire an additional 130 new employees in Austin. Over the next seven years, TCS plans to invest more than US$ 100 million in Austin. In the same year, Tata Consultancy Services (TCS) has expanded its strategic partnership with Star Alliance (airline alliance) to provide predictive and real-time business analytics, improve customer experience and accelerate digital transformation.

In December 2020, Infosys partnered with Rolls-Royce for aerospace engineering in India.

In the same year, Wipro collaborated with Verifone for a multi-year contract to drive agility across its (Verifone) cloud service offerings.

In December 2020, Finacle software, part of EdgeVerve Systems, (a subsidiary of Infosys), and RBL Bank, announced a collaboration to migrate the bank's on-premise deployment to a containerised ecosystem, which is managed by Kubernets and has been certified by Cloud Native Computing Foundation (CNCF). Same year, the company launched Infosys Modernisation Suite to help organisations accelerate their cloud modernisation needs.

Total number of employees grew to 1.02 million cumulatively for four Indian IT majors (including TCS, Infosys, Wipro, HCL Tech) as on December 31, 2019. As on 2020, the total workforce in Indian IT Industry accounts for 3.3Mil under direct employments and those under third-party subcontracts could be even larger.

There were 11,89,826 active companies as on June 30, 2018," the corporate affairs ministry said. Out of the total number of 17.79 lakh registered companies in India, 5.43 lakh were closed as on 30 June and 1,390 were classified as dormant, which means 66% active companies. India's major IT hubs are Bangalore, Hyderabad, Chennai, Mumbai, Visakhapatnam, Trivandrum, Vadodara, Patna, Mysore, Indore, Jaipur, Mangalore, Lucknow, Coimbatore, Chandigarh, Bhubaneswar and Kochi.

India has the advantage of having the largest number of technology graduates, notably English educated in the world. India currently has over 60 technology start-ups that are unicorns. Even after the 10 strong unicorns that have cropped up already, which are currently raising funds over a billion dollar valuation.

Industry bodies like NASSCOM, TiE have been bullish about the Indian start-up ecosystem's growth and believe the country is set to hit 100 unicorns by 2025. But it will be getting there much sooner. In the first quarter of 2021 alone, India has seen $11.85 billion in private equity and venture capital funding.

There are a total of over 650 unicorns in the world, with cumulative valuations hitting $2,173 billion. China and the US alone account for 80% of the world's unicorns. In fact, China is also home to the world's most valued unicorn – ByteDance, with a valuation of $140 billion. There's a lot of money in the world, but on the other side, it speaks significantly of the depth of the Indian market.

The constraints and setback

India has a global recognition for its largest pool of technology graduates educated in English that too in the age-group of 25-40, which makes it the largest workforce across the world. Her education model is considered to generate more workers than employers, with a history of slavery to servants to workers or employees, but not entrepreneurs during the last seven to eight centuries.

If we analyse the business success factor in IT and BPO sector, mostly the income is from export and tax-free, the profit is the difference from a higher contract rate to the actual hiring cost, both based on hourly work. IT and BPO are highly manpower-intensive, which is so costly and deficit in countries where the beneficiary end-users or clients are based, and India is a highly admired country for people working for extended hours to fulfil the delivery deadline. No doubt it creates millions of employment especially from middle class at relatively much higher salary disproportionate to national wage index. This advantage has no alternatives, but it limits India's scope to create more entrepreneurs than employees which is secured and risk-averse.

The above report indicates about the growth strategy that India's government and private sector focus largely in areas where the country is already strong, ie IT and BPO. It has many diverse strategies to drive Disruption and Innovation which is proven to be the future accelerators of economy, but are mostly vague and without clear directions. The major threat for taking low cost labour despite a competition from other low-cost labour countries like Philippines, Indonesia or Vietnam, but the increasingly alarming application of automation and robotic technology that can trim down the workforce content in future. Indian IT & BPO majors shall rise up to this challenge.

The largest Technology talent pool in the world, almost all they are imprisoned to the workstations as cyber workers, largely those IT and Software giants to be blamed. Though many of them had a mindset of disruption and innovation, these talent brokers failed to identify them and raise them to invent unknown things which did not exist before. They boast about large HR departments who administer mostly the recruitment, attrition, wage revision and internal placements and promotions but hardly their imaginative skills towards discovering products and applications for an unknown future. The best technical talents were recruited from campuses by major MNC and Indian corporate and glued them to workstations in IT Parks, which in fact destroyed their hidden potential to disrupt and innovate. Such wholesale campus recruitments do not attract outstanding technical skills in US or Israel and if at all anyone recruited from campuses are too expensive as compared to India. It is a notion that only large corporate and organizations can invent new technologies, which was proved wrong by so many start-ups in the past few decades.

The major technology companies in India are largely into Software and Programming, unlike US and Israel where they are into research and innovation, enabled by AI, ML, IoT and Robotics. For over the last three decades, Indian companies were recruiting the frontbench talents from technical and science campuses, training them and bolted to a workstation to do software programming for their clients. With its nature of long shift or double shift required to fulfil the delivery deadlines, it becomes next to impossible to nurture their creative and innovative thinking because the same work repeated for years. For them, the HR duties are limited to recruitment, attrition, wage-revision and relocation. Despite quite a large number of technology graduates who are so expensive to work as software programmers, this was not the case in US or Israel who outsourced the labour-intensive programming to India, sparing their technology graduates to research and innovation.

Examples from US and Israel

In contrast, most of the technology graduates are recruited by IDF elite forces like Unit 8200 and Talpiot for incubation and mentoring on Disruption and Innovation under a strict and tough military training.

In 2019, Israeli high-tech export continued to grow, and reached an all-time record of 45.8 billion dollars, about 46% of all Israeli exports,29 Bil from High-tech goods and 17 Bil from software and R&D. Intel and Teva contributes to 50% of total high-tech goods. In 2019, the number of high-tech employees grew at a growth rate of 8.4%, to 321,000, up from 295,000 in 2018, and for the first time crossed the 300,000 threshold.7 Also for the first time, the ratio of high-tech employees in the workforce exceeded 9%, and today stands at 9.2%.

India with an estimated employment of 4,3 Mil in technology sector, which is a meagre 0.318% of gross population; in contrast Israel employs 321,000 ie a 3.57% of total population which reflects the dominant number of technology graduates in the country. As the wage structure for them in Israel is fifth highest in the world and also so scarce, they are largely engaged into highly rewarding sectors as innovation start-ups than IT and BPM sectors.

According to a survey conducted by the Central Bureau of Statistics, Israeli high-tech is in need of an additional 1,250 thousand tech professionals. A survey conducted by the Start-up Nation Central (SNC) and the Israel Innovation Authority estimates this number to be even higher, reaching approximately 1,850,000. The shortage of human capital is driving a rapid increase in high-tech salaries compared to the general average salary (annual growth rates of 4.3% and 3.1%, respectively), with Israel having the fifth highest wages for software developers in the world. Hence scarcity of technology skills is a stumbling block to Israel's start-ups, which extends immense opportunities for India.

The potential of Indian Military to incubate and develop start-up Innovators:

How is Indian Military in AI and Innovations? Though the military operates in total discretion from media and public, we know that it has expertise in following areas where AI and innovations have wider applications, especially after close partnership with Israel and US-India 2+2 Defence deal in 2020. We all know in random that Indian Military is equipped with more advanced computer system than our private or government sector, they have advanced sensitive knowledge of enemies and a good in-house cyber-security, besides very discrete organizations like RAW, DRDO.

A. Laser-sensitive missiles and bombs, capable of sensing the target and hit with 100% precision, as successfully used in Balakot and other cross-border terrorist bases.

B. LaserTechnologies considered vital for hitting missiles, drones and other targets with precision.

C. Advanced navigational aids and avionics on US-supplied fighter aircrafts to India.

D. BEKA, an Air force to Air force navigation gives us access to US; a geospatial intelligence that connects satellite mapping to strike the target with 100% precision.

E.LEMOA allows the militaries of the US and India to replenish from each other's bases, and access supplies, spare parts and services from each other's land facilities, air bases, and ports, which can then be reimbursed. LEMOA is extremely useful for India-US Navy-to-Navy cooperation, since the two countries are cooperating closely in the Indo-Pacific.

F.COMCASA allows the US to provide India with its encrypted communications equipment and systems so that Indian and US military commanders, and the aircraft and ships of the two countries, can communicate through secure networks during times of both peace and war.

G.Indian Military has acquired the capability to defend enemy's missiles in the land, air and sea, sensing any assaults in advance supported by AI enabled satellite mapping. It is now acquiring a network communication system from Israel, which enables the fighter pilot, naval officer and a military officer, even those ground soldiers to communicate each other's movements as well as enemy's positions.

H. India's Military is specialised in Electronic and cyber warfare in all sectors of land, air and sea, which is designed, operated and serviced by highly skilled engineering and technical experts capable of wide areas of modern warfare innovations. Besides it is one among the few military powers which is highly crisis-tested and undergone constant training and exchanges with most technologically advanced powers like US, Russia, France, Israel and recently the Quad. It's next normal is the digital warfare.

When tension escalated across LAC with China in second quarter-2020,Mike Pompeo called up External Affairs Minister S Jaishankar in the third week of June, National Security Advisor Ajit Doval has been in touch with the US NSA Robert C O'Brien, and Chairman of the US Joint Chiefs of Staff Gen Mark A Milley has been in touch with Chief of Defence Staff Gen Bipin Rawat. The US Secretary of Defence Mark T Esper called up Defence Minister Rajnath Singh in the second week of July.

Skyroot is the first private company from Hyderabad, to formally work with the Indian Space Research Organisation (ISRO) to test and qualify its small rocket, capable of lifting up to 2,000 kilograms. The company was founded by former ISRO scientists Pawan Kumar Chandana and Naga Bharath Daka in 2008.

Skyroot Aerospace is now the first Indian private aerospace company to successfully test a fully cryogenic rocket engine, named Dhawan-1 in honour of eminent Indian scientist Satish Dhawan. The engine runs on two high-performance rocket propellants (a combination of fuel and oxidiser to move the rocket), Liquid Natural Gas (LNG) and Liquid Oxygen (LoX). In this case, LNG is the fuel which is mostly made of methane and LoX is the oxidiser, both of these elements mix and produce energy to power a rocket.

These propellants can be stored at extremely low, also known as cryogenic, temperatures of less than -150° celsius. Therefore, it is called a cryogenic engine. Skyroot's cryogenic engines are 3-D printed, which is reducing the manufacturing time by 95% and increasing efficiency of the engine compared to conventional methods. Conventional engines have several components welded and limitations on the contours that can be manufactured. These engines give out higher efficiency compared to a conventional alternative engine, still being the cheapest satellite launch vehicle in the world.

Finally a word about business patriotism, education without patriotism, values and purpose is like taking a wrong path to reach a destination totally unknown to us. The foundation of a Military training and incubation nurture the business patriotism in every new start-up.

Talpiot- The elite unit of IDF

Israel is an example of how a Military elite unit can take responsibility of incubating Start-ups and Innovations. The idea was initiated by Prof. Felix Dothan and Prof. Shaul Yatziv of the Hebrew University, who submitted the idea to the Israeli chief of staff Rafi Eitan. The idea was to harness human creativity, which peaks early, to develop new technologies for the army. The program is sponsored by the Israeli Air Force and IDF Administration for the Development of Weapons and the Technological Industry, and run under the auspices of the Hebrew University of Jerusalem.

Talpiot program is an elite Israeli Defence Force (IDF) training program for recruits who have demonstrated outstanding academic ability in the sciences with a leadership potential. Graduates pursue double higher education while they serve in the army, and they use their expertise to further IDF research and development in technological leadership positions. The program was inaugurated in 1979 after Israel suffered large casualties during the Yom-Kippur War against Egypt, Syria and Jordan in October, 1973.

During their initiation period, the cadets study for their B.Sc. in physics and mathematics, some of them in computer science – according to their choice at the Hebrew University in Jerusalem in Air Force uniform, while also undergoing different periods of field training designed to familiarize them with all branches of the IDF-infantry level 04 basic training, combat engineering course, armoured corps course, artillery corps course, instruction in military tactics etc. At the end of the course, which lasts 40 months, the cadets receive the rank of first lieutenant and a B.Sc. and become integrated in R&D in the IDF and Israel Military Industries, or alternatively, in various combat positions, if they so choose. In addition to the three years obligated by the Israeli law, the service includes six years of standing army service in a wide variety of positions. The total program, including military service, is nine years. The idea was to replace numbers with quality and smartness.

The first class had 25 cadets. Later, the class was increased to 50–60. The applicant pool consists of nearly ten-thousand top scorers in a test taken by all graduating high school seniors. 150–200 potential applicants are then subjected to a two-day series of tests. These include further IQ exams, as well as group-tasks designed to test one's social dynamics, all conducted under the supervision of trained psychologists and military personnel. For example, teams of applicants are given a specific task then the instructions are changed while the test is in progress, such as shortening the allotted time or changing the assigned tasks. Final acceptance into the program entails a high security clearance rating, given by the Air Force.

Three decades after Talpiot was founded to modernize the Israeli army, the program has created an unforeseen by-product, a legion of entrepreneurs that has helped turn Israel into a technology juggernaut with largest number of companies listed on Nashdaq, other than the U.S.

The Talpiot Program Contents

The soldiers of Talpiot begin their military service at Hebrew Uni but housed separately. Study for their bachelor's of science in physics, mathematics, and computer science, the courses are taught at an accelerated rate, almost 40 % faster. Also they are trained in military strategy and complete an officer's training course. They spend their summers doing 12 weeks of basic training – same as the paratroopers.

Talpiot soldiers take special courses rotating with each force of the army: intelligence, navy, and air force – to learn about the weapon systems from the inside. They sit in cockpits of fighter jets and shoot off weaponry to gain a real understanding of its operational and technological needs.

During the second year, they devise a project of their own choosing for three months. This is where a lot of early versions of innovative tech have come from. Talpiot graduates undergo military training alongside their academics, they observe first-hand the theatre of war, the need for technology to create an edge and how and where they can help. They master the art of problem solving. A common theme emerging across multiple graduates is that the graduates learnt to take on the impossible projects. They are trained to not be afraid, but to face challenges with guts and nerve.

Today majority of the Start-up Innovations in Israel have their founders either from Talpiot or Unit-8200, who command a premium either in employments or innovations.

Israeli Innovations

Big problems were proved to be the biggest business opportunities! Israel has no enough food to feed its people, with its arable land being only twenty percent, and could not import food due to the Arab boycott. In 25 years, Israel increased its agriculture yields 17 times, where according to Simon Peres, the agriculture 95% a science and 5% farm work. As neighbouring countries were too hostile, it followed a rule that what we are today is not enough for tomorrow, a continuous increase in everything being produced. The below list is the top few agri start-ups with the so far funding:

- Kaiima (Genome Multiplication), founded by Doron Gal in 2006 Funding:$113 Mil.
- Evogene (Seed breeding and Plant Genomics) founded by Dr. Hagai Karchi and Dr. Rafi Meissner in 2002, Funding:$94.5Mil.
- Playtech (innovative plant sensors, which helping the plant's growth) by Sarig Duek in 2011 Funding:$.44.3 Mil.
- Tevel was founded by Yaniv Maor in 2016 in Robotics and drones for harvesting and aerial manuring secured a funding of $30Mil.
- Cropex founded by Issac Bentwich in 2013 is a cloud-based software integrated with wireless sensors, which boosts crops yield received a funding of $23.4 Mil.

Intel Inside

Intel is the largest private sector technology employer in Israel with 30,000 jobs. Intel's Habana's Gaudi accelerators deliver up to 40% better price performance than current graphics processing units used for machine learning workload to AWS. Intel acquired Israel's Habana in 2019 for $2 billion to boost its artificial intelligence capabilities and to strengthen its portfolio of AI-based accelerators for the cloud and data centres. This is Intel's second largest acquisition in Israel after Mobileye, a driverless cab in 2017 for a whopping $15.3 billion. In May, Intel said it acquired Israeli smart-transit start-up Moovit, a mobility journey planner app for $900 million. Habana's Gaudi processors are specifically designed for training deep learning models that include natural language processing, object detection and machine learning training, classification, recommendation and personalization, Intel said.

Habana's Gaudi processors are designed to address these needs by delivering cost efficiency and high performance. Intel 8088, the first PC CPU form IBM was designed in Israel; also most of the Windows NT O/s by Microsoft Lab in Israel, besides the Pentium MMX chip technology by Intel-Israel. The home to the largest Intel development centre in the world and the Israeli team's contribution to the company's global technology development including the 7th and 8th generation Intel processors, the firm's factory in Kiryat Gat which even teaches Intel's Santa Clara head quarters, is considered one of the most advanced and highest quality among Intel labs around the world.

Mobileye is a vision based advanced driver-assistance that alerts against collision and mitigation, where for autonomous cars, it supports with OrCam My-eye, a compact artificial vision devise that is blind-sensitive. Recently Mobileye partnered with Transdev of France to operate a customised public transport system by developing self-driving shuttles by 2023 Fleets of autonomous 16-passenger vehicles in France, then rest of Europe.

Cisco-Israel is the company's largest overseas labs, besides India and China. Michael Laor, a technology graduate from Ben-Gurion Uni developed CRS1 a router that can download up to 92 terabits (1 terabit is trillion, equals to million megabits) which is far higher than the present global requirement of any institution. Laor was serious about return from Cisco CA to Israel but Cisco retained him as the director of R&D centre in Tel Aviv.

Rafael Advanced Defence System Ltd-RADS

Israel's biggest problem is its landscape encircled with hostile Arab countries who declared its removal from world map. When the country is too short of people, it makes another problem with its small military where it cannot afford human loss. This problem led to an opportunity of modernising the military with technology and automation. RADS is a leading military contractor which developed advanced UAVs and missile shields to protect the country against attacks.

As a leader in ground-breaking technologies, it is committed to maintaining the highest levels of excellence and professionalism. Roughly 67% of its employees have advanced degrees in engineering and science, with over 300 PhDs. Over 2,500 employees volunteer in 50 community projects, including enrichment lessons for students excelling in science and technology, design of special accessories for the mentally and physically challenged, coaching weaker students, and many more community projects.

It has capabilities in a variety of fields, including image processing, mechanics, electronics, software, aeronautical and micro-electronics, components and subsystems, such as rocket motors, warheads, pyrotechnics, Electro-Optics and Signal processing, RADAR & RF Technologies, Propulsion & Explosives, Unique Technologies like Acoustic Warfare, Directed Energy, Active Protection, Big Data and Cyber Technologies besides Basic Technologies. Each year, Rafael invests over 8% of its in R&D.

The company, one of the country's leading weapons manufacturers, sees these technological developments as a step toward a more interconnected and intelligent future battlefield that connect in real time the plane, the helicopter, the drone, the tank, the soldier, the half-track on every front, at all times, constantly, said Rafael CEO Yoav Har-Even. Such interconnectivity was once impossible within the military to work with one another.

RADS Iron Dome (I-Dome), a missile defence interceptor system and UAVs demonstrated a miraculous winning performance during the recent Israel-Hamas war in Gaza strip, without any loss of its solders. I-Dome interceptors destroyed almost 2200 rockets fired by Hamas in the sky itself, which was controlled by AI enabled commands. In 2020, RADS signed a contract with Raytheon to produce I-domes in US.

Israel Aerospace Industry-IAI

When France discontinued defence partnership with Israel after the War of Independence in 1948, it was left with no option but to go for self reliance. Starting with indigenous versions like AI Kfir, a prototype of Dassault's Mirage-III and Nesher (Hawk) another derivative of Mirage-5, AIA was capable of challenging against any Russian fighters of Egyptian and Syrian Air forces. In 1980, AIA launched its modern fighter jet called the IAI Lavi, to be a superior assault aircraft, integrated with advanced avionics and onboard electronics.

The Start-up Nation

Israel is known to be a "Start-up Nation" with Tel Aviv being the "Silicon Wadi". It has the highest per-capita of start-up innovations an VC Capitals in the world and in numbers, it ranks after US and China. More than half of Israeli exports come from technology sector. Hugo Hagen, Bayer's local chief, says the company has invested heavily in Israeli firms and is looking for more: The Israeli 'culture of innovation is amazing'.

Recently, tech giant Oracle said it will set up a new data centre in Jerusalem that will function as a regional cloud provider for Israeli clients. The data centre, which is planned to be functional this year, is part of Oracle's global plan to set up 38 cloud regions worldwide by the end of 2021. The data centre will be set up together with Bynet Data Communications on its server farm in Jerusalem, spreading across an underground facility of thousands of square meters, over four floors and at a depth of 50 meters (160 feet) below ground level. The centre will "be designed with the highest industry standards, and will be one of the most secure in the Middle East," the company said in a statement. The centre will provide advanced cloud services to companies on the Israeli market from a variety of sectors like the defence industry, government, banks, insurance companies, infrastructure, technology and retail.

US tech giants Amazon and Microsoft are also planning to set up public cloud-based regional data centres in Israel, to provide cloud-based services to government ministries and other public entities in Israel. "Many organizations, including government, security and other enterprise organizations that are subject to laws and regulations find it complicated to migrate to a public cloud because the servers are not located in the country in which they operate," said Eran Feigenbaum, vice president of Product Development, Oracle Cloud Infrastructure. "A cloud region located in Israel provides a solution to this challenge, certainly when it comes to a cloud that was built in the first place to meet the most stringent security requirements." Israel has the largest number of companies listed in Nasdaq, after US and China and mostly from technology and military sectors.

Israeli start-ups raise record $1.44 billion from investors in January, 2021. Six start-ups raised more than $100 million each last month; data is 'vote of investor confidence' in Israeli tech during COVID-19 pandemic, Start-Up Nation Centre-SUNC.

The six mega-rounds that were announced during January 2021 were:

- Rapyd Financial Network (Fintech): $300 million, D Round
- Drivenets (Network Infrastructure): $208 million, B Round
- OwnBackup (Enterprise solutions): $167.5 million, D Round
- K Health (Digital health): $132 million, E Round
- Resident Home (Ecommerce): $130 million, B Round
- Melio (Fintech): $110 million, D Round

Israeli cyber-security company Armis has announced the closing of a $125 million financing round in Q-1, 2021 led by Brookfield Asset Management at a company valuation of $2 billion. This latest financing round comes a year after US venture capital firm Insight Partners acquired control of Armis for almost half the current valuation - $1.1 billion. The latest financing round brings to $300 million the amount raised by Armis.

B2B sales contact data company-Lusha announced today that it has closed a $40 million Series A financing round from US fund Providence Strategic Growth (PSG). Its community network has already expanded to over 520,000 sales professionals and 167,000 sales organizations.

Israeli Innovation Authority-IIA plays a pivotal role in the nation's economy, accounting for almost 15% of GDP and nearly 50% of industrial manufacturing. Irs role is to manage and grow this ecosystem, providing grants and incentives to fledgling and high-risk ideas and entrepreneurs. The authority's budget totalled NIS 2.25 billion ($694 million) in 2020 and it provided grants to about 1,600 innovation projects in all technological fields at all stages of product development.

Fintech start-up Earnix, a developer of artificial intelligence software that allows banks and insurers to personalize offerings to customers, said it has raised $75 million from investors in 2020-21, at a pre-money valuation of $1 billion. This cloud-based platform combines AI with advanced analytics that does modelling and simulations, and enables banking and insurance clients to give highly personalized price and product offerings to their customers in real time.

Theator, a start-up based in Palo Alto, California with an R&D site in Tel Aviv, aims to bring AI to surgery. In first quarter-2021, it raised $15.5 million in a Series funding round to grow what it calls its "surgical intelligence" platform. To date, Theator has raised $18.5 million. The idea behind surgical intelligence is to power a "next-generation" operating room using AI and computer vision to extract and analyze key moments during surgery, giving surgeons significant insight into both their own operations and those of their colleagues.

Adam Neumann, born in Israel founded WeWork a office sharing platform in 2010 which was a dazzling unicorn valued at $47 billion, and SoftBank's founder Masayoshi Son had openly hailed Neumann's vision. SoftBank says WeWork holds potential, especially in markets like Japan, where office space is costly and workers' commutes tend to be long.

Dynamic Yield, run as a standalone company in Israel under McDonald's, personalises customers' experience by changing offerings on the chain's Drive Thru menu displays, according to time of day, weather, customer traffic and trending choices. The start-up, whose customers include IKEA and Lacoste, has businesses with more than 300 brands globally.

In 2021 March, Baring Private Equity Asia-BPEA and Israel-based Lumenis said they have entered into an agreement to sell the surgical business arm of Lumenis to US medical devices maker Boston Scientific for $1.07 billion.

The First Digital Bank is owned by Shashua, the co-founder of Mobileye, a maker of self-driving technologies that was bought by Intel Corp. in 2017 for $15.3 billion, and OrCam, a maker of devices to assist the visually impaired. "The artificial intelligence revolution is here and has now reached banks as well," said the founder of the bank, tech entrepreneur Amnon Shashua. "The banking industry is thirsty for innovation and competition." The branchless bank will operate by integrating human bankers, who provide around-the-clock customer service through online chat and a call centre, with advanced artificial intelligence-based technology that aims to "create a customized service experience for each and every customer," the statement said.

Robotically assisted surgical devices (RASD) are not actually robots, but the devices cannot perform surgery without direct human control. RASD enable a surgeon to use computer and software technology to control and move surgical instruments through one or more tiny incisions in the patient's body in a variety of surgical procedures or operations.

The Hominis Surgical System developed by Memic features miniature humanoid-shaped robotic arms. It is intended for benign hysterectomy, or the removal of the uterus for non-cancerous conditions along with the removal of one or both fallopian tubes and ovaries. To remove the uterus, the Hominis Surgical System uses minimally invasive surgical instruments inserted through the vagina (transvaginal approach) and a video camera inserted laparoscopically through a small incision on the abdomen for visualization of the instruments inside the patient. The transvaginal approach requires fewer incisions on the abdomen compared to conventional laparoscopic hysterectomy. During the procedure, surgeons in the operating room control the instruments from the Hominis Surgical System console. Approximately 600,000 hysterectomies are performed annually in the US. The transvaginal approach as opposed to abdominal hysterectomies is documented as resulting in better clinical benefits, including less patient pain and scarring, shorter recovery times and reduced infection rates, compared to other approaches to hysterectomy.

EDGE, a UAE-based advanced defence technology group, has signed an accord with Israel Aerospace Industries (IAI), the nation's largest aerospace and defence company, to jointly develop an advanced system to intercept drones and other threats tailored for the UAE market.

The parties have signed a memorandum of understanding to develop an advanced Counter-Unmanned Aircraft System (C-UAS) solution, making use of IAI's existing products to detect, identify, classify, and intercept a broad range of UAV threats. A subsidiary of EDGE, SIGN4L, a provider of electronic warfare services and solutions for national security, will be working with IAI to develop the tailored anti-drone solution. EDGE, an Abu Dhabi-based conglomerate of private firms and government owned bodies, has 25 subsidiaries and employs 13,000 workers across five main sectors: defence platforms and systems; missiles and weapons; cyber defence; electronic warfare and intelligence; and mission support.

IAI develops and manufactures advanced systems for air, space, sea, land, cyber and homeland security. Since 1953, the company has provided technology solutions to government and commercial customers worldwide, including satellites, UAVs, missiles, weapon systems and munitions, unmanned and robotic systems, and radar. The firm is one of Israel's largest technology employers with offices and R&D centres in Israel and around the world.

"The artificial intelligence revolution is here and has now reached banks as well," said the founder of First Digital Bank Amnon Shashua, who was also the founder of Mobileye and Orcam, acquired by Intel. The branchless bank will be operated by integrating human bankers, who provide around-the-clock customer service through online chat and a call centre with advanced artificial intelligence-based technology that aims to "create a customized service experience for each and every customer," the statement said.

Some of the major start-ups acquisitions during 2010-15.

In June, 2013 Google acquired Waze a mapping start-up for US$.1Bil. In August 2013, IBM acquired Truster, a data security firm for an undisclosed value of US$.500Mil-1Bil. Same year FaceBook bought Onavo, a mobile analytic startup for $180 Mil. Cisco bought Intucell for $.475Mil. Rosetta Green by Monsanto for $.35Mil. Besides Adapt Tv for $.405Mil AOL bought Waze for $.966Mil.

EMC acquired Scale10 for $.250Mil IN 2013. OPKO Health bought PROLOR for $.480Mil. Apple bought Anobit Tech for $.390Mil. ICQ was the first internet-wide instant messaging system founded by Yossi Vardi, who is most respected in the Israeli High-tech industry which was acquired by AOL in 1998 for US$.400Mil.

Yossi invested in 80 start-ups which twenty seven failed. In Israel, not failing is a shame that you have not attempted anything new. Co-working start-ups are very common in Israel which helps everyone to lean from other's failure and get inspired of their success.

In 2012, the total M&A deal exceeded US$.9.75 Bil., an 88% increase from 2011 according to IVC Research Centre database. Israel attracted a VC per capita twice as US and thirty times as EU combined. There are seventy VCs active in the start-up market of Israel. Israel account for six Nobel winners during 2000-10 and employs 135 engineers, scientists and PhDs/ 10,000 people, the ever highest in the world. Remilk, that makes milk products without the use of cows has raised $11.3 million from Tnuva, Tempo and Hochland a diary company from Germany.

Waze reports traffic congestion that saves time on road as well as fuel consumption, which was founded by Uri Levine and later acquired by Alphabet in 2013 for $1.1 Bil to complement its Google Map navigation. It works with IOS (I-Phone) as well as Android. It alerts the user on traffic signals, speed sensors, road work and road condition.

Forescout Technologies by Advent International for $1.9 billion, the Checkmarx acquisition by Hellman & Friedman for $1.15 billion, the acquisition of Cyber-security firm Armis by CapitalG and Insight Partners for $1.1 billion, and the $1 billion acquisition of smart transit start-up Moovit by Intel Corp. In 2020, nine companies held IPOs on the TASE, raising an aggregate of $345 million, compared to none in 2019 and 2018; in 2020, seven companies held IPOs in the US, raising an aggregate of $1.2 billion, compared to five companies that raised $407 million in 2019.

Top initial public offerings in 2020 included those of JFrog, an IT and enterprise software firm, on the Nasdaq; Lemonade, an AI-based insurance firm, on the New York Stock Exchange; and life sciences firm Nanox which raised $165 million on the Nasdaq. Two Cleantech firms, Ecoppia and GenCell, held initial public offering of shares, raising $82 million and $61 million on the TASE in same year.

Israeli start-up Arbe Robotics says its ultra-high-resolution radar system can provide a perfect vision for autonomous and semi-autonomous cars. The system recognizes objects, including people, up to 300 meters away, giving a driver – or an automatic braking system – ample time to stop. Unlike other advanced imaging and sensing systems, Arbe's technology also works in low-visibility conditions caused by bad weather or glaring sun, and can detect cats, dogs and other small objects, as well as hidden and unseen dangers, such as a child walking between closely parked cars. Arbe systems are developed in partnership with major global automotive manufacturers and will be available in some vehicles from 2022. This device understands very fast, within nanoseconds, where there are objects, and do the ultra-high-resolution frame only on areas in the environment that have some information that is relevant.

Michal Mor and Shir Ahuvia, two knowledgeable women approached the IDF officials with an artificial intelligence-based shooting device named Smart Shooter that makes rifles smart, more accurate and deadlier. Mor has an MSC in Industrial Psychology and Human Factors Engineering from the Technion – Israel Institute of Technology. She worked for RADS as a team leader for R&D groups in the missile division. It is called Smash Fire control system, equipped with a camera, electro-optics, computer vision technologies, real-time embedded software, and image processing algorithms. It gets fitted on the barrel of any standard assault rifle. Surgical precision can save lives on both sides. If you miss that first shot and hit the wrong person, hell breaks loose and gets punished in Military court.

Israeli company StoreDot announced in January, 2021 that in a landmark achievement in the electric vehicle industry, it had managed to develop the world's first car battery that can be fully charged in just five minutes. Electric cars, which are a major part of global attempts to tackle the climate crisis, have faced the challenge of batteries taking hours to fully charge, giving rise to "range anxiety", the fear of a battery running out mid-journey and the driver getting stranded at a charging station. Charging an electric car could become as quick as stopping to refuel a gas-run vehicle. StoreDot has raised $130 million to date from investors including US$.20 Mil from BP Ventures of BP plc, Samsung Venture Investment, Daimler AG, the maker of the Mercedes Benz cars; and electrical and electronics maker TDK Corporation. A five-minute charging lithium-ion battery was once considered to be impossible, StoreDot CEO Doron Myersdorf said.

Dr. Michal Tzuchman-Katz, a paediatrician and a software engineer is the co-founder of Kahun. After physicians submit their patients' symptoms to Kahun's website, the software scours the wealth of information available in medical texts and creates a "knowledge graph" that can map out 5 million relations between symptoms and diseases, findings, labs, complications and risk factors. The software is an AI engine that uses the knowledge graph created to substitute a physician's thinking. It assists them in making their diagnosis, points them toward a recommended course of action, and "backs them up with medical sources" by linking the information provided to the original medical sources consulted. It prescribes to tests, or further lab reports and imaging that is required to narrow down the diagnosis and the software has passed with an 80% score by the US Medical Licensing Exam.

K-Health raised $132 million in its third year of funding, has developed a free mobile app that enables users to insert their age and gender and ailments to get an immediate initial diagnosis of what could be afflicting them.

Jasper is an Israeli start-up operating in the US that targets the growing, affluent and under-recognized sector of consumers who cannot get a credit card from traditional lenders. The pandemic is forcing millions of people to stay home and ramp up their reliance on electronic payments, but the financial institutions that issue credit cards are making it tougher, not easier, to get credit. In the US, 21 percent of credit applications were denied in 2020. Among those being turned down are high-earning recent graduates, immigrants and other creditworthy working professionals who have not been paying enough bills long enough to get the credit rating scores used by traditional card issuers. Jasper uses technology and alternative data instead of the industry's long-established credit score when approving applications, looking at where applicants are going, rather than where they have been.

Kubota Corp., Japan's leading robotics company, has taken a stake in Tevel Aerobotics, an OurCrowd portfolio company adapted to AI, whose flying robots pick fruit from trees, cutting costs and waste. Future Family is a fintech-driven digital health startup that replaces the $50,000 average cost of starting a family through IVF with a $300 a month plan. NanoLock Security is a fast growth start-up projecting an increase of 600% increase in 2021, protects the vast and rapidly expanding $.15B market of IoT devices which is growing by 24% a year. By 2025, IoT devices market is estimated $.14B worldwide each with a potential security risk from hacker's entry into networks. NanoLock blocks advanced threats to IoT and OT enabled devices from external fraud and cyber attackers.

The video game market is worth over $.150B a year, more than three times the global film industry. TetaVi embeds a broadcast version studio in to your mobile which is customized for the TikTok generation, creating a 360 degree immersive viewer experience with life-like holograms which enables precision and realism in video games. This AI supported TetaVi turns every phone into a portable video studio.

enVerid is focused on saving the planet by minimizing energy use in buildings. Now the company has launched a new ceiling-mounted, in-room filtration system for classrooms, common areas in offices, auditoriums and retail stores. It removes 99.99 percent of viruses, including Covid-19. Another start-up Trellis is helping Pernod Ricard to improve its supply-chain palate, by providing accurate grape yield, quality, harvest time and procurement cost prediction, with significant savings.

In January, 2021, Israeli special purpose acquisition company-SPAC ION Acquisition Corp 2 filed to raise $220 million IPO on the New York Stock Exchange with the aim of taking Taboola, an Israeli tech company of content recommendation platform used by online advertisers, which was merged with ION at a valuation of $.2.6B.

In 2021, the anti-cancer drug developed by Biond Biologics, which the Israeli startup will try on humans in clinical trials with French MNC Sanofi, for an upfront payment of $125 million in cash and up to $1 billion in potential development takes a multipronged approach to fighting tumours, activating three kind of cells in the immune system at the same time.

Dr. Gabi Iddan from missile division of RADS-Rafael Advanced Defence System invented "Pillcam" a pill-shape camera, once swallowed will capture images of intestine which is a simplified diagnosis to Gastro-intestine disorders which is today used in sixty countries. Former recruits of IDF-Unit 8200 and Talpiot were the founders of CheckPoint, Compugen, Anobit, recently bought by Apple, and XIV later acquired by IBM.

With cars becoming increasingly dependent on computing power, the car is really becoming a computer," said Yuval Engelstein, analyst at Start-Up Nation Central, which tracks tech companies in Israel, home to a growing automotive technology sector. "But you need really fast computing power because this is the brain of the car, and it has to work in real time, and in better than real time. This technology has to become cheaper in order to scale. Braodmann 17 is a start-up that provides a cheaper and hyper-efficient software at a lower the cost of the sophisticated artificial intelligence and machine-learning applications behind these new driving features, allowing them to be fitted to more non-luxury vehicles.

As on 20th January, 2021, At least 10 Israeli companies are seeking listings in the United States at valuations ranging up to $5 billion, as cash-rich investors with few opportunities flock to technology. Israel accounts for 31% of global investments in cyber-security sector, second in world after US, as National Cyber Directorate says; Israel has 33% of global sector unicorns. It posted a 70 percent growth in funding in 2020, raising a record $2.9 billion in 100 transactions. Exports of cyber-security products in 2020 totalled $6.85 billion, up from $6.5 billion in 2019. Last year saw more than 20 acquisitions of Israeli cyber-security firms for a total of an estimated $ 4.7 billion.

Story of a Start-up's Failure

Israel has no oil and it was impossible to import from OPEC during the Arab Boycott. It was an opportunity to explore and discover cars which can operate on electric power. A young software executive with SAP Shai Agassi came out with an idea with a battery powered engine mounted on a Renault saloon and named the start-up as 'Better Place'. With support from Simon Peres, the idea prototype was submitted to major car companies but got rejected as Israel has neither volume nor any cross-border commerce. Finally Shai decided to go with seed funding and listed in NYSE, it secured more than $.900Mil funding. Later it collapsed due to mismanagement, but it was a good lesson for latecomers like Tesla which did not repeat any mistake that Better Place had made.

Despite initial concerns during the Covid-19 pandemic, Israeli high-tech companies raised approximately $9.9 billion in around 578 deals in 2020, exceeding 2019's results by 27% in value and 14% in number of investments. The biggest checks being high-tech sectors like cyber-security, fintech and IOT. Despite a slow beginning, investments boomed towards end of 2020. VC funds continued to be the major source of capital in Israeli tech, with foreign funds taking the lead. In December, 2020, Jared Kushner, advisor to Donald Trump divested his stake in Kushner firms and filed papers to sell at least $100 million in bonds on the Tel Aviv Stock Exchange in Q-1, 2021. Pagaya is a global fintech company on artificial intelligence (AI), raised $.102 Mil Series D funding round led by the Singapore Sovereign Wealth Fund-GIC in June, 2020. Fintech has shifted from competition to collaboration with banks and start-ups bringing new wave of innovation to global banks.

From 2012 to 2017, 1,000 new start-ups were established per year, with an average of 500 companies added per year net after deducting closed ones. US and Israel have proved themselves how Start-ups could drive the GDP so abundantly.

7 DRDO+ISRO+CDS to Nurture a 'Brain Unit'

Unlike civil services, military is known for audacity, courage, daring, boldness, fighting, physical and mental fitness, challenging life situations, where academic knowledge and civilian experience hardly matter. This culture is too complementing to the attributes required for disruption and innovation, where one shall not be filled too much with past knowledge, but a rare gift of a creative dream and vision of what does not exist in an invisible future. If the military fights against an existing and visible enemy force, this new eccentric breed fights to break an existing norm, to improve anything already existed and also wrestle by stretching out to create something unknown that did not exist. They share more common attributes with the people in the uniforms than those civilians.

Teaching Children how to Think

Our present schooling is about 12 decades old, made to produce industrialized model of graduates. Two thirds of the students are analytically weak, not suitable for research, who wrote poorly, and the entire course is designed to prepare them as workforce. If this continued, what will be the fate of our country when those in our early schools who will retire after fifty years? If creativity, collaboration, problem solving and critical thinking are the essentials of today's jobs, schools have to reinvent for the twenty-first century learning, as future is not at incremental improvement anymore. Learning has to change from instruction to construction, that is learning through doing, especially with a computer support which can liberate those 23 percent of world's children currently not in school. They have internet, video games and about five hundred cable channels to learn in a world with an extreme shortage of qualified teachers.

Imagination and creativity reach their peak at one's early age of schooling. More years spent in the classroom moulds this mind to a more rigid and structured format of what is taught and instructed. Gradually this so called imagination and creativity die and disappear, if not it conflicts with the classroom discipline, norms and teachers. As a result, children become segmented two groups- those frontbenchers and rest backbenchers and drop-outs.

Indian Military does not attract the brightest talents from campuses, where for those talents the private sector makes their most desired career destination. Military always needs men who like a job because it is tough and difficult unlike the government or private sector which provide an insulated and risk-free working atmosphere. Hence the military's need for creative men is pressing.

Experimenting of new things, almost 90 percent of all experiments have proven to be successful. To merge science with defence towards innovation of new weapons, a sharpness in Maths, Physics, chemistry and Computer science really support. AK-47 rifle invented in 1947 still continues to be the most widely used assault weapon for soldiers, which until today did not go through an up-gradation or cost effective research which means its potential to improve and modernise. Inventive engineering, different dimension of infantry thinking, refuting evidence, confusing the enemies about our strike strategies and redirecting them to wrong targets, etc are simple and possible areas that a military lab can think about. Next it can connect the space science with a satellite program to support an electronic warfare. Drafting young entrepreneurial and innovative minds to such military intelligence and innovation creates a cutting edge over the enemies, not alone most advanced weapons.

These elite cadets after graduating the military training program, shall be commissioned to Navy to flying the artillery and sailing the infantry forces hence capable to engaged into every aspect and function of the military.

With diverse exposure and specialisation to Navy, Army and Air force, operating tanks, vehicles and fighter aircrafts, the cadets operate variety of fighter planes like F15 of Boeing, F16 of General Dynamics to the latest of F35 supersonic from Lockheed Martin where they come out with new ideas of what all additional weapons, radars, lasers, shields and avionics that can connect to a satellite mapping program to make sure highest striking precision, speed and absolutely a zero-loss of men and equipments. When military equipments are available to all allies as well as it is open to even rivals through grey markets, finally the difference and winning factor become the officers and technology.

Recent Israel-Hamas Conflict in Gaza

Casualty of civilian lives and destruction of residential properties in a war stand for a court trial in Israel hence IDF is accountable for such miscalculations, where it does not matter for guerrillas and terrorist outfits from enemy's side. In the recent Gaza war with Hamas, IDF caused deaths of 160 terrorists out of total 230 lives mostly in the guerrilla hideouts, where the toll on Israeli side was just eleven including two paramilitary soldiers and one Indian lady caretaker.

When Hamas fired about 2200 rockets to Israel, IDF destroyed almost 99 percent of them in the sky with interceptors fired from I-Dome, where an AI supported shield screen detects the incoming objects and commands its destroyers by sensors. On the assault part, Heron UVS drones spots the precise locations of hide-outs and ammunitions and fire Patriot and Spike missiles sensed by AI and satellite mapping. If I-Dome is developed by RADS, drones were from IAI and the Israeli version of Patriots as augmented by Elbit System. These AI-enabled Drones also destroyed the 20-km long tunnel which transports weapons received in Egyptian port for Hamas in Gaza.

Was it a war to test the hit rate of Israel's I-Dome, Drones and missiles? As there were hardly any soldiers deployed in the war fronts, it was almost an electronic and digital war fought by RADS, IAI and Elbit. This could be an attesting pot for how the technology can fight war without human loss. Hezbollah, ISIS and such non-state actors are well adapted to using drones as suicide bombs, where recently Pakistan based extremists used similar ones across the LOC to drop weapons to its fighters in Jammu & Kashmir.

In similar form or not, with the diverse specialisation of our Military into electronic warfare, cyber-security, AI-enabled satellite mapping precision, missile shield, laser-sensitive weapons, drones, the modern warfare is minimum of manpower, and maximum of electronic and digital technology. Continuous modernization and code sharing with other militaries of most advanced technology, our military cannot be anyway of inferior officers. That is our strength and opportunity to nurture and incubate a world-class team of disruptors and innovators.

Brain Units

The mission shall start with selecting and recruiting just 300 student cadres of highest IQ, reasoning and intuition, with good brain in Physics and Maths or Electronics and Computer science. The screening shall go through various tests and interviews like academic and personality traits like attitude, courage, behaviour, passion and values, besides ability to overstretch mentally and physically, adjusting to camp life, ration and turbulent backpack travels. They adapt to military uniform, haircut and training, with syllabus studies in university colleges which enable them to qualify double degrees- one from University and next from military school. Combined, it makes a distinct advantage for a cadet with a high degree of instinct and intuition that guide them to think and do only what is right and appropriate. Army, Air force and Navy shall adopt 100 each cadets after their military induction by CDS or DRDO. Later at their half way course, they carry-out exchange programs to experiment how their learning, discoveries and innovations can be adapted to each other military divisions.

A team of these 'brain units' are drafted to our ordnance factories to improve and innovate the existing weapons they make, like reduction in the materials to make, stealth capabilities, strike rate precision, and speed in rounds and replenishment of shells, etc.

It could be also an improved and more efficient RF communication and signals, shielding and protecting a vessel or tank from an incoming destroyer, faster communication among land, air and sea forces, and also between border soldiers and aerial surveillance, bugging into enemy's computer system and commands, sensing radars and missiles, and laser sensitive assault weapons.

These cadets are under direct supervision of selected motivator-cum-mentors, selective technology experts with outstanding leadership attributes, who will assign tasks, training and laboratory experiments besides specific objectives of inventing new weapons, new technology and upgrading existing ones. They are trained not what to learn and what to think, but how to learn and how to think. These training schools will receive visiting trainers and mentors from US Marine, Navy Seals, Talpiot and Unit-8200, as well as similar schools from UK, Japan and Australia for exchange programs.

Unfortunate that the political leadership or their advisors are not fully aware of these technologies absorbed by Indian Military and their capabilities, without which it is impossible to get into equal partnership with US and Israel. This gives us a significant edge over PLA which consist largely of less educated, low-thinking labour soldiers. As the future warfare is changing to electronic and digital, the days of seapoy, havildar and subedar cadres are history, who are moulded to only obey orders and follow what is instructed, but not good at thinking, discretion, instinct and intuition. It is not just these men in numbers, but also those officers who create and enjoy a company of orderlies than educated and intelligent subordinates. Naturally they cause highest casualties, loss, rescue and delay during any confrontation which decides on winning or losing the war. The future military will employ more of science and technology graduates. This should differentiate our military edge over the conventional PLA or Pakistan forces.

These "brain units' are to consider not only to improve present weapons over the direct enemy countries, but also the equipments they are likely to receive from their allies. It is not an easy task which makes their responsibility much harder and demanding.

The Battlefield in Kurukshetra-Missiles & Interceptors

It was in 3067BC, one of the biggest conventional wars in history took place in Kurukshetra, fought with a total of 3.94 Million soldiers among them only twelve survived. Despite very large numbers of horses and elephants, arrows were the most advanced weapon of very high assault capability and human casualty. We are familiar with how Agneyastra (arrow of fire) was intercepted with Varunastra (arrow of water or rain) in the sky. Such other weapons were so large in use and every offensive arrow countered with a defending interceptor from opposite side.

Today the most winnable equipments in a war are assault missiles and shielding interceptors; for which the basic technology dates back to nothing but our assault and intercept arrows. One can imagine that these arrows were the ancient prototypes of the present cruise missiles. How surprising to see that it is Israel, or the second oldest of religion and language mastering the innovations in Missiles, Interceptors and I-Dome defence shields, which was originated by the oldest religion and language about 51 centuries back. A missile technology mastered in ancient India, modern India is far behind US and Israel. Had we been to a relentless research of this ancient science, the AI would have been its extension, which enables a precise strike-rate, networking the military intelligence, fighters and the men on the ground. Also what we see the remote controlled unmanned Pushpak aircraft in Ramayana drags us back to the use of AI during Ramayana war.

ML is riding too fast in setting loose data in order and can discover the realities of the history. Here we need a serious adaption to technology by connecting human brains to internet.

From a Cost to Contribution

Military spending is one of the highest costs in most of the government's budget which keeps increasing every year fearing a war and defending borders. More money spent on military, the country is left with less money for other welfare purposes like education, infrastructure, healthcare, food, etc. Despite all these, military spending cannot be avoided and even reduced. Because what is not sure is a war or its preparedness makes a country war-deterrent. Now this spending is changing from soldiers on ground to technology and equipments.

ISRO once a cost to the nation has successfully created its own revenue by providing satellite launching pads for so many foreign countries, besides gaining on crop losses with weather forecasts. Today ISRO is first-choice of satellite launching for more countries in the world. Benchmarking $.450Mil that costs a single space shuttle mission by NASA, ISRO could accomplish the same for as low as $.108Mil and to place a space probe in Mars orbit at $.74 Mil.

DRDO has helped Indian military with its own inventions of various ballistic missiles- anywhere from land, air or sea to destination across land, air and sea with target-tested precisions. It also improved our armoured off-road vehicles, launch vehicles, surveillance, radars and naval outreach. All these capabilities result a great replacement for imports.

The cost of US military is absorbed partially by their defence contractors like Boeing, Raytheon, Northrop-Grumman, General Dynamics and Lockheed-Martin and the cost-sharing with partner forces. Another military power- France has their arm exporters like Dassault and Thales to earn income to support their military cost, Russia also has large artillery and infantry equipment exports to give relief to their massive military cost. Of late China and Iran entered the arms export market to earn an income to support their huge military budgets.

Israel is another striking example of increasing their arms export to give a relief to their defence budget, which is the world's highest per-capita. Its government owned defence contractors like IAI and RADS earn large export income even from moré advanced countries like USA, France and Sweden that includes mostly micro-electronics, lasers, drones missile shields, surveillance radars, communications, besides AI enabled support systems for electronic and digital warfare.

'Atma-Nirbhar Bharat' an initiative of India's import substitution has given more self-reliance in our defence needs, by producing or assembling those imported technology and weapons indigenously, where not only our Public sector defence contractors like HAL, BDL, BEML etc had entered Joint ventures, the private sector like Tata, Reliance, Adani, Bharat Forge and M&M had also formed JVs with most US, Russian, French and Israeli companies with a goal to increase our self-reliance as well as to boost our exports. This will result in substantiating our high military cost with import reduction as well as export income. Next is establishing a research and innovation facility under DRDO+ISRO+CDS which will make sure of indigenous development of electronic and digital warfare equipments and also the patents for improving our civilian lives.

Military Intelligence

Increased warfare technology can bring down injuries and casualty in human lives. Every loss of life has to be compensated heavily by the nation which still cannot replace the loss to the family. Indian armed forces and para-military face huge loss of lives against fighting enemy infiltration, terrorism and extremism which is possible to bring down with modern electronic warfare assisted by early warning, radio-frequency sensing, remote surveillance and commanding.

Integrate all complementing units of three sections of defence- army, air force and navy with DRDO, engineering, production, intelligence, innovation, espionage, technology with human capital which controls the rest. First, considering the future potential, India requires an independent Minister for IT and AI, a specialist who can envision an unknown future that do not exist and who can align with our Military intelligence and technology. No doubt our peacetime military can spare its AI specialists to incubate and innovate new start-ups for Military as well as civilian purposes.

If modernisation and improvement of equipments are to be addressed, physics (material science) and maths becomes the fuel for innovation. To make an aircraft more lighter, means higher the speed and cheaper the fuel consumption, better the arsenal capacity, and flexibility against enemy destroyers, where material science and weight to size calculation are the basics. The similar way, how an existing tank can be made lighter with better dimensional stability and vibration resistance, how an armoured vehicle can be improved in terms of speed, less fuel and off-road driving comforts, how an assault rifle can reduce its weight and the time required for its magazine replenishment? It is physics and maths.

When it comes to shielding high-combat fighters, aircraft carrier vessels and airbases, computer science gives significant edge in hacking and bugging as well as satellite imaging and RF surveillance. AI and robotics supports deployment of radars, drones and domes, remote-command assaults, laser-precision strikes and satellite-mapped missiles and shields etc, and connectivity linking the forces on land, air, sea with intelligence helps exchange of information about enemy positions minimum loss of lives and weapons.

India has an upper edge in air force and navy against her bordering rivals where highest casualty is in the land force, no matter across the LOC, LAC, low-visibility and snow-filled mountains and Bastar-Dantevada forests. An example of where our military has to go for innovation is to improve our fighting strategy in these sectors. The 'brain units' will help enormously and effectively in this area, which in terms of cost is too little as compared to loss of lives and equipments besides the consequential compensation to families. AI, remote surveillance and satellite mapping can do away with physical soldier presence across the border. This shows the new opportunities for innovation in the Indian Military, which is just a fraction of the amount we spend on lives lost in protecting our borders, fighting terrorism and internal extremism.

If Lockheed Martin dominated the defence industry during twentieth century, it is the technology industry going to invade the twenty first century with automation, unmanned aerial vehicles, drones, AI-enabled interception, sensors and lasers, missile shields, hacking and other technology-enabled assault methods which will take away a large portion of defence budgets. Already defence contractors like Northrop Grumman and Raytheon are in global partnership with RADS and IAI of Israel for technology integrations like I-Dome and AI-enabled advanced drones.

What motivates Start-up Innovations?

We have seen that the enterprise value of a successful start-up scaled to a Unicorn status is much larger than any listed company in manufacturing or banking sector. For example:

Amazon was valued at US$.1.7Tril in 2020, where the value of the holding of its founder Jeff Bezos was estimated to be $.180 Bil (10.58%), which means Amazon had built $.1,520 Bil (1.52Tri) for others.

Google is the third most valuable company worth US$.1.Tril of which founder Larry Page and Sergey Brin together own $.100 Bil, which means Google has created 900 Bil for others.

Microsoft was valued at US$.1.2 Tril. Of which founder Bill Gates owned just 1.35% and his wealth is $.124Bil in 2020. Co-founder Paul Allen who died in 2018 was holding 1.34 Million shares in Microsoft. Steve Balmer the 30th employee in Microsoft is worth $.75 Bil mostly the shares he owned in the company, and the rest two-third of the value it created for others.

Facebook was valued over US.$600Bil, where its founder Marc Zuckerberg was worth about $.95.7Bil, means it had built 85% of its value ($.505Bil) for others.

See Apple, the first company to surpass US$.2.0 Tril in 2020, but its founder Steve Jobs is no more, and co-founder Steve Wosniak sold his shares, who is worth roughly $.100Mil today. The entire wealth of Apple Inc is today owned by others. It contributes almost 8-9% of US GDP of 24 Tril.

Gordon Moore, co-founder of Intel is worth $.12.8Bil, where the company valuation of $.271 Bil, which shows the wealth it distributed among others.

Started in 1997 by Reed Hastings and Marc Randolph, Netflix is valued at US$.243Bil in 2020, with the wealth of Hastings at $.5.0 Bil and Randolph at $.100 Mil.

Jack Ma owns 5.3% worth $.24.8 Bil of Alibaba though his total fortune is $.65.6Bil, where the rest of its remaining value of $.465 Bil is spread over others.

Tencent owns WeChat and Tencent Music, is the world's seventh largest valuable company worth $.761 Bil/2021, where its founder CEO is rich by $.55.2 Bil.

Ren Zhengfie, founder and CEO started Huawei with $.5,680 in 1990s, is rich by $.35.4 Bil out of its value $.656 Bil in 2019-20.

Naspers a VC invested $.32 Mil in Tencent in 2001, which is 31% ownership worth $80Bil in 2019. A $.20 Mil invested in Alibaba by Sotbank is today worth $.60Bil.

Byjus Learning App is today worth $.8 Bil, started with an idea of Online coaching. Accel Capital made the first investment of $.8,00,000 in Flipkart and increased it to $.100Mil, which Walmart acquired for $.16 Bil in 2019.

Mobiley is an electric self-driving cabin which was acquired by Intel for $.15.3 Bil in 2017. These are examples of how an idea can create much larger wealth for the GDP than any manufacturing and banking institutions, which still much larger than the GDP of many developing countries. If GDP is a measure of a nation's economy, the future of the world will be dictated and influenced by the countries driving successful start-up innovations.

Israeli Unicorns

SUNC-Start-up Nation Central report in 2018, Israel had 18 Unicorns in total, founded by Israelis. The 45 unicorns on the list today have a combined value of $92.6 billion and have raised more than additional $41 billion to date. As on 2019, the country has 6000 start-ups, 900 hubs, 350 MNCs, 100+ mentors, 400 Investors and 320,000 talents.

Though there was a steady rise in Chinese investments during 2014-18 especially in the tech sector, it started declining during the last two years to 10% of the total. After three years of robust investment from China in well-known Israeli VC funds, such as Catalyst, Carmel Ventures, JVP, and Singulariteam, in 2017 those investments dried up completely. The very robust business co-operation between US and

Israeli technology sectors, China could not easily penetrate much into Israeli VC opportunities where US stands as not only the investor but also as an equal partner in acquisition and collaboration.

Google runs a most optimistic project called 'Next Billion Users (NBU)'. NBU is an initiative by Google to build products for the next wave of internet users, especially from countries, which have mobile-first internet users and also face data, network and hardware constraints. Surprisingly NBU works on unknown inventions of future, which do not exist today. Google Pay was one of the most successful innovations by NBU which made the lives so easy for millions of users with digital payment. Gmail captured almost eighty percent of the global email network

As already explained in detail about the application of Maths and Physics in research and innovation, Dell and HP, Apple and Samsung keep innovating their products made from a number of materials other than metals, largely engineering plastics and recyclable alloys resulting a drastic reduction in weight and thickness with a higher structural stability. Material science and maths make so essential to Intel's research and innovation programs. It is amazing to see how aircraft companies like Boeing and Airbus innovate with an equally structurally stable plastic composite developed by companies like GE and DuPont to replace metals to every possible level. It is nothing but Physics and Maths! In passenger aircrafts, weight reduction helps fuel economy, more passenger seats and increase in speed and flying flexibility.

With deep roots into nurturing start-ups, IDF-Unit 8200 and the Talpiot play significant roles into incubating the Israeli Start-up ecosystem. This drives Israeli technology start-ups with a business patriotism, where the country's foreign diplomacy has a strong influence on its home grown business and industry.

Reset the Purpose of Education

Post-independence, our education model was founded on three pillars-Secularism, Pluralism and Socialism which were right model at by that time. To fulfil the present needs, these purposes are due to be redefined to Patriotism, Values and Purpose (Goal).

Education without patriotism, values and purpose is like taking a wrong path to reach a destination totally unknown to us. In contrast except in Jio and Tata Group ventures, mostly those seventeen largest unicorns in India still have sizeable ownership from Chinese investors like Alibaba, Tencent, Fosun, Steadview Capital, Sailing, CEECF, Didi Chuxing, China Lodging, SAIF, Hill House, Foxconn, Meituan-Dianping, etc. When India regulated to reduce the Chinese ownership, it still keeps growing through off-shore channels. Such restrictions are unlikely to be successful by regulation unless a business patriotism which is possible with the help of a Military training, mentoring and incubation.

Not only that India has to remain the world leader in IT and BPO sector, but also very important to rise her Innovation and business start-up indices. India's premium technology universities like IITs, IISc and NITs and other private campuses like BITS and VIT are recognized by world ranking employers. If many of our migrants who made great fortunes with Global Technology MNCs and Innovation start-ups in US and Europe are from these institutions, there is also an equal or higher potential in nurturing those talents towards digital technology innovations. Most of the global corporations select graduates with academic brilliance and also on social skills and values.

To Nurture Social Skills

For organizations, training job skills is easier, but training social skills and values are more difficult, which play a pivotal role in capabilities and performance. On the other side what an employee learned in campus is short-relevant until two or three years at workplace, where it is the job related skills and social skills take him forward and grow. From the dawn of 2020, the job market demands, not only a brilliant academic score, but those core social skills required in modern workplace. These core social skills are essentially a high emotional maturity, with good perseverance and resilience, which could make them so outstanding if achieved at their early twenties.

It is so essential that the campuses shall drive their future aspirations both towards ambitious career jobs as well as to research and innovation. Once the universities and military join hands, the combined initiative could drive a new innovation culture for the benefit of the nation. Every year delayed, we miss so many potential disruptors and innovators.

Ray Kurzweil, cofounder of SU-Singularity University and today's best known evangelist on Innovation said, "digital technology is growing exponentially, but our intuition about the future is growing linear". This is the tumbling block for the future innovation. Greatest thing in life is to keep your mind young.

Needless to say, when technology plays an integral role in our future livelihood, an all time importance in STEM discipline- Science, Technology, Engineering and Maths is required to meet the future challenges.

8 Once Four Start-ups; Today the World's First Trillion Dollar Companies

If those most influential companies of 20th century were GM, Ford, GE, Boeing, Walmart, Sony, Toyota, IBM and Microsoft, Those most influential companies of 21st century on the planet are Apple, Amazon, Google and Facebook.

Also these companies are either already or in the race to become the world's first trillion-dollar company without anyone to challenge them. NYSE and NASDAQ did forgive for their sins that destroyed other companies. These magnificent four infiltrate deep into our lives so completely that they are the most impossible to reject. Their technologies helped us achieve a rapid speed in our lives and businesses during the last two decades that none others could equal. To live today, we have no other way but to understand and absorb these technologies. If twentieth century companies thrived on defeating competition and expanding new markets, these new companies progress on collaboration without copyright protection.

These companies changed the existing rules of rich and poor countries, liberated a huge population from poverty bar and empowered them to a buoyant middle class workforce by driving them to afford and possess a higher quality of living, education, healthcare and housing than the combined output of all those biggest companies could transform until then. This led to a multiple growth in most other manufacturing sectors from automobiles, electronics, home appliances, housing, computers and smart phones.

Until twentieth century, global companies did not need to look beyond US and Europe for doing well. Even the policies and strategies of consumer product companies considered the top 2 Billion of world's population as their customers. They expected this to be the rules to remain same for rest of our lifetimes.

In the wake of 21st century, these above rules got re-written with the real meaning of technology to down cost rapidly and the cell phone spearheading to penetrate into the bottom segment of 5 billion especially in Asia and Africa. Internet enabled this revolution to networking across the world to a level of at no extra cost today. Internet and AI empowered millions to work from any remote corners in collaboration with each other. Dramatic progress in life extension, is resulting to a new reality of more grandparents than grandchildren by 2030.

The global economy which was once powered by consumers from US, Japan and Europe is going to be driven by consumers from Asia and Africa with a substantial increase in global wealth generated and owned by women. A decade later, there will be more robots than unskilled workers and more currencies than countries with shopping being swept away by e-commerce than retailers.

AI and ML has enabled your personal habits and preferences as data storage which simplifies the process of ordering your food, clothes, shoes and groceries, with category, size, colour and price bar, and on completion of the ordering, it automatically debit the bill amount to your credit card or bank account without the need for a cashier or helper. These four technology giants achieved the trillion-dollar bar in a span of twenty years, as against a long period of four to five decades for those big firms in the 20th century.

It is very interesting to see that if the global companies of twentieth century followed a policy and strategy of incremental growth, ie about ten to fifteen percent growth over base year, these new technology giants adopted a path of exponential growth of a rapid pace at the rate of 10X ten times its present size otherwise known as "Moonshot Goals".

Market Cap of five largest US companies in FY-2006 and FY-2018

In 2006			**In 2018**		
Exxon-Mobile	:	US$.540Bil	Apple	:	US$.888Bil
GE	:	$.463 Bil	Alphabet	:	$.773Bil
Microsoft	:	$.355Bil	Amazon	:	$.748 Bil
Citigroup	:	$.331Bil	Microsoft	:	$.723Bil
BoA	:	$.290Bil	Facebook	:	$.534Bil

This above chart explains the difference between incremental companies and exponential companies. It is worth knowing the top five of Fortune 500 list in 1980 were Exxon-Mobile, GM, Mobil, Ford Motor and Texaco in order. In 2000, this list made little changes with GM, Walmart, Exxon-Mobil, Ford and GE, where none of them remain within the top five in 2018.

Once computing meant IBM, communication meant AT&T, voice was synonymous with phone and video with television, where Internet has dissolved these boundaries and distinctions.

The Big Fours

01. Amazon

Amazon is the biggest store on Earth, with practically no inventory. It is worth more than other retail giants like Walmart, Nordstrom, Target, Tesco, Gap, Carrefour and Ikea combined with its market cap of $.1.56 Tril in 2021. In 2016, US retail grew by 4 percent, where Amazon grew 40 percent with the help of Internet. A humble beginning as an online book store in 1994 by Jeff Bezos with a start-up fund of $.250,000 from his parents, Amazon gives an attractive price advantage and shopping comfort to the customer, where its cost of capital declines while every other retailer's increases. It also employs largest number of advanced robotics in its warehouses, while increased dependence on drones in delivery.

From the wake of twenty first century, retail started booming like never before. In 2005-06, Sears was valued at $14.3Bil, Target still higher at $38Bil and Wallmart at an all-time high of $158Bil, where the online start-up retailer-Amazon was at $17.5Bil. With the spread of e-commerce, online ate too much into offline, a decade later Sears lost its value by 94 percent to its exit from business, Target improved to $55Bil, Wallmart rose to $244Bil, but the Everything Store-Amazon accelerated to $700Bil. This resulted tremendous changes to the lives of billions. Online transaction was replacing offline trade, saving hours in driving, finding a parking and visiting showrooms. Today the trend is 'everything online'.

Off late it opened Amazon Go grocery stores where customer can simply pick their items and walk out where sensors will scan your cart and app and will bill your bank account automatically without cashiers. At larger volume and lower margins, Amazon reinvests its pile of profit back into its business which avoids tax elements. Its invasion of retail trade led to the decline of values of major mall properties like

Simon Property Group and Taubman Properties. One of its major cost is the shipping, but its important objective is to reach more and more households in less and less time.

Amazon focuses in e-commerce, Cloud, digital streaming, VR and AI. AI drives the Amazon search in areas like product search and feel, selection, ordering, payment, tracking and delivery. Amazon challenges others who keep raising prices faster than inflation as they are ripe for disruption. It already announced about entering business delivery, which fell the stock of FedEx, UPS and DHL with a combined value of $.200Bil, by 5 percent on next day. As the world's largest internet company, it operates from its world headquarters based in Seattle selling more than 12Mil products.

With over 1.3Mil employees in US, Amazon is the second biggest employer after Walmart registering a sale of $386Bil in 2020, an increase of 38% over previous year, with over 200Mil Prime subscribers. It recently acquired MGM Studios for $.8.5Bil to produce its exclusive movies to its cinema platform which is in competition with Netflix and Disney Hotstar. Though AWS generates 13% of its revenue, it is most profitable division of Amazon with almost 35 percent of the Cloud market. Its dominance in Cloud is largely contributed by its robust cash flow generated from its e-commerce business, far exceeding Google, Microsoft and IBM.

The average lifespan of big US companies being thirty years and with already twenty seven years over, Bezos says that his job is to extend the life of his company as much he could. The company has also faced accusations of putting undue pressure on suppliers to maintain and increase its profitability. It is also criticised for not sharing annual profits with its dedicated suppliers squeezed with stressed margin and delayed payments.

With so much activities into logistics and delivery, Amazon operates thousands of fleets and drivers, which gave them access to other's delivery partnerships. With extended fleet of third-party deliveries, Amazon has become one of the world's largest five logistics and delivery companies.

Amazon Go is a physical stores ecosystem that disrupts their e-commerce business. To enter the store, you need to scan your Amazon Go app in your smart phone, where not any sales staff but robots will assist you to pick your choice of item and once you complete your shopping, you exit without anyone checking you, where your bills are auto-debited to your credit card with no cashier. The showrooms are AI-powered with sensors and cameras which enable your face recognition, tracks your movements and buying pattern, which will be stored for future use.

Jesse Levinson from Stanford with Tim Kentley-Klay co-founded Zoox, an autonomous car in 2014 in Foster City, CA, which Amazon acquired in 2020 for $1.2Bil. Zoox is creating an entirely new autonomous vehicle targeted at the robo-taxi market. The company›s approach is centred around the fact that a retrofitted vehicle is not optimized for autonomy. Zoox has applied the latest techniques in automotive, robotics and renewable energy to build a symmetrical, bi-directional battery-electric vehicle that solves the unique challenges of autonomous mobility. Without a driver seat, it claims, "built for riders, not drivers". A 133 kWh battery equips Zoox vehicles with the power to drive all day. Its lighting system tells other road users what Zoox will do next.

In compliance to its Climate Pledge footprint, Amazon ordered for 100,000 electric delivery trucks, drone delivery and plastic-free bio-degradable packaging. With so many customers, it tracks and stores their personal data, whenever a transaction and payment is completed, not only the bank account and credit card details, but also the income, buying patterns and habits, preferences and frequencies, etc.

With great plans for commercial expansion in space, NASA has granted a total amount of $415.6 million in November, 2021 to Jeff Bezos' Blue Origin, aerospace company Nanoracks, and defence contractor Northrop Grumman to design space stations and commercial destinations in space. NASA hopes to find a replacement for the International Space Station (ISS) that has time till the end of this decade to retire. NASA plans for a "robust low-Earth orbit economy" includes coordination with private industry to formulate and design commercial destination capabilities that will work not only for potential government but private sector needs as well. It will be called 'Orbital Reef' and it will be developed by Blue Origin and Sierra Space. Orbital Reef will be a "mixed-use space business park" that will support all types of human spaceflight activity in low-Earth orbit. It will feature reusable space transportation and advanced automation that is expected to help minimise the cost and complexity of users onboard the space station.

02. Apple

Apple ranks to be the most profitable company in history which sits on a cash pile which is close to the GDP of Denmark. When technology companies are known to serve the untouched rising billions at prices at decreasing levels, luxury will not complement to the industry, but as an exception Apple represents to be a luxury possession, through i-Mac notebook, i-Pad or i-Phone. It is popularly accepted the fact that an i-Phone in hand is a pride identified to a lifestyle, which complements with a Rolex on wrist, Cartier Sunglass on eyes, Mont-Blanc in the pocket, Tumi leather business bag where every other handset makes a misfit. On the other hand, the production cost of i-Phone is too low, unlike the other luxury icons. Apple is a rare example how a cheap product can be too luxury brand.

If i-Phone enjoys 19 percent of the global smart phone market, it swept away almost 87 percent of the sector's total profit in 2016. When Dell and Asus continued to drop the prices of their notebooks and HP was struggling to hold its higher price tag, Apple ruled the roost with a substantial premium in its notebooks. Why? Its language of luxury is simplicity which was never been such a premium luxury in the past. Its simplicity is light and sleek, and so easy to use. It is in contrast to the normal rule of price based costing or cost based pricing, but how a product can be sold at unheard margins despite being so cheap in production cost?

When other Club-4 members were disrupting into new and unknown technologies, Apple always works for expanding from its present borders. Realising the fact that technology life cycles are too shorter than brands, it starts with a new selected team to work from its present edge; ie, when a new i-Phone is launched and sets a new record in sales, it is already ready with its improved succession model. When this innovation is repeated, it leaves hardly any space for another competitor to disrupt the market. When no other technology firm ever solved the problem of being aged and outdated, Apple keeps itself above the rest by defeating its own benchmarks. As a result, the competitors of i-Phone always follow behind the leader.

In 1976, Apple Computer Co was founded by Steve Jobs, Steve Wozniak and Ronald Wayne in a garage at Los Alto, CA which is today known as Apple Inc, 1 Apple Park Way, Cupertino, CA. For initial capital, Jobs sold his VW minibus and Wozniak his programmable calculator.

Steve Jobs was an audacious eccentric like mostly other disruptors, who believed in 'make a dent in the universe". When i-Phone was launched in 2007, it destroyed 100,000 jobs at Nokia and Motorola. Nokia was at its peak, with 30 percent of Finland's GDP and quarter of the country's total corporate taxes. It is higher than the daily trading at Russian stock market, and also the market cap of Boeing, Airbus and Nike combined. With poor sales performance, Woznaik left to become a teacher in 1985 and four months later Jobs was terminated, Apple got a new CEO John Sculley from Pepsi. Failing a partnership with Intel on its processor with WO/S, Macintosh helped Apple to touch $.10Bil in 1988 after relentless innovations to have own Mac O/S. Sculley was replaced by two more CEOs, during when Mac O/S failed with just three percent market share making it a stressed company. In 1997, Steve Jobs returned as an advisor to CEO, soon to become the CEO who sold all his shares in NeXT and invested in Apple, and by next year the birth of legendary i-Mac. Next year, Apple returned to profit after three years.

From 2000 Apple launched i-Tune and converted Music to MP3 digital format followed by i-Pod on Internet, a portable MP3 player. In 2007 Apple introduced the touch-screen i-Phone capable of operating on Internet, with a number of features like music, chats, cameras, e-books and further upgraded with play-store, games and learning apps which were sold and serviced though App Stores to experience the products and to buy additional apps. In 2010, i-Pad was launched an intermediate between I-Mac and i-Phone.

i-Phone X is sold at $999 price tag, which is 170 percent higher than its cost of $370, a profit margin of Ferrari at a Toyota volume. Still it enjoys 92 percent customer retention than 77 percent of Samsung. This profit is not much as compared to its user segment's profit by using i-Phone. Apple redefined the way businesses are carried-out. Today smart phone is the connecting factor between sellers and buyers across the world.

iPhone was launched in June 2007, which was like a maternity hospital that caused births to so many technology platforms like e-commerce giant Amazon, relationship app like Facebook, search and related engines like Google, entertainment like Youtube, hospitality giant like Airbnb, Online taxi like Uber, so many food delivery businesses like Zomato, Ubereats and Swiggy, WeWork office sharing, and many other new born technology businesses, connecting seller and buyer directly without middlemen, job and education portals, flight booking, online banking etc that generate trillions of dollar revenue and many times more market value, to the benefit of billion livelihoods, especially those underprivileged society, which history had never witnessed and surprisingly at free of cost to Apple or PlayStore. In this digital technology era, companies do not protect their patents, making them accessible even to competitors. I-Phone and i-OS have become the heart and nucleus for all these companies, who cannot imagine running their businesses without it and surprisingly they make more profits than the owners of i-Phone.

During these years of Steve Jobs, Apple was a successful innovation firm, but after he resigned in 2011 due to ill-health, Tim Cook reigned over as CEO. Tim was more a scale-up specialist as how Jobs was a start-up innovator, under whom Apple went on multiplying its revenue, profit and value to become the first ever company to cross $1 Tril in Market value. A strong proof of its innovation, it is surprising to note that more than half of its revenue and two third of profits come from products that did not exist three years ago. Next it keeps coming out with new technologies, features and apps, not ever asked by its customers but embraced by them in total. Apple virtually redefined the way of doing business and helps other businesses to make more money than itself. The company announced in 2021 about its new autonomous car to be launched by 2025. It is the world's first company to cross the market value of $3Tril in 2021.

03. Google

Few companies in the history have ever been so successful and admired as Google the company, that has transformed the internet and become an indispensible part of our lives. Along with the internet search, its founders invented a new way of making billions of dollars from digital advertising. Their main domain of free search, supported by revenue from digital advertising, Google dramatically expanded to more transformative projects; data centres, You Tube-free internet videos, open-source cell phones, Cloud, digitalising books, driverless cars, Life extension etc. Its key success factors are the engineering mindset, transparency, agility, relentless experimentation and audacity in risk taking.

"Our Mission is to organize the world's information and make it universally accessible and useful, and dedicated to improving human lives". That is what Google stands for! It is the 'extra-terrestrial intelligence' search engine, far exceeding the human intelligence to learn and remember. Once depending on encyclopaedia for most of the information we required, today we have everything and anything trust-worth, available on Google Search, just a fraction of a second. Google is driven on AI super-intelligence.

Founded in 1998 by Sergey Brin and Larry Page, two PhD students in Computer Sciences from Stanford, CA. When both founders approached investors mostly technology people, they could not understand the terminology called 'search'. They launched Google News in 2002 and Gmail in 2004, followed by Google Map in 2005 and Google Chrome in 2008, the most surfed platforms in respective segments. In 2011, Google entered the Cloud market, with earnings of $.13Bil in 2020. It makes its revenue from online advertisement, a whopping $.95Bil in 2017 and commanded a cash flow of $38Bil. No other companies had expanded its business as much as Google as technologies continue to converge, the scale of disruption will only increase. In 2021, Google was valued at $.1.68Tril. It handles 3.5 bil search queries a day. Google turns every recruit to be part of their dynamic, creative group- the Three Ts- talent, tolerance and technology, as most new jobs requires creative analytic skills, predominantly what we call the social skills like collaboration, negotiation, persuasion and social perception.

The core businesses of Google are Search, Gmail, Youtube, Chrome, Android, Adsense, Google Drive & Cloud. Its other new projects are Waymo, Google Ventures & Capital G, Google X, Nest and few divisions like Space and CALICO-Life Extension Science. G-mail has a virtual monopoly in global e-mail network, with a massive 80 percent market share.

Autonomous car is a separate high priority division where Google integrates Sensors, Waze-a traffic sensing technology with Google map which could take the car market to another direction, application and volume.

Banking was unknown to Google, but by next year it is entering entirely to this new territory-the world of banking. The tech giant is creating checking accounts in partnership with Citigroup and the Stanford Federal Credit Union as part of a project named Cache, an account checking app that will collaborate with most leading banks. Google's

G-Pay is the largest browsed money transaction app in the world but once it scales up to billion users, Google will find an ad-revenue model without charging the users. Not to rule-out a possibility of entering e-commerce in next couple of years, mostly through acquisition.

In July 2007 when Marissa Mayer, the vice president of Google Search Products and User Experience until the end of 2010 led a delegation to India, one of the local engineers asked, "we have heard of our roadmap for products, but what is the roadmap for revenues"? She answered, "that is not the way we think; we are focused on our users. Once we make them happy, we will have the revenue". Absolutely right- Google thrives to make its users happy at free of cost, where its revenue comes from digital advertising.

Larry Page is dedicated to new businesses like Autonomous cars, Space exploration and Life extension. When the world is busy with electric cars, Google is in the development of driverless cars, driven by AI-enabled robots and sensors which are not only carbon-free, but can save human lives and accidents. Google Map is expanding its search beyond earth to explore numerous planets, moons and the International Space Station using a new Google Map feature. Under a separate company called CALICO (CAlifornia LIfescience CO) Life Sciences LLC, it converges AI, Genomics, lab tests and DNA to arrive individual health reports and treatments which will together help extension of one's life by a decade or more by better understanding of human biology. Its autonomous, driverless cars completed test drives and is in the regulatory process before hitting the market. It does not require steering, brake pedals, accelerator and other components that drivers use for controlling movements. AI and sensors will control the car, ensuring hardly any accidents and traffic violations; no drink, no phone, no sleep while driving. Driverless cars pose a severe loss of driver jobs to robots which cause far less casualties. When robots cause a rare accident, we tend to blame them but not the drivers who cause more accidents. This can risk the relevance for vehicle insurance business. Google developed LaMDA-Language Model for Dialogue Applications aims to replace robotic conversations with AI with more natural dialogues. It is an open-ended conversational AI application.

Google is most trusted name where people disclose every detail about themselves and their family until it knows all and everything from bank account, credit card, food habits, medical test data, illness and medication, buying habits to cloth and footwear sizes leaving us in a helpless situation that we cannot reverse back all that we shared. This trust we placed in its mechanism makes Google the most influential among the Big Fours.

Google has a unique and best team to work on these missions. It recruits the most brilliant brains in Electronics and Computer Science and provides training in motivation, collaboration and innovation, but relatively the highest remuneration packages. Google acquired several companies, but Youtube and Waze are the noteworthy ones. For FY-2021, Google reported a revenue of $256Bil.

04. Facebook

Facebook was founded in 2004 by Mark Zuckerberg, Eduardo Saverin, Andrew McCollum, Dustin Moskovitz, and Chris Hughes, roommates and students at Harvard as a relationship connectivity platform for their colleagues. In 2020, it boasts 2.8Bil monthly active users, seventh largest internet users, and largest downloaded app in the world. Its main income at $39Bil is from online digital advertisement.

What's-App was founded by two former Yahoo employees named Jan Koum and Brian Acton, which was acquired by Facebook for $.19Bil in 2014. What's-App has a monthly user base of 2Bil worldwide in addition to 2.85 Bil of Facebook. Instagram which was also acquired by Facebook for $.1Bil in 2012 has almost a billion users worldwide. Almost 85 percent of the time we spend on our phones is on Facebook and its subsidiaries-What's-App, Instagram and Messenger which makes our phones are no longer a communicate devise but a Facebook one.

Facebook is gaining influence faster than any enterprise in the history. Its business is relationship which makes anyone happier, especially when we discover someone we knew twenty years ago in college. Over the last six to seven decades what made us happier were things like cars, cameras, TVs, stereos, video-cams, cell phone, etc, it is Amazon, Google and Facebook making us happier in e-commerce, search and social media in the last two decades. One example, if millions of soccer fans took 150 years to engage the world together, Facebook and its two siblings- What's-App and Instagram achieved the same milestone before it turned twenty years.

When Coronavirus spread across the world in 2019-21, none of the world's most advanced nations or the UN/WHO establishments were prepared to control its spread rate and finding a cure. Though Facebook and What's-App when invented, did not foresee the coronavirus resulting lockdown and isolation but as a blessing in disguise, both platforms played the most crucial role of relationship and messaging, which prevented large number of consequential disasters like suicides and psychological disorders. During the months-long shutdown causing isolation for millions, Facebook and its subsidiary What'-App were the most blessed remedy to engage them with relation and connectivity at no cost. But when the pandemic was brought under control and life was back to near normal, the facebook and what's-app habits only continued to scale-up. If Facebook had a global subscription of 2.23Bil in 2018, it surged to 2.9Bil in 2021, an increase of almost 32 percent in two ears. Similarly What's-App active users went up from 1.5Bil in 2019 to over 2Bil in 2020-21. Despite this increase in subscriptions, the number of times a day spent on these platforms were multiplied with a manifold increase in the time engaged.

05. Tesla

On $754 a share as on Sept, 2021, Tesla achieved a market value of $.755Bil, which is more than Toyota ($252Bil), VW ($149 Bil), BYD ($112Bil), Daimler ($89Bil), Great Wall Motors ($73Bil) and GM ($71Bil) combined ($746 Bil). Once it achieves 10Mil cars in next four years, the share price is expected to cross $.3000, ie above $.3Tril value by 2025. Besides EVs, Tesla is spending sleepless nights on Energy Storage and SpaceX mission. Its new venture "Starlink"- a satellite broadband internet service is to take a high-power, high-speed internet globally with a reach-out potential across remote villages. Hyperloop is a new driverless mobility system from Tesla, which can scale down the high-speed rail travel hours by 60 percent without environment hazards, while it also poses a serious threat to the air travel.

In the last week of October 2021, Hertz ordered one hundred thousand S-3 model electric cars from Tesla to boost its rent-a-car fleets which took Tesla to become the fourth company to join the $1trillion valuation club ahead of Facebook. Founder Elon Musk owns 20 percent of the company shares. If Apple is a low cost-high luxury product, Tesla is a high cost-high luxury brand.

All these companies which are known for destroying the existing businesses and transforming the world to a new trajectory, know well that a fierce disruption is taking place in some small garages by small teams of entrepreneurs which will destroy them and make their business irrelevant in a short future. If the success factors are vision, passion and will, the failure is the fear and setting limits.

Almost every major car company has a future dream in electric car. The number of models has increased from two in 2010 to forty-one in 2019 worldwide. Ford is working on forty models by 2025 with an investment of $11Bil. Mercedes is outspending Ford with $11.7Bil on 10 electric models and forty hybrid variants, outstripped by VW with $40Bil to electrify 40 electric vehicles by 2030. Worldwide, global automakers have already committed more than $300Bil, which is in addition to the dream visions of new comers like Tesla into electric cars and Google into driverless cars. This future vision is certainly going to extinct many regional automakers by displacing several thousand jobs. When this change leads to closing down the many of the fuel stations and fast food joints on our highways, which has created huge real estate wealth will remain as heritage monuments in coming decades. On the other side, parking in the malls and food joints will add new business services like power ports for electric and driverless cars.

Humanity, Equality, Peace and Democracy

Relationship makes us more human with empathy to each other, which unites our society with happiness and peace hence it reduces frictions, violence and crimes. Countries that trade with one another, are unlikely to go for war. FB is a powerful media that blossoms and breeds human rights, exchange of knowledge and culture besides grooming democracy. As a result, youths tend to agitate and turn away from religious extremism, suppression and censoring. More equality, human rights and democracy, the world has less relevance for arms race and defence spending. If Coke, McDonald's and Marlboro were the ambassadors of compassionate capitalism and democracy, today it is first FB, followed by Google and Internet.

The digital economies proved to be less religious and fanatic people. Higher the education and financially secured, people are less intolerant towards other faiths and skin colour. The discrimination which existed in employments in industrial and government sectors in the past, does not exist in technology sector where job skills and social skills are considered as the only merit for recruitment and growth. As youths are more regular and adhered to use these four engines, they are found to be extremely friendly and tolerant to other nationals and faiths than those aged who are less exposed. As a result, religion becomes less divisive in countries where digitalisation is surging. That is its power of integrating and uniting. As these companies do not move against any government or political ideologies, they are extremely compassionate to humanity, especially the next billions with a purpose to touch and improve their lives that exceeds all other conventional and tangible goals of profit booking and shareholder returns. Over the last two decades, religious affiliation in US has come down by 25 percent. When our society is transforming with an exploding progress in digital technology, our planet has become more economically developed, united, safe and peaceful than ever before.

Apple was a machine, Amazon a store, Google a search engine and Facebook a social network. In the beginning they competed each other, later they enjoyed the advantage of collaborating each other. Today, what is Amazon or Uber without Google and Apple? Google and Facebook together earn 25 percent of the world's total advertisement expenditure. Today all these four technology giants are enjoying miraculous benefits of collaboration than competing and weakening each other. The internet connectivity in 2017 was 3.8Bil, which is expected to touch 8.2Bil in 2025. On a simple measure that if a smart phone can result an increase in a common man's average income by twenty percent, its impact on a national GDP is so abundant that no other economic sectors can equal.

If Amazon is the largest search engine without a warehouse, Facebook is the largest resource for relationship, Apple the most innovative company and Google is the most trusted pool for information search. Together these companies make billions of lives better, comfortable and worth living.

Uber Technologies

Ten years ago, the idea of getting into a stranger's car, or walking into a stranger's home, would have seemed too risky and dangerous, but today it's as common as ordering a book online. Uber and Airbnb are household names; redefining neighbourhoods, challenging the way governments regulate business and changing the way we travel and stay. The word Uber is an American generic, meaning greatness, or great things.

Uber posed a severe threat to taxi owners; which attracted several local government resolutions for its ban. But the company with its wide public acceptance in such a short time, mobilised its customers to voice out against such regulation. A survey of US Auto Association in 2016 revealed that three out of five drivers felt scared to ride in self-driving cars and only one in the five would entrust his life to a driverless car. The courage in a driver-driven car is that the driver is also at risk in an accident, but nothing like that in a driverless car.

Its services include ride-hailing, food delivery, package delivery, couriers, freight transportation, and through a partnership with Lime (LimeBike), electric bicycle and motorized scooter rental. It boasts as much as 2Mil driver partners, still adding another 50,000 every month. It has a service coverage in 85 countries and 700 cities. With 'Customer Obsession' as its core value, Uber achieved $78Bil value in 2019.

Microsoft

After ruling the technology list for over two decades, Microsoft lost its sheen with a number of new start-ups entering the fray. Its assault into cell phone market with the acquisition of Nokia for $7Bil in 2013, did not make any impact as its adoption of W/OS- Windows Operating System failed against i-Phone's IOS and Google's Android. For almost a decade, Microsoft did not have any worthwhile innovation other than its extended versions of W/OS in personal computers, besides "Azure" Cloud Store. With its dominant place in personal computers O/S, Microsoft is valued at $2.28Tril in 2021.

Google and Facebook are accessible for everyone from anywhere at free of cost. With millions of users at their sites, it gives enormous advertising opportunities to other companies at a cost which they can never achieve at such a scale on any other media. This generates a truly democratic and ethical means of income for both, which is generously spent on business expansion and new innovations that touch millions of lives. Though Facebook increased the friendship and relations many folds, teenagers are 40 percent less likely to hang-out with friends than before. P&G and Intel have a benchmark of $2.3 Mil value per employee as against $20.8 million per employee for Facebook.

AI and IoT help to track behaviour of individuals from their past purchases and habits, which is scaled up in such a way that when they browse for a particular product, the page opens the images of similar category of products which suit to their interest and preference. For example when we open the travel destination, it shows the airline operating to that region, hotels and car rentals including other tourist spots near around. Facebook can identify and serve up the right customers at a big scale because it connect data to identity, where one posting by an individual to a group of twelve friends can further get connected to each one's social circle in a multiple effect. Amazon has 350Mil credit cards and shopper profiles in store perhaps the highest than anyone else on our planet, which helps them to know what we like, and connect us to our preferred shopping patterns and behaviour. Apple also knows our data at our purchase point, which links the same to our identity. Google started with early days of its internet search from the Microsoft Internet Explorer. If Microsoft was first to bring Internet Explorer, a PC-centric platform, Google took these technologies at an escalated degree with Google Chrome- a mobile centric platform. This brought a rapid shift from PCs to smart phones that resulted a huge growth for smart phones like Apple, Samsung and other Chinese brands at the cost of PC manufacturers like HP, Lenovo and Dell. Under the present CEO Satya Nadella Microsoft successfully repositioned itself from a 'devices and services' provider to a 'mobile and cloud' company.

Story of Wealth Creation

Jeff Bezos the founder of Amazon, owns 10.3 percent as on Sept, 2021, which is \$.176 Bil that makes him the richest person on earth. This means that Bezos contributed a wealth of \$.1,534Bil for other investors. Corporate history had never seen such a robust Cash Flow that Amazon boasts, with one of the highest borrowing capacity at lowest rates.

Steve Jobs and Steve Wozniak the co-founders of Apple owned 65.4 and 34.6 percent respectively at its founding, which Jobs sold almost all his stake to fund his future start-ups- NeXT and Pixar and Wozniak followed him selling his stake later. Ronald Wayne who joined the founders Steve Jobs and Steve Wozniak as co-founder sold his 10% shares in Apple for \$.95Bil in Oct, 2021. This leaves almost the entire wealth created by Apple with new investors.

Bill Gates is worth \$.129Bil as on October, 2021, where he owns 1.3 percent of Microsoft shares (\$.24Bil) with the balance wealth accounted by his philanthropy- Bill & Melinda Gates Foundation. Former CEO of Microsoft Steve Ballmer owns 4 percent amounting to \$.91.2Bil and balance $.2,159Bil rests with others.

Larry Page and Sergey Brin together owns 11,4 percent of Alphabet, the parent company of Google, which make them worth $.192Bil with $1488Bil created to other investors. Marc Zuckerberg, the founder owns 14 percent of Facebook which makes him rich by $.110.6 Bil, while creating a remaining wealth of $.1,100Bil to others.

This is the might of innovation start-ups which creates massive wealth for their nation and are not greedy to charge the users despite having monopoly in sector businesses, besides enriching human lives.

IBM and HP

In technology sector, the first and one of the most respected names is IBM. It started as CTR Corporation-computing, tabulating and recording in June 1911 New York as a public listed company. After Thomas Watson joined it as General Manager in 1914 and becoming its president next year, IBM achieved a fast-track growth story and was better known as "Big Blue" as an American Icon. Very soon it achieved the corporate respect for its superior quality of salesmen training and customer service, which helped them winning most corporate clients when the company launched its Cloud business in last decade. When the computer business was facing tough competition from low-price competitors, it turned into integrated computing and maintained its leadership position until 2000. In the related industry, IBM is highly respected for its organization strength and culture which helped the company to sustain two financial turndowns. In 2021, The Big Blue reported a market value of $91Bil with a revenue of $.74Bil in 2020-21 reporting a net profit of $2.3Bil. IBM has a global workforce of over 346,000.

From its founding IBM defined its core values as "Excellence in everything we do, Superior customer service and Respect for individuals" which not only remained unchanged but also by what the company lived. But as companies grow old, they do not continue to be any career accelerant any more, it once was.

IBM has adapted to the new market changes than HP or Dell. It is one among the top four providers of Cloud storage with Amazon, Microsoft and Google, but with a distinct advantage of customer preference and acceptance, despite not being the biggest because IBM core culture since its inception was 'Superior Customer Service' and it is difficult to find a customer who had not experienced that service at least once in history. IBM enjoys highest number of customer calls for its Cloud service than its competitors.

In the recent past- post 2020, IBM adapted to creating a consulting division with four specific areas of expertise- IBM Strategy Consulting, IBM Experience Consulting, IBM Operations Consulting and IBM Technology Consulting, which drive digital adoption of AI, Hybrid Cloud and Security. IBM has a global delivery network of over 55 thousand fully cloud trained consultants of which 70 percent are with an in-depth industry experience across regions and practice including people with technical skills in its Red Hat automation platform ie, scale-able with speed. IBM demonstrated a rare quality of disrupting its core businesses like Office Equipments and Personal computers by adapting swiftly to technology services, software, consulting, life science and cloud.

HP-Hewlett-Packard Co was founded in January 1939 in Palo-Alto-CA by William R.Hewlett and David Packard. It introduced its first computer HP2116A in 1966 and it was known for technology innovation and product expansion in coming years. It maintains its leadership in the medium-high market with laptops, printers and accessories. It is worth $33Bil, with a revenue of $.57Bil in 2020 reporting a net profit of $.2.85 Bil in 2020 and a total workforce of 55,000.

The exploding dynamics

First internet has made information globally so accessible and free of cost. Next, mobile phone and network expanded it to global spread. Third, cloud computing shot up the computing power and storage, and a range of advanced tools and apps are so affordable at a ‘pay as you use’ basis. The user segment is expanding too rapid the next five billion people are to be online soon, making impossible things possible.

Adapting these dynamics, every economy sector from retail, healthcare, delivery, financial services, defence, energy, education, government, media and research to marketing makes significant benefits from quality, cost, speed, cycle and scale. It makes research and experimentation cheaper and faster with lowest cost of failure. It makes co-working and collaboration easier across a single premise, remote, or inter-continental. It replaces the old doctrine of aversion to risk and mistakes with speed and challenges.

The "Knowledge Worker":

- Know the product from the user perspective, though never asked for it.
- Moves from technical expertise to product excellence to business success.
- Designs not concepts, but builds prototypes.
- Always questioning norms, thinks that he is to solve the problems.
- Not afraid to fall, but confident of getting up quickly to next trial even if it fails.
- Doesn't wait for instruction, sometimes ignores directions if not agreeable.
- Self-directed and open-creative, freely collaborates and judges idea on its merit.

They are the teachers and mentors at Google and Facebook from whom even the founders take lessons. During recruitment, their culture gets first consideration, because it goes with success hand-in-hand. Companies can train work skills but not values, hence it is closely watched how an individual's values and culture are aligned with the company values and culture. Next is the mind power of imagination and innovation followed by social skills and project works during academics. Today the fastest growing job category is the "Knowledge Worker". As knowledge is not conflicting with any existing knowledge, but is totally collaborating with new ideas, it will create new products and services in future. Major companies which produced goods and services for the wealthy segment till recently, now had turned to the new rising billions with a smart phone. The days of incremental progress and improvement are not anymore relevant, with the twenty-first century which is running fast levelled to 10X growth targets.

Until twentieth century, wealthy businessmen used their surplus reserves on charity to provide food, housing and education, where the present age entrepreneurs took a step forward by helping the poor to grow food, make money, put back its profit into crops, employ ten others, which in the process, transform the entire farming. One such early entrepreneur was Mohamed Yunus who founded Grameen Microfinance in Bangladesh.

Rules are challenged

Like any large companies, such a rapid growth rate through a number of leadership and policy changes, tend to slow down to bureaucracy and complacency which result in lack of agility, innovation and speed. Intel had a monopoly with its Pentium microprocessor, which Apple replaced with its own in-house developed processors. Microsoft lost its race to Apple in Mobile internet and its Bing search against Google search. Jeff Bezos admitted that his leadership role in Amazon is to incite and insulate the company against losing its relevance. His words indicate a possible downfall for even today's prominent technology giants to those new garage enterprises in Silicon Valley. IBM and HP witnessed a common setback, later followed by Microsoft, when success breeds complacency, older employees becoming redundant and smart youngsters leaving them to either becoming start-up founders or employees with new technology start-ups.

For decades it was one or two big cities contributed large share of a country's GDP, where most of the largest corporations were located. It was because these companies attracted talents from all over the country for jobs. In contrast, with technology sector becoming the largest employers, they relocate and out-reach to talent locations and remote-working, which result great savings in allowances and perks linked to cost of living index resulting a reverse migration.

Nothing works better than when these workers attain an emotional maturity at their twenties especially in favour of women who react smarter and resilient than men. Women listen better, explodes less, summarise critical issues, relevant facts, and make conclusions that helps to move to the next task. With more girls getting smarter and attracted to university degrees, no surprise if the future belonged to them. They are more adaptable to use the master tools that did not exist a decade ago. For a same age of twenty five with equal education and training, women employees show much higher emotional maturity and resilience than men.

With ideas becoming reality at an unprecedented speed, Apple, Google, Amazon and Facebook are too agile with due consideration to what worked yesterday is out of date today and forgotten tomorrow. If Microsoft took 22 years to reach a billion users, Gmail only twelve and Facebook just nine. If Big companies adhered to process, these new workers break the existing processes but with an unquestioned sense of ownership of their project and business. Steve Jobs, Bill Gates and Mark Zuckerberg were all college drop-outs, but their campus experiences helped them to succeed. Facebook first became viral among college students because it spread out of a real need of the campus. Their campus friends were so helpful and valuable in their later lives. These companies share a unique university culture in contrast to any of the twentieth century companies.

Salary cheques and cash compensation for senior managers in big companies do not make anyone super-wealthy, except for a good lifestyle. External talents are recruited for an average of 20 percent higher salaries than their peers in the company, but these new recruits are likely to quit in a short while. In contrast, start-ups are known for people-first with better pay and recognition including ownership stake and incentives during success. They work with trust and bond with the founder and if the boss is not fighting for you, either he is a bad boss or probably you are a bad employee. Today big companies no longer attract young talents, where Exxon or Walmart is not the preferred place for young university graduates. To become successful, you need to ask for help from others; also to help others without even asked or not. Asking for help is not an offense anymore.

In big companies it is very common that if the CEO comes from sales, the company tends to respect sales than other functions. If the CEO is from Finance, accountants rule the company. Entrepreneurship is largely a sales function, selling ideas to attract talents, investors and customers. It is meeting people who do not want to see or hear you and treat you bad, and still chasing them again until your idea is sold. In Google, people sell ideas, strategies and plans and work relentless to achieve the goals, without an incentive for first three to four years until they exit or make a fortune. In start-ups, tides are either too high, or too low but nothing in between.

Highly rational and intelligent people are smart in foreseeing risks and chances to fail, hence not good serial entrepreneurs, but it is the guts to disrupt and break the norms that make one an entrepreneur. With the life expectancy is increasing so rapidly and companies living shorter and shorter, an adult gets misfit in two decades after working in three to four companies.

These technologies brought an end to brands, which were dominating in the business and industry sectors for decades. Innovation was a peace deal after WW-II, which helped us to get better cars, superior appliances, electronics, TVs, cameras, music and video players and even apparels. In 2015 Tesla was the largest sold EV car in US despite being twice the price of its competitors.

For decades employers faced a critical problem in recruiting, where most of the job aspirants submit fabricated and inflated CVs to suit the job description. Internet and AI are capable of gathering detailed data about candidate right from family, campus, past police record, experience and reasons for change, etc which help the employers to have a realistic history as well as the skills which comply with the actual job requirements. Also CEOs cannot cook-up the balance sheet to cover up a weak performance.

So common with all the founders of these technologies, they do not look smarter and handsome; in fact their rooms looked brighter whenever they are out. Their eagerness and audacity, conflicting and eccentric nature make serious discomfort for others around them.

Start-up's Patriotism:

Losing the manufacturing economy to China and the service sector partially to India, today the US GDP would have remained in par with the Chinese GDP of $14.72 Tril. Without these four technology giants, US GDP is likely to further slip down to second position in coming years. They are too fair and transparent in business, treating their people so happy with respect and still more committed to benefiting the society than most other established companies. It is so unique that their profits come not from their users, but from other sources like advertisement, cheap capital, technology and agility. Except Apple, other three companies despite their monopoly never raise their price to the customers. They created incredible market value, shareholder return, thousands of high paid jobs, employee and customer pride and innovation, together placing their country- America at top.

New ventures are important to inject new energy and ideas into the economy and a source of wealth creation for the founder as well as the investors. "Microsoft Millionaire" is a well known phrase in Seattle where at least such 10,000 millionaires were in the area in 2000. Technology companies are abused for job loss, but have created more new jobs than those lost, which did not happen when industrial and banking sector adopted VRS and job cuts in the process of computerisation and automation. Two decades of large job loss when US industries relocated to China, we did not see any rise in US unemployment rate because the US technology sector substantiated this loss with disproportionately more new jobs in their respective sector, at much higher wages taking its GDP to new horizons, largely by raising the middle class segment. According to Forbes-2021 survey of best employers, the first nine companies were from technology sector by leaving the tenth slot to BMW.

Besides, if US ever existed for decades to establishing and spreading democracy and American capitalism against communism, dictatorship and religious regimes in the world, it is so surprising to see how these companies spread and establish the message of equality, human rights, harmony, relationship and compassion which are the strong pillars of democracy. In another two decades, the world could possibly become a USD-United States of Democracies.

Why Business Education and Experience?

Gordon Moore and Robert Noyce, the founders of Intel and Andrew Grove, Intel's legendary CEO, Larry Page and Sergey Brin, founders of Google and Marc Zuckerberg, the founder of Facebook, Michael Dell and Adolph William "Al" Schwimmer, the co-founder and CEO of Israeli Aerospace Industries were all Jews. Most of them did not have any formal business education or experience which they considered an advantage than a liability. The first and foremost principle they believed was to focus on the user's benefit- how it will touch and transform their lives and if they create great services and applications, it will show the track to make money. This resulted in the world's best search engine, microprocessors, connectivity, defence systems and affordable computers. Intel, Google and Facebook hire as many talented software engineers as possible to create their University Labs and liberate their minds with total freedom, authority and trust towards 10X moon-shot goals to achieve, where the most valuable asset is intellect. Today our memory is not in our heads anymore, but they are all compressed in our smart phones.

If the burning instinct of disruption and innovation were the audacity, daring, eagerness, challenging, courage and a creative dissatisfaction, these same instincts were the dynamics of Chutzpah, a child to adult growth tradition in Hebrew. If Business education and experience were the guiding factors in twentieth century corporations, none of those successful start-up founders did have the same, which was considered an asset than liability.

How the Big-4 works?

These smart companies recruit the creative smarts, mostly engineers with disruptive minds. If twentieth century companies adhered to a formal dress code, discipline, structural hierarchy and timing, these twenty-first century firms believed the opposite, with full freedom in thinking and working in an equality structure. If clean desks and offices without paper mess is the culture enforced by those companies in the past, messy offices and accumulated papers are not sinful if it is required for their easy reference access.

Established and traditional companies face great difficulty in attracting high skilled smart employees such as data scientists and internet professionals. Contrary to this, about 98 percent of recent data science graduates opted to work for Google, Facebook or LinkedIn and such other start-ups, by leaving very less talents for other companies.

Within five to ten years after inception, everyone laughed at the free access and service provided by Google and Facebook, but these companies surprised everyone with their new innovative revenue model of digital advertising which raised the value of Google to $400Bil by 2015 and Facebook and LinkedIn together to $.200Bil. In 2002, Google had a revenue of less than $.500Mil, which after ten years surged 125 times when kept registering a revenue of $500Mil every three days or annual income of over $60Bil.

The managers first go to their engineers for their ideas before concluding their projects and business plan of 10X growth unlike the incremental targets of B-school managers. Business training and experience are not pre-requisites for these engineers as such background tend to think and look at the future from an intuition derived from their past experience and knowledge. Campus recruits are preferred because of their ability to dream the future from a zero base. It is a strong belief that these smart engineers are the source of new technologies and products to be invented for the future. No matter if you fail as long as it gives new lessons to do the next important. Their primary objective is great services for mankind where money will figure out later.

Google and Facebook follow the Academy or University culture where the greatest asset is intellect, as a model for their offices which are to support research and knowledge. Peter Drucker predicted that the future workplace will be of 'Knowledge Workers', which by all means become true in these corporations. These workers look at every product or technology from its user perspective than the amount of money it can generate. Both these companies consider Internet to be the most ideal platform for their searches.

As these founders did not have past management education or experience, they seldom guide their engineers what to do and what not to do. The only choice was to have best smart creative engineers, give them full freedom to think and work and by talking to them for ideas. As a common rule, they were guided with a strong user-bias which absorbs a user perspective in their work to achieve an audacious goal of touching the billion lives.

Small teams get more results than big ones with a deep focus on goals, hence these companies determine who have the passion and biggest impact and more and more assignments are given to them. Today's small teams are making bigger impact on the humanity, which once either government or large corporations could do. The most serious and urgent works always tend to go to the busy desk. Title makes a manager, where people make one a leader and true leadership comes from passion.

People Asset

If character of a company is the sum of the characters of its people, these four companies set their standards to strive for sterling character of employees with no space for any lapse for integrity. Best culture attracts and enables people to do too many challenges with a work-life balance. Best culture is aspiration and each failure makes others in the company stronger and winning. By giving them a sense of ownership of what they do, they are granted to do it so well without supervision. A culture of 'Yes' is felt around their workplaces. VCs invest not by any MBA-trained business plan, but by the quality, vision and passion of their team. For them no matter the plan could be wrong, but people have to be right.

Giving what the customer wanted, was the formula what companies followed during twentieth century. Today their vision is to giving what the customer does not yet know what he wants. Giving what the customer wants is phased out to giving him what he does not yet know what he wants which shows how they are customer-centric. Google's successful products have been based on strong technical insights, which apply design or technology which drives down the cost or adds the usability in big way. Technical aspects outsmart business reasons, hence first they benefit the customers and later once scaled-up, it opens the door to revenue. Century back, Henry Ford said "if I asked the customers what they wanted, I would have gone for faster horses not for Model-T car".

If companies in the past century were comfortable with 8-10 percent quarterly growth which was sufficient for bonus and promotion, today the word 'growth' is not enough but what is required is 'Scale' to grow and again scale quickly to be global. In technology, where cycles are getting shorter and shorter, and competition is killing, competitive advantages do not last long hence nothing less than 'big-fast growth". Past companies prioritised revenue over growth, but these new ones go just the opposite. The global phone network took nine decades to reach 150Mil users which gave a century-long life for AT&T, but Facebook hit a billion users at its eighth birthday, which doubts its present dominance no so longer. Bill Joy, cofounder of Sun Microsystem said "no matter who you are, the most smartest people work for someone less smarter".

When Andy Rubin suggested to close-down Android, Sergey Brin came with an opposing idea to retain the division and scale-up quickly in the splintered Mobile O/S space. Apple launched i-Phone on its own i-OS to be exclusive over scaling opportunities, where Android started opening to all which helped Google to shift the platform from PC to mobile device, scaling-up to a multiple number of users in tune with the growth in smart phones.

Businesses of the twentieth century largely kept a close eye on competitors, who were careful to risks and grew incremental. Being close to competition gives comfort like testing opponent to a winning strategy. By doing so you grow just above the opposite, do not raise the bar above your potential. In general, people have a tendency to think of what already exists. Though competition makes you sharper, the new generation firms think of what is not thought and yet that you really need.

Recruitment at Google

The new recruits are selected based on their potential to do certain jobs, but smart ones create new roles and expands their capabilities. Passion and the nerve come as the first trait they look in a candidate, which makes them to rise quickly from defeats and do same or next one again. As everyone is good at something, Google looks for how passionate he is to what he is good at, which reflects his output. It is essential to have something exciting in a candidate to build a fulfilling career. Your skills, interests, and goals are the result of your life, your experiences, your triumphs, and your failures. Google believes that "If we hire you based on your skills, we'll get a skilled employee. If we hire you based on your skills, and your enduring passions, and your distinct experiences and perspectives, we'll get a Googler".

Resume shall describe about aligning your skills and experience with the job description. If you're a recent university graduate or have limited work experience, include school-related projects or coursework that demonstrate relevant skills and knowledge. Keep it short. We don't have a lengthy requirement, but concision and precision are keys — so desirably avoid your resume moving onto multiple pages. If any covering letter, avoid repeats from your resume, draw a direct line between your passion and our position and how you make a difference from others. During interview, we ask open-ended questions to learn how you solve problems. We want to understand how your mind works, how you interact with a team, and what your strengths are. Emotional maturity, resilience and collaborative skills are equally important.

One can change himself, he can adapt, also he is more comfortable and do better once forced to do more. The best motivation to keep them is to listen and recognize their views, as they want to be heard and felt relevant and valued than compensation. Nothing makes more valuable than an emotional maturity and resilience with force, especially for people in their twenties as their minds becomes so disruptive, explodes with new ideas, challenges and drive. The resilience and emotional maturity at twenties, make them hard nuts capable to withstand setbacks and failures, as well as rise up quickly to learn lessons and to begin with next idea. Obviously they are not exposed to alcohol, narcotics and smoking, also no workplace politics, rumours and gossips, they seldom discuss people or events, but mostly ideas and vision, which make them ideal examples for our campuses in nurturing their students. Once the entry process is so focused, hardly anything to regret later!

Whichever areas the founders as well as CEO do not understand, for example finance, technologies and space, autonomous cars etc, they rather trust those smart creatives on those subjects. Rather than worrying in CPAs, EBITDAs, ADR, ROI, ROCE etc, they care for what matters like cash flow and revenue. Reaching to best idea and decision is by consensus, but after conflicts. As Gen Patton said “If everyone is thinking alike, then somebody is not thinking”. Even an engineer is encouraged to disagree with the founder or the CEO and free to come with his own conflicting ideas. It looks impossible until it is achieved, as records are made only to break again. This raises the bar and stretches the human ability beyond what was believed as unbreakable.

In terms of user benefit, if Google serves as the largest search engine, Facebook is the most searched relationship network, but in terms of revenue both are largest in digital advertising. Googlers who leave the company keep a seamless relation so that they can always reach-out Google Venture for mentoring and funding.

Experimenting passionate projects

Google allows all its engineers to engage themselves with 20 percent of their time in experimenting new passionate projects. This gave birth to Gmail, which is the world’s largest email subscription. In twentieth century, we had seen 3M, the most innovative company of those days and even today, which allowed 15 percent of their time to explore new ideations and Post-It Note was invented by Spencer Silver, a chemist which became a runaway success. Today 3M has 20,300 patents, mostly through its idea lab. As such US has almost 5 percent of its population engaged in sectors like R&D, innovation, new product development and creative discoveries. Companies are competing for skilled workforce, in contrast those smart and skilled workforce do not compete for employers.

A specialist brings an inherent bias to solve problems which fails when a new problem requires a different expertise which will get solved better by a smart generalist. Hiring generalists is far better than hiring specialists. Google and Facebook believe that one should work with another he does not like, because a workplace of people liking each other lacks diversity and conflict of ideas and viewpoints. People from different cultural background and regions see the world different. Such differences in perspective generate insights that cannot be taught. So the person should have passion, intellect, talent and character to success and excel. Technology firms are too used to have difficult situations of conflicting ideas and most of them being audacious and strong-willed, it continues until they agree at a decision level, not necessarily any of their ideas, but surprisingly a new idea than they conflicted. One may think that he can win exchanges and negotiations as he is right with his data and analysis, but if one has to change other's mind, he has to touch their hearts, not by argument. The new workplace does not foster friendship from being comfortable and liking to each other and agreeing to each other, but more a new form of colleagueship and partnership from disagreeing each others on ideas, internal discomfort, and even conflicting towards fulfilling the set goals. As every Google recruitment is signed by Larry Page, employees come first and foremost and everything else being next.

If companies in the past sold their goods and services to consumers at a price, the new-gen technology firm take another route. Their major business areas are money earners where other businesses use their platform for a price. Google or Facebook do not charge their clients on its major business of search or connectivity, where both earn huge revenue from companies who use their search formats for their digital advertisements. They do not earn a single dollar revenue by expanding their markets; it takes the dollar from other companies by helping them to reach-out to customers. Apple charges their customers one-time when they buy i-Phone, but everything else like thousands of Apps and games at its playstore come free for unlimited and lifetime use. Amazon is free to search products and movies, but customers have to pay only for what they order with most of them delivered free and everything returnable. Business is taking a new turn from its traditional model. If banks and companies of last century treated humans as a source to buy their services or products to increase their profits, these twenty first century firms look at the entire humanity as beneficiaries at no cost, but to scale-up their business, like how smart phones are growing almost equal to the global population.

i-OS and Play Stores are where other business platforms like Google, Amazon and Facebook took birth, but Apple did not protect its patent or charge others for using its technologies. Google search was so vital to Uber and Amazon which became largest search platforms for taxi and online shopping but did not claim any royalty. While starting and scaling themselves, they allow even their competitors to use their technology to start and scale. This model was never heard or seen among twentieth century corporations. Today convergence of these technologies allow anyone to start-up and scale without much investment, but with an audacious idea which could tomorrow erupt to become an extinctive threat for the mother companies who know that reality. For such an extinction or failure, they do not accuse anyone, but themselves.

If Amazon connected sellers directly to buyers face to face that removed distributors and retailers, Airbnb and Uber created a special space for themselves as middlemen platforms between customers and hotels, apartments or taxis. If both of them brought a new model of removing liquid assets like properties and cars unlike Marriott or Hertz, Amazon removed logistics and supply chain from its system unlike Walmart or Nike.

Academics and scholars who once decided about education policies, teachers with masters in teaching were ruling our classrooms, which today is dangerously under disruption with new online coaching supported by animation, VR and technology. Qualified scientists and researchers with biotechnology, surgical and other healthcare specialisation were inventing better methods in treatment, analysis and surgeries, which are also under serious disruption as recent innovations are advanced by engineering graduates and drop-outs. The automobile sector is no more a specialisation for automobile designers and engineers, where the future vehicles have nothing as automobile technology, but a computer on wheels. When we read this book today, already so many existing business rules and models are under threat by naughty boys and girls from outside the industry. When specialisation cares about how to improve, more efficient, less priced and least risky, these quirky and reckless ones come with alternatives and choices. These new disruptive companies hire them, pay them better and allow them all freedom to think, do and achieve with no more instruction and bureaucracy. They change the present rules with no more teachers to teach in the future, no more soldiers required to fight a future war and no more drivers to drive tomorrow's car, thus finally our present is on exit, leaving its space for a new future already born.

9 21st Century Skills and Emotional Maturity

If competition was the rule of business in the past century, collaboration has become the new rule for the present century. Now more than half of the desired core skills considered so important for many of the jobs are not that crucial for the same jobs in the wake of 2020. Academic brilliance and syllabus depth are important but make to fifty percent merit for recruitment. What is equally important is the social skills of the employee, means emotional intelligence, attitude, behaviour, collaboration and mentoring skills. Nothing makes better than attaining an emotional maturity, perseverance and resilience at an early age of twenties which otherwise acquired through ten to fifteen years in future work experience, in other words, a biological advancement of fifteen years by age. Being average in classroom was once a close-door future, but today it is not a sin. World's most successful entrepreneurs and innovators were not the most brilliant students, but most of them experienced a classroom conflict with a tendency to break norms.

This makes more clarity on how the future workforce needs to be nurtured and brought up. How to make them achieve these social skills during their early twenties? How to accelerate the absorption of these attributes at early age of twenties, which otherwise attained at late thirties? This can result a very positive impact on national economy.

Too much knowledge and intuition based on this past knowledge led to most of the decisions and policies in the past. Today we experience a reality of most of the things we thought and believed to be right are proven wrong. This poses a threat to adopting decisions based on what was right in the past. Only thing is that when our world is turning totally towards future, which is almost unknown and uncertain for us, those whom we considered to be intellects and policy makers are not the right brains to drive our future anymore. This makes wasting time and money on their advices as they are assured failure than success. This poses a big challenge that most of our government technology and innovation missions are with wrong hands of bureaucrats, politicians or business leaders than technology wizards with a vision.

If we have to induct these lessons one attains from a ten years of job training and work experience to a technology graduate in his early twenties, we shall create a check point of such learning which makes one to attain high emotional maturity, perseverance and resilience. The future workplace demands high degree of Collaborating, Leveraging and Reconciling, but no more competition.

Name any of the successful innovators from history, what is so common with them without exception, was that they did not fulfil the aspiration of their parents about their future. In general parents wish their children to study well in schools, to be toppers in their majors at ivy colleges and to get employed in best known companies, universities or government positions. To break such aspirations of parents which have come from their life experience and knowledge, a disruptor requires an equal or close-by maturity and determination to choose what his line of future. What may look like disobedient or disrespect to the parent's aspiration, it is the passion, willpower and self-conviction that guide him towards his determined future. Here, it is very essential that this disruptive mind requires a much higher emotional maturity, willpower, perseverance, resilience and social skills, which helps him from choosing from alternatives, choice of options and to follow a decision most appropriate for the business. Therefore, the founders have to attain an emotional maturity of late thirties at their biological age of twenties. This chapter is dedicated to how to attain that level without ageing.

Last century, most of the jobs were regional, where the employers as well as the employees were from a specific region, religion, country or language. By the turn of this century, employment changed to global than regional, where it was difficult to address the culture conflict between the employer and employee. This brought a significant change in the requirement, which was once the academic brilliance considered as a decision factor, changed to how the candidate's values and character leverage with the values of the organization. This has become so important because training job skills are easy, but training values are next to impossible. Today when it comes to future jobs, it remains a strong decision factor in favour of social skills.

Off late, region, nation, religion and race are no more any limiting factors for employment as before. It is collaborative culture which rules every workplace. With a company of US origin, design at Israel, research and engineering in India or Taiwan, with manufacturing facility in China, business had expanded global beyond national and regional boundaries with working from office or remote working. This diversity of culture, knowledge, pooling ideas and execution leads to innovation like never before. Accelerating technologies like AI, Cloud, automation, Big Data and quantum computing made it instant sharing, at decreasing cost and time with high-speed performance. This keeps bringing down the costs to almost free, making things available more, and making our planet more liveable than before.

This makes imagination more precious than knowledge, where we are shifting from a knowledge economy to an imaginative economy, where the difference is made by smart people who are capable of addressing to new challenges which can accelerate the lives of millions and solve problems to new opportunities. Therefore it makes so imperative to have a smart workforce in their early twenties, with the intellectual maturity, perseverance and resilience of those in their late thirties. Now the question is how to attain these attributes at a young age? Obviously these lessons are not taught in universities but from outside the classrooms.

The Playschool lessons of Emotional Maturity

When there is a new idea which can change our planet, it requires a strong passion and drive to make it a reality. In the process, we have to be totally focussed as ‘obstacles are those frightful things when we take our eyes off the goal!’

Success is more permanent when you achieve it without destroying your principles. It takes one or two years to learn how to speak. I takes beyond a lifetime to learn what not to talk.

The hardest battle you’re going to fight is the battle to be just you. In a day if you do not come across any problem, obviously you’re travelling on a wrong path. The task of a leader is to get his people from where they are to where they have not been. Accept them as what they are; transform them to what they are capable of!

Weakness of Attitude becomes weakness of Character. In our new garage workplace, those five attributes of success are Cohesiveness,

Communication, Strategic foresight, Agility and Authenticity. What is important in a conversation is "reading what is not said". The more you speak of yourself, the more likely you are to lie.

Engage & Conflict with ourselves; which help us to realise where we were wrong! It will also help us to discover a very versatile person, whom we hardly knew. When we are in the business of disruption, most of our assumptions are proved to be wrong. The way to avoid mistakes is to gain experience, and the way to gain experience is to make mistakes. Good judgement comes from experience; often experience comes from bad judgement. Efforts may fail; but don't fail to make efforts.

To grow, you have to exit off your comfort zone. Until you can change, you remain what you are! Strive not to be success; rather to be of values. If you cannot change your fate, then look at changing your attitude. Too much of praising, it is the personality that disappears.

The reward when you complete a task successfully, is the strength to begin with your next duty. Strength comes not from success, but from struggles and failures. Good leader takes little more than his share of blame, a little less than his share of credit. A candle loses nothing if it is used to light another one! Generosity is giving more than you can; pride is in taking less than you need.

Fight is not a desirable approach if the objective is to win! A ship in the harbour is safe; but that is not what ships are built for. More the noise man or machine makes, less power there is available. When it is easier and beneficial in making collaboration than competition, the best way to win enemies is to make friends with them. When the only tool you have is a hammer, it is surprising how all your problems begin to look like nails. If you can always do a job well, then it is beneath your capabilities.

A diamond goes through a process of extreme heat and abrasions before it attains shine; so was with any legendary leader. Barriers to Innovation are usually in our mind. It is easier to suggest a solution, when you don't know too much about the problem. Great men never feel great; small men never feel small. Many of the life failures are people who did not realize how close they were to success when they gave-up!

Once you say you are going to settle for second, that is what happens to you in rest of the life. The illiterates of the 21st century will not be those who cannot read and write, but those who cannot learn, unlearn and relearn. Life is what getting prepared for mostly what is unlikely to happen.

A long dispute means that both are wrong! Courage is the discovery that you may not win, and trying when you know you can lose. You grow up the day you have your first real laugh-at yourself. If we keep doing what we're doing, we are going to keep getting what we're getting. A man doesn't begin to attain wisdom until he recognizes he is no longer indispensable. Only thing we know about future is that it will be different. Knowledge has to be improved, challenged, and increased constantly, or it vanishes.

Victory is sweetest when you have known defeat. Ability will never catch up with the demand for it. It is not always good for one person to have too much power for too long. Towards meeting the purpose of creating a customer, business has to focus on two basic functions- Marketing and Innovation. Marketing and Innovation produce results where all the rests are costs and activities.

Live as if you were to die tomorrow; but learn as if you were to live forever! Those who give-up for a purpose, really win! To the extent others can be wrong, we also can. True measure of a man is not what he does, but what he makes. Journey of life is not as smooth or sweet as you wish to be! Know more than others, work more than others and expect less than others!

What you do may seem insignificant; but it is important that you do it. Freedom is not worth having if it does not include the freedom to make mistakes. You have a right to perform your prescribed duties, but you are not entitled to the fruits of your action. Never be associated to not doing your duties! You tend to get more of what you give.

It is a hard truth that nobody wins in a war! War does not determine who was right and who was wrong; but what is left. The dreadful thing in a battlefield we realize that most of the scratches are not caused from enemies but from own camp!

Experience is a comb that Nature gives to man after he is bald. More he gets bald, he looks for someone to share his comb!, a Thai proverb. When the going gets tough, the tough gets going!

Agility and Innovation are keys to future success. Don't hit at all, if honourably avoid hitting. If you hit, do it strongly. In business there is only invaluable person, not such indispensable person. Once we accept our limits, we tend to go beyond them. Intellectual solves problem, genius prevents it.

If you cannot explain it simply, you have not understood it well enough. Nobody cares how much you know, until they know how much you care. To be prepared for war is one of the most effective means of preventing it.

Work expands until the time for its completion. Time is what we want most; but what we use worst. It is not enough that we do our best, sometimes we have to do what is required. You will not get a second chance to make a good first impression. An effective executive is someone who can change the tires while the car's still running. Without knowing the problem; it remains more difficult to solve.

Any book so easy to read and understand, is more difficult to author. To simplify the design is more difficult, whereas it is easier to complicate. The ordinary way of doing business, is neither the right nor the best way. The less complex an article is, the easier it is to make, the cheaper it can be sold, and therefore the greater numbers may be sold. Successful generals study the battlefield and look for that one bold stroke that is least expected by the enemy.

Trust is hardest to earn and easiest to lose where money comes a distant second! Once an organization earns customer's trust, the most difficult thing is to maintain and preserve it. Trust is termed as the DNA of the company, where quality and service are product related. Trust is an intangible factor; where product, quality and service are tangibles. Trust is not that easy to copy as quality or service. Trust safeguards a company during market downturns. Irrespective of their businesses, the culture at companies like Coca-Cola, McDonalds, 3M, IBM, Boeing, Google, Facebook, Nestle and Amazon are centred around trust.

Competition is very killing; customers have more choices. Those who cannot win their perception, tend to extinct. If you want something new, you have to stop doing something old. Be a little cynical. Things are mostly the opposite of what really they look. Creativity is the input to innovation and change is the output from innovation. When rules changes faster and business cycles are shorter, investing in people and technology make lasting solutions.

To be successful, you have to be willing to fail. Any strategy without a differentiation will fail to succeed against competition. The day soldiers stop bringing you their problems, is the day you have stopped leading them. Win without boasting, lose without excuse.

Great works are performed not by strength, by perseverance. Only those wisest and stupidest of men never change. Money never starts an idea, it is the idea that starts money. Life is too short to hang out with people aren't resourceful. If people are not laughing at your goals, your goals are too small! Roots of Education look bitter; where its fruits are so sweet! A dignified defeat is more honorable than a success of betrayal.

It is not what you produce; but what you stand for? Products are short-term; but purpose stands forever! It is not that relevant what companies make and sell; but their core values & purposes! Business cycles are getting shorter and shorter day by day, whereas core values & purposes remain lasting & constant. Hence be clear about what you stand for and why you exist! Visionary leaders die; products become obsolete; visionary companies go on forever! Every new business in Tata Group starts with a Business Patriotism- import substitution, local jobs and state revenue than the profit it generates.

B-School doctrines, "optimizing shareholder wealth" or "maximizing profit" were not the dominant driving force or a primary objective through the visionary companies. The core values are important; but still more important is how deeply these values are lived, behaved and practiced in the day to day business activities of the organization. The difference between stupidity and genius is that genius has its limits!

William McKnight transformed 3M to a company that turned innovation into a systematic and repeatable process lasting so successful even today after his lifetime. J&J withdrew Tylenol capsules (US$.100 Mil by earning) on customer safety over short-term financial setback. Darwin Smith, CEO of Kimberly-Clarke closed the capital blocked giant paper mills and launched Kleenex to become world's No.1 paper based consumer products company for over twenty five years, outperforming the stock market by a factor of four over this period.

George Merck rationalised the price for Meetizan, a medicine for blindness and itching more affordable so that additional 30Mil could be benefited. "The better we remembered, the larger they have been". Bill Allen CEO of Boeing, so successful in bombers and fighters during Second World War, found collapsing after the war. Allen found a great opportunity in commercial aircrafts that changed the future of Boeing. In absence of a competitor, Boeing looks internally through the eyes of a competitor. GE creates an atmosphere of a creative discomfort especially in its research and product development.

It should be inspiring message to those inside the company. It has to be so relevant for a century from now as it is today. It should help to think clearly of what you could do but are not doing. It should help to define what not to do. What you stand for and core purpose should be properly expressed as truly authentic to your company. HP do not follow a culture of imitating others, where its every product offers something new values or benefits to its customers than others.

Records are good achievements, but not to be celebrated because they are to be broken. No matter how good you get at something, you could be still better.

In life or work, set benchmarks against yourself, wrestle with yourself and keep defeating yourself. Anything achieved or any good work accomplished, can be performed still better. Good CEOs beat their own past records and set ambitious targets for coming years. Once we relax on a good performance and relish its glory, sure there is a fall waiting in front of you.

Great companies like 3M, HP or J&J did not start with a Vision statement; but with a set of personal core values and a drive for progress. 3M till now had nothing as core values.

Customers were central to Wal-mart and J&J; but not for Sony or Ford. Employees were so central for HP and Marriott; but not to Disney and Nordstrom. Products and services come first for Ford and Disney; but not with IBM and Citicorp. Risk taking was central to Boeing and Sony; where not for Nordstrom and HP. Motorola and 3M start with innovation; where not with P&G and Amex.

Apple, Microsoft, Intel, What's-App and Google keep inventing new features and formats and integrate them into their products resulting great market acceptance. The conventional practice of launching any new product or product extensions was following a detailed market survey, but these technological innovations are offered much in advance or without the customers being asked for.

Organizations must renew themselves every 3 years. Apple transformed the way of managing business. A leader shall not leave behind a carbon-copy successor to encounter and win the changing rules of the future. Kites rises-up against the wind- Churchill. The true leader is someone who gets up from defeat. If people are not laughing at your goals, your goals are too small! Roots of Education look bitter; where its fruits are so sweet! A dignified defeat is more honorable than a success of betrayal. The future challenge of technology and innovation is in serving the poor. Technology has no value unless it's benefit can reach-out the poor masses in cost or value.

Mobile phones were bought for talking, then added messaging that not being asked, then added with data also without being asked, followed by camera, play store, apps, etc without being asked for. An industry providing what all can be given without the customer ever asking for, but created a big market of adds-on. Today more it's made smaller, it has more power inside. Companies with defined values and mission with a purpose beyond profit, do not perish.

Get your ego and emotion out of the situation. The more you screen things through your ego, the farther you get from reality. Avoid wishful thinking; reality is not what we wish to be, it is mostly what it is. Everything around you that you call life, was made up by people who were less smarter than you!

Power Negotiation

Like how these companies are accommodative and sharing with their employees, they are also compassionate in negotiating with their BPO vendors, associates and founders of acquisition companies. In every negotiation, they follow a win-win approach and shared benefits for which they first win the trust of the other party, behave truthful, and win their hearts. Some of the rules and formulas followed in negotiations are as described below:

1. Avoid wishful thinking. Reality is mostly opposite to what we assumed.
2. The more you screen things through your ego and emotion, the farther you get from reality.
3. What is important in a negotiation is to read what is not said.
4. If you cannot beat your enemy, make friend of him.

5. The more noise a man or machine makes, the less power it is left with.
6. If you are not clear of what is to be achieved, it is more difficult to achieve it.
7. To the extend we are wise and right, others can be equally wise and right.
8. Listen more of what others talk.
9. It is resilience and perseverance, the two most crucial winning factors in a negotiation.
10. Biggest obstacle to success is mostly ourselves, but it is always blamed on others.
11. It takes one or two years to know what to talk; where it takes a lifetime to learn what not to talk.
12. The difference between stupid and genius is that the latter has limits.
13. To be successful, you have to be willing to fail.
14. Giving up for a purpose, you really win.
15. If we know the problem in depth, it is easier to find a solution.
16. Anyone can be generous with solutions as long as he does not know the problem.
17. Ours is a world where people don't know what they want, are willing to go through hell to get it.
18. A long dispute means both are wrong.
19. Fighting is never an option if the objective is to win.
20. Revenge is always a weak pleasure of a narrow mind.
21. Best remedy to anger is delay until you are calm and have control on emotions.
22. Look at what you are left with, not what you have lost.
23. To fall a tree in six hours, a smart cutter takes four hours to sharpen the tools.
24. When the only tool you have is a hammer, it is surprising how all your problems begin to look like nails?

25. Avoid screening things in a lawyer or accountant perspective, but an intellectual and commonsense wisdom.
26. You cannot win by silencing a person.
27. Avoid any pre-determined outcome of the negotiation and face reality as how it comes on its way.
28. If a settlement is not reached and it takes to an ugly turn of arguments, it is advisable to defer the meeting for another date with a revised agenda, so that the relation does not break.
29. A meeting shall begin and end with words of respect and recognition for each other.

Interestingly, none of the founders or senior managers in negotiation team are experienced as senior managers or negotiators, but with a rare emotional maturity of perseverance and resilience at relatively a younger age with an ability to envision its future scale-ability. Those technology giants of the twenty first century are fine examples of win-win negotiations and collaborations, not the killing competition of previous century corporations.

Lessons from Henry Ford

"Life will give you many unpleasant tasks to do; your duty will be hard, disagreeable and painful to you at times. But you must do it!" – this was the most inspirational word for Henry Ford from his mother. Being greedy for money, is the surest way not to get it; but when one strives for the sake of service by believing to be right, then money abundantly takes care of itself. To manufacture at the highest quality and to sell at the very lowest price is possible by scaling up the volume that can meet a wider market demand, which today we call as '10x' law of scaling up.

Strength is never just weight – either in men or machines. The most beautiful things in the world are those from which all excess weight has been eliminated.

When one my cars break down; I know I am to blame. Price is what you pay; value is what you get. The less complex an article, the easier it is to make; the cheaper it may be sold and therefore the greater numbers may be sold, reaching out even those who could not afford it. Everything always can be done better than it is being done. Doing better and faster solves nearly every factory problem.

Everywhere the demand for creative men is pressing; we always need men who like a job because it is difficult. If I had asked the public what they wanted, they would have asked for a faster horse, but not for a car! The only real mistake is the one from whom we learn nothing. The time for a business man to borrow money, if ever, is when he does not need it. Find resources within itself instead of borrowing.

When Henry Ford started with car production, a belief was deeply implanted to the public that cars were the rich man's toy and he made a luxury product to a necessity so affordable for public. To achieve this goal, every activity, process, method and procedure were innovated, automated and simplified.

The reasonable man adapts to the world and the unreasonable one persists in trying the world to adapt to himself; then all progress depends on the unreasonable one. Your game is most vulnerable, when you're ahead. Never give up! A horse never runs so fast as when he has other horses to catch up and outpace.

Beware of what you set your heart upon. Surely it will be of yours! Fighting is not the option, if you have to win a war. Technical or academic knowledge makes 15%, but human relation and leadership make 85% of the success in business.

3M Corp runs an innovation culture that allows its employees to spend an average of 30% working hours on inventing new products and concepts that can be developed to Product Innovation resulting mass consumer demand and enhancing their lifestyle. In 3M, Andy Wong discovered an optical comfort system which can minimise glare and reflection of external light on the TV screens, Computer monitors and Mobile phone displays. When he could not complete the project within the assigned period of time and was decided to close down, Wong requested for an extension of two more years to its completion. It is 3M Optical System that runs to a big profitable business. Most other brands of 3M like Post-it, Scotch-guard, Scotch-Brite, Thinsulate etc were innovations which opened up new markets and end-uses, which did not exist before.

3M Corp created a new market for branded products when its core business of mining was nationalised. Today 3M is an excellent example for innovation, where Optical system, stationary products like Post-it, Scotch-tape and marking pens, cleaning products, Auto-finish, etc. Thirty percent of 3M's annual sales is expected to come from new products introduced within the last four years.

DuPont is another company that keeps innovating into new products. It has 50% or more business coming from such products like Kevlar, Teflon, Nylon, Lycra and Corian, all patented by DuPont. All these products created their own new markets and applications which did not exist before. So GE with Lexan or Noryl.

Another example is P&G where innovation is embedded into all its operations and activities, which not only spends on new product developments, but also how these products can fulfil massive market demand by raising the lives of millions. Kimberly-Clark revolutionized the market with Kleenex which remains as the market leader, when the timber and paper business were not doing well.

Future success of Business depends on not on Cost based pricing; but Price based costing. More than half of Apple's revenue comes from products that did not exist 4 years ago. Apple spends US$.1.765 Bil on R&D against US$.9 Bil of Microsoft and one/ third of what Microsoft spends on Sales & Marketing. When Apple launches a new gen I-Phone, customers respond so excited for its advanced features and technology; by this time Apple directs its R&D to design its next gen product. If things are not failing, you are not innovating enough'. Our greatest glory is not in never falling; but rising every time we fall.

Apple is fighting hard with Android; Google is struggling with Facebook on revenue front: where both Google and Apple now wrestle each other! But all of them work in collaboration than competing.

When work is too easy and comfortable, then there is something seriously wrong and untraced. If you are with people who are so comfortable around, agreeing each other, it is dangerously going to fall. One does not convert a man by silencing him. Too much of appreciation and praise, the personality disappears. Without deviation from the norm, progress is not possible. It is so alarming that our technology has exceeded our humanity. If it scares you, it might be a good thing to try. Unless a business creates value for others, it will cease to exist. An optimist can see opportunity in every calamity. A pessimist can see calamity in every opportunity. Dirtiest and still the merciless operations are always carried out by the most honest men.

Visionary companies are more than successful or enduring; many of them had severe setbacks, almost close to bankruptcy but still recovered back to exemplary performance. Disney faced a serious cash flow crisis in 1939 that made them to go public; later the company nearly ceased to exist in 1980s. Disney does not make movies to make money; it makes money to make more movies. Of late under CEO Robert Iger (2005-19) Disney returned to be one of the most respected and largest media companies with acquisitions of Pixar, Lucasfilm, Marvel and 21st Century Fox.

Boeing Co broke in 1930s, 1940s and again in 1970s when it laid off over 60,000 employees. 3M started with mining and manufacturing and went out of business in early 1900s when mining was nationalized. HP faces serious cutbacks in 1945 and later in 1990, its stock dropped below its book value. During 1945-50, Sony's products failed repeatedly for five years. Ford Motor Co posted one of the largest losses in US business history ($.3.3 Bil in 3 years) in 1980s. Citicorp (founded in 1812) struggled with Global loan portfolio. IBM was close to bankrupt thrice in 1914, then in 1921 and again in 1990s. UBS went nearly closed in 2008-10 with almost $1.00 Bil fine in US, but recovered by the next year. BankAm was crashed in the 2008 financial crisis but bounced back soon. If you want to fail, it does not take time to think; if you want o succeed, it takes a lot of time to think. Surveys will not reveal how the dreams of tomorrow should be shaped because nobody knows tomorrow. As people enjoy the company of comfortable men around, they like to hear more of pleasant side of the reality and not the adverse facts which leads to total failure. During the WW-II, Churchill appointed a team to bring him only bad news of allied forces as he wanted those unvarnished truth. Hitler was surrounded by his confident team, thought he was still winning till late by hearing glorified news about the war.

USD.1.00 invested in general stock fund in 1926 would have grown to $.415 as on Dec, 1990. If $1.00 invested in comparison companies would have grown to $.955, where the same $1.00 invested in a visionary company would have grown to $.6,356 which is more than 15 times the general market. In comparison, Google, Facebook and Amazon had grown so exponentially at a 10x times with a short span of 2 decades.

Imagine how world would have looked and felt without Ford's Model-T and Mustang, Boeing 707 and 747, 3M's Scotch tape or Post-It, P&G's Tide detergent and Gillette Fusion, Amex cards, ATMs by Citicorp,

J&J's Band-Aids and Tylenol, GE bulbs and Appliances, HP calculators and printers, Motorola pagers and cell phones, IBM 360 computers, Marriott, Merck's Mavacor and Sony Trinitron and Walkmans? Imagine how many kids and adults grew up with Disney Characters, McDonalds and now Google-playstore? A US rural highway without Marlboro billboard and Wal-Mart store? These companies made an indelible footprint on the world around. Surprisingly these companies differentiated themselves into a special category than their competitors.

Comfort was neither an objective nor a situation in any visionary company like Boeing or P&G, where they install a visible mechanism to create discomfort in order to obliterate complacency and saturation, and thereby stimulate improvement. They assigned managers the task of establishing strategies to alert as if competitors waiting to steal away its business any time.

No matter how much they achieved; no matter how far they are placed over their competitors; they are guided by a creative dissatisfaction of own performance as 'not good enough'. Comfort is neither an objective nor a situation in a visionary company; where they install a visible mechanism to create discomfort in order to obliterate complacency and saturation and thereby stimulate improvement, innovation and change even before external world demands it.

Southwest automated flying, Ford automated car-assembling, IKEA automated furniture industry and McDonald automated hamburgers. By 1993, McDonald sold over one hundred billion of those identical Hamburgers. The automation led to shorten the cycle of cooking and serving, hence the same restaurant could serve more customers without increasing space. McDonald saves on labor cost; does not require waiters, kitchen staff or cleaners. There are over ten thousands of firms in furniture industry; but only one IKEA! After so many decades into packaging, it is surprising that Tetrapack does not have a worthy competitor till date.

Once the market leader in 1980s, IBM suffered volume against simplifiers like HP, Compaq and Dell in mass segment, where Apple secured the lucrative premium segment. In terms of sales and profit, GM performed admirably but failed miserably in terms of public perspective and customer esteem.

GE had 8 firms controlling 90% of the market, DuPont had 64 firms controlling 70%, International Paper with 24 firms controlling 60%, Five brands of GM with 60% US market share, Otis had 6 firms controlling 65% and Nabisco with 27 firms controlling 70%, besides GM with 6-7 brands holding 60%, which suffered severely with top heavy bureaucracy, slow speed in decisions, strategy and execution, sleeping over their past glory and larger debt than they could repay.

There is so much competition that if you make a mistake, your competitors quickly get into your market share. On the other side waiting for competitors to make mistake, does not happen very often. Lost is lost; any attempt to reversing to the past is against optimism and hope. We are made wise not only by the recollection of our past, but by the responsibility of future.

A global network of everything connected to everything already exists. But to make a direction towards future, we require a vision of the future, which data alone cannot take us there. Data and information are knowledge, an edition of the past, but it needs individual wisdom, intuition and judgment to envision the future. Once we depend too much on these data and information, it leaves less space for creativity and imagination. As a result when our minds are filled with this knowledge, it weakens the leadership judgment. Excessive data masks the reality.

More information has been produced in the past 30 years than in the previous 5000 years. The total of all printed knowledge doubles in every 4-5 years. One weekday edition of NY Times contains more information than the average person came across in his lifetime in the 17th century in England. More than 4000 books are published around the world every day. The average white collar worker uses 70Kg of copy paper a year, twice the amount he consumed 10 years ago. A knowledge worker with today's workplace technology, performs 10 times efficient than a worker 10 years ago.

As a result, memory finds it difficult to recall an information when needed. To a question, what is more helpful in developing the theory of relativity Albert Einstein answered, "figuring out how to think about the problem". Half the battle is getting to the essence of the problem.

Anyone who stops learning is old - at 20 or 80, but one who keeps learning is young. It takes a long time to grow young. There are only the young and the experienced. Courage is conviction, it is mercy and compassion, it is also what which makes us stand on the side of truth and do what is right.

If you win, you do not have to explain; if you fail, you are not there to explain! Our lives begin to end the day we remain silent on things that matter. Don't compare yourself with anyone else in this world. If you do so, you are insulting yourself.

Life is a cycle; to balance it you have to keep moving forward. You have not lived today until you have done something for someone who can never repay you. Those who will risk going too far can possibly find out how far one can go. It is only after we lost everything that we become more adventurous. Going for it is more important than winning or losing. The difference between stupidity and genius is that genius has its limits! A business that makes nothing but money is a poor business. Commonsense is to know what not to talk than what to talk, also what not to do than what to do. For evil to flourish; it only requires good men to do nothing. Two men keep talking, together will not go far.

Talented people with bad values can do far more damages than virtuous people with lower talent. Future opportunity is not with your customers, but with non-customers. If you keep focusing your eyes to the sky, wings start growing by itself. If you are in the right track of innovating, you tend to be misunderstood. The reward when you complete a task successfully, is the strength to begin with your next duty. Between too much of appreciations and praises, the personality disappears. Revenge is always the weak pleasure of a little and narrow mind.

Growing old is mandatory, growing up is optional! This gives enough insight for those brilliant graduates in their early twenties an emotional maturity, perseverance and resilience of what they are going to achieve by forties. They make our future leaders, who will change the world by raising a billion lives. As our world has enough of regional problems like poverty, illiteracy, hunger, water shortage, banking, connectivity, access to government services, transport, housing, inflation, healthcare etc, these young and brilliant future leaders will challenge and solve these problems which will open up new business opportunities.

One cannot rise up unless knocked down. Youths between twelve and eighteen are very prone to do stupid things, more eccentric and experimental trials. In an innovation start-up, one cannot command smart people to do hard tasks. In order to succeed, we should be able to inspire people who are smarter than us, who outrank us to solve problems we cannot solve. We shall not occupy any slot below what we are and less than our potential. Life is too short be wasted with silly and meaningless engagements and with wrong people. One shall nor live smaller than what he is. There is an increasing demand to raise our limits stretch to new oceans in space. Breaking barriers, we tend to stretch beyond our limits.

Managing V/s Leading

A manager drives, where a leader leads.

A manager does things right; a leader does right things.

Managers Monitor & supervise, where leaders empower, energise and excite.

Managers generally control & govern, where leaders facilitate and accelerate.

Manager delegates work where a leader delegates responsibility.

If a manager is hesitant to problem & taking risk, the leader face realities and initiates risks.

If a manager is problem focused, a leader is solution focused.

Managers largely perform to comfortable and present job; leaders perform to new tasks & develop subordinates to do present jobs.

Managers are self-centred, steal credit for other's success; where leaders are people concerned, create winners, share credit and develop successors.

If a manager passes failures on to others and hides ignorance therefore, less open to learn from mistakes and failure; where a leader accepts failures, admits ignorance and learn.

Manager misses focus on shared values. As the leader pools intellectual capital & shared values.

If a manager tends to focus on own growth, a leader develops and turns-out competent successors.

Manager tends to reserve authority and delegates responsibilities, where a leader delegates both.

Managers focus on incremental growth, as leaders focus on innovative growth.

Managers adapt to new situations where leaders transform future of business.

Managers fight competition, but leaders leverage competition.

If managers focus on activity and operations, leaders focus on Objectives and end result.

If managers try for a self-side negotiation, for leaders it is for win-win negotiation.

Manager thinks targets where leader thinks of logistics.

Managers encounter environments, as leaders change environments.

If a manager puts himself at front, a leader puts people at front.

Managers tend to become too indispensable, where a leader takes himself dispensable at any time.

If a manager behaves with authority, a leader takes parenting with responsibility.

If a manager brings surveillance to workplace, a leader energizes and enriches workplace.

If a manager possess good knowledge, a leader has good knowledge with deep intuition.

If a manager thinks inside the box, a leader thinks outside the box.

Manager does more of assigned jobs, where a leader does more of un-assigned jobs.

A manager is sensitive to competitors, but a leader is sensitive to customers.

Manager drives human resources to performance but a leader drives human resources to human capital.

Managers are more of responsibility-driven, where leaders are of value and purpose-driven.

Managers focus on efforts for self-growth, where leaders focus on efforts for other's growth.

Managers respond to ideas, where leaders shapes ideas.

Manager looks for comforts and easy at work, where a leader creates and encounters challenges and crisis at work.

If a manager operates from low-risk position, a leader operates from a very high-risk position.

Managers are Comfortable if others accept his ideas, where leaders encourage others to conflict with his ideas.

If managers promote stability, leaders press for change.

Management is taught in B-school, where leadership is learnt and mentored at work.

Malcom Forbes said, "too many people overvalue what they are not and undervalue what they are. Victory is sweetest when you have known defeat". In business there is only invaluable person, not such indispensable person. When you cease to dream, you cease to live.

Abraham Lincoln said, "Don't worry if you are not recognized, but strive to be worthy for it. I do not think much of a man who is not wiser today than he was yesterday". According to Roosevelt, "There is only one quality worse than hardness of heart and that is softness of head. The most single ingredient in the formula for success is knowing how to get along with people". If we become increasingly humble about how little we know, we become more eager to search and discover. One cannot do today's job with yesterday's method and be in business of tomorrow.

As Henry Ford said, "If money is your hope of independence, you will never have it. The only security that a person will have in the world is a reserve of knowledge, experience and ability". When two persons in a business always agree, one of them is unnecessary.

Few quotes from Albert Einstein:

- Before one think of future, it is just before him.
- A person never made a mistake, never tried anything new.
- If you cannot explain it simply, you have not understood it well enough.
- Imagination is more important than knowledge.
- Intellectuals solve problems, geniuses prevent them.
- It is so alarming that our technology has exceeded our humanity.
- Intellect will not make a scientist, it is the character.
- Once we accept our limits, we tend to go beyond them.
- A life is worth lived, once it is lived for others.
- Intelligence is not knowledge, but imagination. For knowledge is limited to own education, whereas imagination embraces the entire world, stimulating progress, giving birth to evolution.

Imagine if Henry Ford decided to live comfortably with his large family farms inherited from his father, the world would have been without Model T20 and its assembly lines leaving the car still a rich man's luxury. Imagine if Ray Kroc did not democratise McDonalds to a world-wide institution, or Walt Disney did not create Donald Duck and Mickey Mouse, how different the life of millions of children in our planet? Imagine if Thomas Watson did not lead IBM to mass computing, imagine if Bill Gates did not invent Microsoft O/S and Steve Jobs did not invent Apple Smart phones, so with Google Search and Netflix. Starting a small internal relationship platform at Harvard, Marc Zuckerberg democratised Facebook to billions. Imagine the power of What's-App when people were isolated, and Amazon Everything Store brought retail to our doorstep during Covid-19 lockdown? Without these legends, world would have been less exciting and liveable today.

Education combined with a military training garners a rare but unique perspective that helps one to achieve a balanced maturity at a young age. Getting direct access and interface with rough and tough military officers, they adapt to a fearless state of mind of being comfortable with corporate leaders of diverse ego in their future career. A good experience comes with age, here one acquires consistency and judgment at a very young age, when mixed with a childish quest and eagerness make a very powerful attribute. As a result, one idea sees in mind, is tested and implemented within short time, without elaborating, detailing and debating. If it fails, they try the next idea. Too much time spent before experimenting, teaches us what can go wrong. This combination fosters a deep sense of purpose and its benefit for the community.

Next decade is predicted to bring more changes than the last century and the world we live will be different from what it is today. Democratisation and demonetisation will result increase in availability with a decrease in prices where technology will accelerate the speed and most of the platform almost free. During this phase of transformation, our new age entrepreneurs will become the change agents.

When CALICO is Google's next big thing in life extension, acceleration of emotional maturity is equally or more crucial, where a ten years of intellectual growth without biologically ageing, can benefit the humanity in a 10x dimension. If CALICO aims to give extended life when a person crosses his downward curve and thought cells get shrinking, accelerating emotional maturity at his early twenties, empower one's imagination stretch and thought stream to new discoveries.

Dream is not what you see while sleep, it is what does not allow you to sleep. When we start something new, the most careful thing is to dare and who dares wins! Winning starts from a necessity without an option of giving up.

10 Future – A Decade Ahead?

If the next decade was an incremental improvement of the previous decade during twentieth century, twenty first century is not an improved extension of the previous century. It proved many of the things we assumed to be right were mostly wrong. Most of the things we wished to happen were turned to be opposite. Until last century, the intuition was one of the most reliable tools for corporate leaders for taking decisions and governments to draft policies. Today intuition proves not to be the right tool any more.

Those ruthless, disruptive and daring start-ups like Amazon, Apple, Google and Facebook challenged all those existing rules. When every US company was compelled to relocate to low-cost regions towards the last two decades of twentieth century, these start-ups born in the last two decades of twenty-first century stabilised US economy to remain at the top of the world. If the first two decades of this century has seen unexpected changes different than in the history, how the world would look like after another decade? As the future is unknown and more uncertain than before, it is still very important to foresee if not to predict it.

Business will relocate to wherever the consumer potential expands. Once companies did not look beyond US and Europe for their growth, but last three decades they were forced to look at Asia which created a huge middle class consumption economy.

In 2030, we can see hardly any movie theatres, not even half of the consumer stores and restaurants, banks, schools and multiplexes where their businesses will move online. There will be more robots than blue-collar workers, more sensors than human eyes and more computers than brains.

Demographic Shift

If once underdeveloped countries depended more on developed countries, today developed ones depend more on developing countries. With economic progress coming from better education of women and couple working, birth rate in developed countries fell below the replenishment level which resulted large number of immigrant workers as well as companies relocating bases to developing regions. With Deng Xiao-ping's one-child policy during 1970s and with its consequential effect, China will have 90 million fewer people in the age group of fifteen and thirty five and 150 million more people above sixty by 2030. One negative consequence of one-child policy was the parent's cultural preference to have boys than girls, resulting 20 percent more boys than girls, a contrast with Russia where girls exceed boys for premature death due to alcohol.

In another decade, US will have a serious problem of more grandparents than grandchildren. By another ten years, one third of American men and almost equal women will retire childless. This opens a great opportunity for migrant workers in skilled areas, besides a large opportunity for human-sensitive robots in elder care. Same time US faces a challenge of attracting immigrants or restricting visas for them. If they are generous to immigrants, the country is at risk of high unemployment, but if it restricts visa, companies are likely to relocate their R&D labs towards talent pool regions like India and China. In contrast, when immigration rules are liberal, US companies stay back in the country, which opens more jobs to immigrants, than to locals. Today immigrants pay huge tax revenues to the federal government. When the number of high-skilled technical and management jobs have increased, those of blue-collar and clerical jobs decreased due to automation.

Higher the population, better the opportunities

There were one billion people in 1820 in the world and it took a century to double it up. It rose to 3 billion in 1960 despite the massive loss of lives in Holocaust and WW-II and 4 billion by 1975, 5 billion by 1987, 6 billion by 2000 until touching 7 billion in 2010. By another decade South Asia will be the most populous region in the world followed by Africa. When every country is on its growth graph, better education especially more number of women into education and work, results less number of children with better and higher quality of life and education.

When the world had to feed such a big population, there will be multiple job opportunities in farming and food sector, also in wide sectors as clothing, education, healthcare, transport, retail, entertainment and many more. If problems become the mother of big opportunities, Israel makes an ideal example for rest of the world to follow. Most of its innovations were born out of a national purpose for its existence.

Migration empowers Innovation

Years before the WW-II, German Jews who fled the threat of Nazi holocaust to US had accelerated the innovation in America. They account for many of the Nobel winners and also caused almost thirty percent of new discoveries. In continuation, America stands as the most attractive destination for migrants than any other country in the world.

Last two decades had proven that migration is a stimulus to innovation and it surges with immigrants than locals. If US is the biggest innovation country, immigrants played a vital role and about 29 percent of doctoral degree holders are foreign born. US has 13 percent of its population made of immigrants, out of 28 percent of the physicians and surgeons, 22 percent of nurses and homecare aides, more than 35 percent of the scientists in NASA. Out of a total 85 Nobel laureates in Physics, Chemistry and Physiology and Medicine since 2000, thirty tree to forty percent of them were foreign born.

Until twentieth century, we were local and linear; a baker's son remained to be a baker, driver's son an auto mechanic or driver, and farmer's son still a farmer. Today children grow many times their parents. Today average American has smart-phone, PC, car, housing, TV and all appliances, which was considered to be luxury and could not be possessed by a rich person in last century.

The founders of Intel, Google, eBay, LinkedIn, Tesla and Facebook which stabilised the US economy to the top of the world, were immigrants. Without them the world economic landscape would have been not the same as today. This achievement is despite the fact that US has relatively very large aged population and very low local workforce. Almost 23 percent of all US high-tech ventures are founded by immigrants, with 40 percent in CA, 42 percent in Massachusetts and

45 percent in NJ. They founded 44 of those 87 unicorns in US as on 2016. Twenty three of these forty four ventures came to US to pursue college degrees, with the largest of them from India, UK, Israel, Germany and Canada. What drives the US Real Estate economy so vibrant is its affluent immigrant community. We generally are negative towards immigrants blaming them for loss of opportunities among the locals, because we are more cautious about what we lose than what we gain. Migration gains many times more than any loss; where we are unhappy of losing $10 than gaining $50.

Immigrants are more innovative than locals, and also is with a sheer degree of entrepreneurship, not alone in US, but in every other nation. Next to US, we see a country called Israel, with the world's highest per-capita in start-ups, which is established with 100 percent immigrants from about seventy countries across the world. To succeed, you have to leave behind everything familiar to start somewhere new. Migrants are more risk-tolerant and creative. Next, immigration takes place at a younger age adding more to the workforce who pay higher taxes to support the idle and aged beneficiaries.

Internet communicates to everyone about the new opportunities and it helps people to migrate to those locations where such opportunities are in plenty, which as a result, US attracts best talents from all across the world.

Migration was blamed by the country of its origin as 'Brain-drain' to the destination country. But it creates large forex remittances to the country of origin. Depending on the country of origin, about 50-70 percent of the immigrants returned to their countries at a later stage where many of them launched start-up as well as Venture capital companies where the idea and experience were originated from their experience abroad with investment from their savings. Such returnees were a real asset mostly for Israel, India and Taiwan especially in IT sectors where requirement of capital was relatively very low. With migration becoming in large numbers, and the immigrants with a better desire to marry and have children than the original inhabitants, the present majority could become a minority in next decade.

Big cities are becoming the Tier-2 innovation centres, where immigrants from rest of the country come and work. This means innovation stems when educated people leave their hometown and migrate to bigger cities. The prosperity of Mumbai is largely owed to immigrants, who made big presence in the city's business and industry. Bangalore and Delhi are proven to be better environments for innovation start-ups in proportion to the number of immigrants. Pune, Chennai, Hyderabad and Kochi are major tier-2 innovation centres in India.

If Britain took three centuries to transform from an industrial economy to a service economy, US took just half its time to do so. China by contrast, took just two generation to move from agricultural economy to technological and service-oriented economy. Next decade, China will have 25 percent of its population over sixty.

If Africa will be the second largest in population after South Asia in next decade, it has the largest landmass as big as US, W&E Europe, China, Brazil and Japan combined and abundant of water resources which makes it most potential for farming and food production that can feed the growing population in rest of the world.

Senior Citizens

With more citizens ageing and with lower birth rate than its replenishment level, developed countries are under threat of more retirees than workforce. Governments were under stress when the young workforce has to be taxed to the welfare of the aged citizens for their pension and healthcare. Senior citizens, especially their lifespan was increasing close to a century, is a big liability for Europe, USA and Japan, but a new entry, China will become the home for largest numbers in another ten years. With this trend, we had seen for last few decades, the future world will have more and more of aged citizens with less and less of working group. This will increase the need for migration.

Opportunities

If we can think laterally, it is possible to turn a problem into a large opportunity. More we focus on opportunities, problems tend to shrink and become less relevant after a decade. Today, business and government focus on those 2.3 billion who were born between 1980 and 2000. They are the present-day's workforce. When husband and wife both work, they make good income but have more commitments like housing, car, children education, healthcare, vacation, interest on loan, etc. As most of them spend more than their income, they become indebted. But most of the companies advertise for catching their attention and offer products and service that suit their needs. Government also pay more attention to the working class as an asset to the country for being the main source of taxes and consumption that drives the GDP.

This age group will rise to 1.4 bil by 2030 from the present 1 bil, an increase by 40 percent globally with 90 mil in US and 113 mil in China and an additional of 6 mil in Mexico, 50 mil in India, 3 mil in UK and 10 mil in Bangladesh. Japan will have 34 percent of its population as aged citizen and Germany 28 percent. If ageing population is a challenge for US, EU and Japan, one-child policy in China destroys the low-wage manufacturing economy which today could be relocated to anywhere in the world with automation, robotics and 3-D Printing.

On the other hand, senior citizens are mostly ignored as liability where government has to pay for their pension, healthcare and welfare. But they are resourceful than working class. They have large savings to ensure financial security after they retire. Together with monthly pension, with all their healthcare and welfare needs being taken care by governments, they make a net income far higher that their limited spending habits.

On spending side, survey reveals that today more seniors are taking vacations with an increase in their lifespan, largely in groups but mostly within their region. This trend will surge in coming years through next decade, they will exceed the numbers of working group. This makes a big business opportunity in air travel, group tourism and hotels more customised to the needs of the seniors. The category and segment what we followed in the past are no longer relevant in future, as seniors are more healthy and youthful with more money to spend. By 2030, a seventy year old live like today's sixty years old.

Business does not see much potential for fashion, clothes, shoes and such products for seniors. When the working class have financial constraints in spending on such products, today the more health and young-looking seniors remain an untapped market segment. Home entertainment is a good area which could engage them. Many people over sixty learnt to live in groups, with daily engagement with others in their age group, either colleague, relations, friends or community. They celebrate their birthdays, anniversaries and special events like family rejoining, children on holidays etc. These are opportunities for event organizers, food catering, wine and gifts. With good earnings and less spending, they do not have to save for future like working groups and they have no mortgage on house, car or consumer durables. Seniors over sixty, are estimated to spend $15Tril a year from next decade.

Seniors also make a big opportunity for start-up innovations. The gray market emerges a big business scope for healthcare, assisted living, homecare and other service businesses like bill payments, laundry and local transport. Japan, Europe, US and in future China will face a huge requirement of elder's care. Until recently, the solution was immigrants from poorer countries which was difficult with government's visa restrictions. Toyota has regular production of senior-sensitive 'human-support robots' which can retrieve medication, bring drinking water, draw curtains, floor cleaning etc. It can also talk so sensitive to the soothing comfort of elders in bed. Japan leads the world in robots for elder care. If US meets its 90 percent paid senior-care with immigrants, Japan needs an additional 1 mil home nurses by 2025.

Today Facebook connects them worldwide and brings friendships and relations and brings them seriously engaged, which otherwise become an isolated and bored life. As they had to depend on somebody to get what they want, it is an unexplored segment for e-commerce business considering the amount of money they have. Virtual Reality enables seniors to be anywhere in the world with a headset and smart phone. Networking technology allows them to share group experience anytime from anywhere to a real-life situation.

With more knowledge and money in hand, about half of all the new entrepreneurs will be of 55-65 age group in next ten years.

Burgeoning Middle Class

Europe and North America remained as the world's biggest middle class for a century or two, where a new middle class emerged in China three decades back and in India during the last decade. By next decade, this new middle class will be home for more than half of the world's consumer buying power. Today China is the largest online shopping setting a world record of $25bil in a single day of 2017 by Alibaba, breaking the Cyber Monday's record of $7 bil in US by far. Macau earns a gambling revenue of five times as compared to $7 bil in Las Vegas. China is estimated to add another 400 mil to its middle class by 2030.

In entertainment and movies, Amazon Prime wrestles with Netflix and Disney Hotstar the world around, which are already on move to have translated versions to Mandarin and Hindi. It will not be far ahead, some of their movies will be co-produced as well as developed in low cost hubs like Mumbai, Shanghai and Chennai. Megamalls like Walmart and Carrefour were considered as lo-cosy stores in US and Europe, but for the traditional Chinese and Indian customers, they were expensive than small retail stores.

The American Conversion

Asia especially in China and India, if parents saw the money to be saved, the new emerging middle class see the money to be spent. Today the Chinese consumers have a strong influence of their American counterparts ie, spend, and borrow to spend, which is in extreme contrast to the ideology that ruled them in the past. Chinese young customers started to believe as if they are Americans which conflicts with their cultural tradition that Chinese save as Americans spend.

In 2020, the proportion of Chinese household debt to GDP hovered around 50 percent, compared to 76 percent in US. Ten years ahead, both could reach the same level. As China's younger generation does not save, US consumers will need to control their spending. China is a communist country, where its people embraced capitalism decades back caused by these wide-spread use and application of the exponential technologies. With capitalism exceeding its ideology day by day, the end to communism is not that far.

The problem and the opportunity

This consumerism leads to a big problem of waste, especially plastics and packaging. If countries plan a sustainable waste policy, it can attract many private entrepreneurs to recycle the waste that turns to energy and by-products. As how government encourages renewable energy with incentives, recycling has a next possible potential to grow with similar incentives.

3-D Printing has a sunrise future which reduces, or almost eliminates waste in manufacturing process. When 3-D Printing gradually replaces the present moulding process of components and assembly-line manufacturing, it has a potential to enhance speed and to cut costs. This revolution in process could relocate the future of manufacturing from China which has an established assembly-line process, to anywhere else in the world, for which large land area is not necessary.

If America is known for the highest consumption in the world, with the new middle class from China and India following the same route, another 2 bil new middle class consumers are to join this high-consumption club in the wake of next decade, ie a 55 percent increase from 2020 to 2030. They can afford for more protein, which means more consumption of beef than ham or chicken. As our planet will be under stress for water, animal feed, farm lands and labour, besides worldwide animal solidarity movements, cultured meet could be a possible replacement to organic meet in future. Today genomic research had made it possible to produce cultured meet adopting the 3-D printing way. Creative methods are on the way to reduce the use of scarce natural resources like water, minerals and energy. The middle class consumers of emerging markets will exceed those in US, Europe and Japan by five to one in next decade, a twofold increase.

Emerging Womenfolk

Women are not to limit their lives within the four walls of their home anymore. Today girls outnumber boys as university graduates and they are already forty percent in technical and professional academies, with an annual higher growth rate than opposite genders. All of them are serious career aspirants with better clarity and determination of what to become in future than their counterparts.

Young women are more listening and resilient by nature than men and hardly argue and conflict in the middle of presenting an idea. During the open house debates, they are very specific in challenging the original idea with improvements and alternatives. They are more creative, imaginative and productive in their projects. They can play good roles in negotiations as a member of the team. They hardly involve in workplace politics, wasting time on unrelated talks and do not take break unless during official breaks. As per a survey by an investment bank in UK, men traded more frequently and took more risks than women, but surprisingly women booked more returns than men in long term. Hence businesses linked to women as consumers, investors and savers provide new market opportunities which will be the winning factors in coming decades. It predicts for more educated and employed women in next decades. Underutilising the women asset, a country wastes almost half its talent pool. Today 70 percent of American women work full-time outside their home.

Women have different spending habits than men. There is a wrong perception that women spend the hard-earned money of men. When it comes to employed and earning couple, if the major spending on non-essentials for women is in fashion, cosmetics and jewels, men have limited habits which can go as expensive as high performance cars and luxury homes and yachts. Men are known for spending on alcohol, sex, casinos, gambling and racing. In this context, women spend less and save more than men.

Educated and career aspirant women restrict the number of children to one or two, which is equal or less than the replenishment rate. More career aspirant and bold ones, either do not get married, or do not bear children. Many of them regret for if married life is an obstacle to their career aspirations, and turn to be divorcees without or with if at all any child. We have enough examples of women unmarried for their lifetime with adopted children or with live-in-partner living or even same-sex partnerships. With the present cost of raising a child, they save more with less number of children. This trend will make the number of schools irrelevant and turn them to real estate assets in future, besides decline in demand for baby food, baby clothes and toys.

From the above reality, there could be more wealthy women than men between the next two decades. As per recent statistics, women live longer by five to six years than men, and with mostly women are younger than men by a couple of years on marriage, besides more men die due to smoking, alcohol, road accidents and sexually transmitted deceases, there will be an increasing number of women inheriting their husband's wealth added to their own assets. For all these reasons, we can see almost 50 percent of global wealth rested with women in another decade. In other words, there will be more men dead than women on the same age in years to come. Already, women make an equal force in sectors like government bureaucracy, banking and finance, teaching, R&D, assembling, retail and healthcare. If Grameen has empowered thousands of women in Bangladesh, India leads in nursing, besides many people representatives in local bodies.

Opportunities

The demand for women workplace wear will surge, also for the cosmetics. Food delivery will keep increasing with less time available for working women to cooking. Day-care and playschools will flourish with special trained teachers with specially designed learning tools for infants. The demand for cars will change with higher numbers of feminine cars in their electric versions of VW Golf and Polo, Chevy-spark, Suzuki Swift, etc largely smaller two-door sedans, besides electric two wheelers. On other hand, wealthy and well placed women are fond of powerful performance cars for weekend and holiday leisure.

It took more than a century for Jeff Bezos to announce a $15 per hour to all his US employees, which Henry Ford declared a wage of $.56 a day in 1914, which is equivalent to today's $126 per day or $14 an hour. Google, Amazon, Tesla and Facebook are so generous in their wage policy in view of attracting and retaining best talents. The future of employment sector will adopt this compassionate capitalism, especially when the technology sector is going to be the largest GDP segment.

With climate change, rising sea water and natural sea-originated calamities on one side, and on the other side we have most of the cities and wealth heavens located in the coastlines, this could result a gradual relocation of cities away from coasts, means a number of new cities taking birth. Many of the ancient cities are decayed and had grown beyond any renovation possibilities for which the only solution is shifting away. Most these cities are congested where the rising middle class waste spending 25 percent of their driving time in traffic, especially for finding a parking. And for sure, it is mostly the middle class which will shape the future of such new cities.

Obesity & Lifestyle deceases

By 2030, the world will have four hundred cities with over a population of one million with half of them being new entrants. With an exploding number of neo-rich middleclass, who will adapt to the present American eating habits of more colas, fast food, hotdog and beef, are tend to become obese, including children. When most of the things and relationship network are carried out online, hardly any reason for them to move out. When obesity rises, it will also rise the numbers of heart problem, diabetes, muscular affliction etc. This could open new opportunities for oversize clothing and shoes, plus-size seating and dietary consulting. With 36.5 percent of adult Americans as obese, the obesity community doubled since 1980, to 1.9 bil overweight in 2016 that is one fourth of global population. Obesity leads directly to diabetes and heart decease and will become the largest health problem in 2030. Genomics and Life extension technology with Big data will address with suitable and simple solutions.

How IBM Watson monitors our health data, predicts deceases and consult, Vinod Khosla, a well known VC estimates that technology will replace 80 percent of doctors in another decade.

More machines than brains

By 2030, PCs will equal with the global population in numbers, where cell phones will exceed by far as every individual, office, school, hospital and government will go online. There will be more sensors than eyes, more robotic arms than human labour in factories. When a new technology replaces the old one, jobs get destroyed and created. This will emerge a new young breed of visionary entrepreneurs, many of them in their twenties with a high emotional maturity and resilience, self-described as leaders who shape our future.

Each disruption results a problem, where each innovation comes with a solution which is the new-wave capitalism. Automation eliminates monotonous and repeat jobs, which liberates human beings to apply their brains than hands. Automation and robotics are likely to destroy many conventional jobs, but are capable of creating more smart and skilled employments.

Quantum Computing

Quantum computers were proposed in the 1980s by Richard Feynman and Yuri Manin. The intuition behind quantum computing stemmed from what was often seen as one of the greatest embarrassments of physics: remarkable scientific progress faced with an inability to model even simple systems.

Google announced it has a quantum computer that is 100 million times faster than any classical computer in its lab. Every day, this system produces 2.5 exabytes of data. That number is equivalent to the content on 5 million laptops. This means that Quantum Computers can perform in seconds equals to what today's super computers perform in weeks. The year- 2021 will be crucial to its commercial viability and growth, where VW and BMW formed a consortium to create the first commercial quantum memory for their vehicles. In 2021, IBM made a remarkable invention of Eagle- a quantum processor with an amazing speed of 127 qubit an hour.

AI exceeding human brains

AI enables a number of opportunities that brings the present world we know to an end, replaced with a new world. Electric and Autonomous cars destroy the present world of fuel-burnt cars, but will open with a new theory of manufacturing cars. Honda launched ASIMO- a humanoid robot which can not only perform to multifunctional services, but to respond sensitively to elder care and customers. Apple's virtual assistant SIRI is embedded to all it's i-Phones. AI is there, all around us from social media advertising to photo tagging and tracking ecommerce delivery, food and ride ordering to satellite mapping. It has an alarming future potential to make human a whole, useless.

AI converged with sensors and robotics, can destroy about 1.7 million truck driver jobs in US with the disruption by autonomous trucks. Added with bus and taxi drivers, chauffeurs and self-employed drivers, this number could exceed 3 million. This eliminates the dangers of road accidents, sleepy driving, honking, light beams, human errors in signalling, with several benefits like computerised signals, fuel efficiency, navigated mapping and less traffic jams. As you drive home, sensors and cameras mounted on police cars and road signs can sense your license plate capturing all your database of car's movements and visits. Your home automation records the time you arrived, Nest thermostat tracks your movements inside your home and your smart TV listens to all your conversations, with no privacy and discretion.

In assembling, a single advanced robot can displace an average six workers. With more robotics deployed into assembling, the lesser skilled people employed in repeat manual jobs were more or less stagnant from 1983-2015 at 28-30 million. During this period, about 300,000 robots were installed, doing the work of 2 Million workers. An average intake of 35,000 robots a year, the impact is too multiple by next decade, where factories will have more programmers than workers. By the same time, the number of skilled mechanics increased from 14 to 27 million and non-routine smart jobs like designers, nurses, teachers and programmers doubled from 28 to 57 million. Surprise to see that Smart Robots in tissue surgeries, performed better than human surgeons.

3-D Printing

When the present $12 trillion global manufacturing gets disrupted by 3-D Printing or additive process, there is no waste or no toxic fume emission by using precisely the exact raw materials unlike the conventional subtractive method. Next the factory is too small and can be regionalised closer to market, dealers and consumers that can save an average of 15-20 percent on transportation costs, reducing the carbon emitted by freight. It has successfully proved to be a better alternative for house construction, with every component printed either in concrete or lighter and durable materials much faster on or near to the site without waste with superior insulation factors. More stronger, but lighter and cheaper alternatives will replace the present materials used in aircraft, train coaches, automobiles, furniture, electronics and defence components which will also be in full compliance to waste-environment-emission protocols. 3-D printed surfaces like Corian, Silicate panels and fortified Gypsum are likely to have greater presence in construction.

It also tried success in healthcare, especially in printed tissue for transplant and organ replacement. Weapon industry in Israel has already brought many variants of assault guns by replacing steel with light-weight alternatives like ceramic, graphite, carbon, tungsten and engineering polymers that give great comforts to soldiers in battlefield.

GE's advanced turbo prop was assembled with 855 individually casted components, which today is made of twelve 3-D printed parts, saving 48Kg in weight and 20 percent fuel efficiency at a fraction of time taken before. In 2014, a Chinese firm printed ten units of single homes in less than 24 hours, below the cost of $5000 each following a combination of 3-D printing and modular design.

Tesla S has as little as seventeen moving parts, which makes it a computer on wheels, and the next attempt is to invent how to 3-D print these parts. Chinese economy was based on manufacturing and assembly of cheap plastic components adopting additive technology which leaves almost 20 percent waste. In the next decade, 3-D printing will replace this with subtractive manufacturing leaving no waste, which poses a severe threat to the world's factory. Such a situation may leave a distressed China which may be forced to call its overseas debts, resulting a global fiasco among those Afro-Asian and Latin American countries deeply indebted to China.

A Collaborative Economy of 8.5 Billion People

Airbnb, Uber and Lyft opened the doors to a collaborative economy, which showed us how to share our idle assets, i.e. properties, services and possessions. These companies are facilitators and do not own, lease or use any of these assets. Interestingly without AI, automation, IoT and big data these shared platforms would have been difficult to imagine. It is estimated that this digitally shared economy will account for nearly 30 percent of total work and consumption.

The emerging middle class is becoming less and less interested in owning houses, cars and hosting guests at home, which can be leased, rented or outsourced at restaurants. Research shows that people who do not own property are generally happier than those who own. The recent surge in human power has not grown to equal with human happiness. As a result, we can see young people are turning away from owning houses and cars, but preferring to lease somebody's property, and ubering cars for a fee than owning one. There is a new growing trend in leasing consumer durables and appliances. Next ten years, spending will be in the form of collaborative and shared consumption. The emergence of networking, search, sharing and relationship platforms bring people together and friendly which spread a culture of 'we' that replaces 'me' or shared than selfish. This culture tends to break all walls of hostility, region, religion, nation and race to a seamless universal culture. Smart phones as the major mode of sharing, this culture can only go forward, never reverse. Four decades back, Grameen Microfinance, a women empowerment mission initiated in Bangladesh liberated millions of poor women out of poverty, which today with the accelerated technology has the capability to expand in multiple numbers, across South Asia and Africa.

The elders have more houses and apartments as investments, but mostly unused and idle. Airbnb connects the owners with travellers, where the idle property earns an income, which is not as expensive as three star hotels to the visitors. This is a contactless transaction between the facilitator, owner, user and bank. Airbnb claims more than four million listing in 65,000 destinations in 190 countries, with a value of $40Bil, which connect and collaborate both young travellers with aged homeowners.

Uber and Lyft are other solid examples of shared economy. Uber works on Google Maps and AI, and Google is seriously into its own driverless cars, which may become a threat to Uber in future. Similarly Uber want to employ robots for delivering Uber Eats as Amazon for their delivery and warehouse, where advanced robotics is a major future for Google. Google complements with Amazon in Search and AI as collaborators, not as competitors.

But Google collaborates with Uber and vice-versa, not as legendary competitors. When you can hire a chauffeur driven car at little more than the cost of a public transport, with no risk of accident, insurance, maintenance and depreciation, why the need to own a car? With such a comfort and convenience culture deeply experienced in the society, today American youths are less bothered of obtaining their driving license and owning cars. This drop is by 15-18 percent from 1983 to 2015. The asset sharing economy is a part of the broader collaborative economy which includes peer-to-peer lending, crowd sourcing, crowd funding, co-working, origin-to-user sales. Today most transactions from original sources like fishermen and farmer to consumer are moving to the shared platforms at no extra cost. This is opening a door to a new civilisation.

Airbnb has attracted excessive number of tourists, but that disturbs the residential neighbourhood, but also degrades the tourism and the tourism economy with more of less spending lower class tourists. Uber discourages the sales of customised cars suiting each one's lifestyle by providing just a car available closer to the customer. On the other side, private cars are used just 5 percent on road, whereas the remaining time it lies idle in the car park, which in contrast Uber car is engaged almost 50 percent time on road. Both depreciates, but Uber with higher odometer. The investment on private car is mostly idle, but Uber car makes high cash flow cycle resulting far better monetisation of asset. Used or not, cars cost huge amount on insurance, maintenance, consumables, parts and depreciation. Purpose of car is to ride, not to keep idle which justifies more in favour of car hiring platform.

Today's businesses have less and less need to own laboratory, factory and even scientific tool, instead all these can be leased and shared. Cloud computing offers storage and management of massive amount of data with unlimited processing, which eliminates the expensive facility of own servers, by saving huge capital investments.

Facebook acquired What's-App for $.19 bil in 2014, a messaging app which did not have any physical assets and less than sixty employees, but the attraction was its 1.5 bil user base with a future potential to expand to entire global population. Next the messaging service was free of cost and it remained free till today and will remain so for ever. Its revenue of over $.40 bil comes from advertising where AI and IoT select the products on digital display by sensing the purchasing habits and buying interests of the users. Facebook believes in connecting all its users, which gives them a richer life.

Digital Republics

Sweden, Norway and Denmark are almost digital economies, with hardly any physical currency transaction and almost all their government services are online. One step forward, The Republic of Estonia, located south to the Gulf of Finland and Baltic Sea is a cent percent advanced digital society in the world, where it's entire 1.3 mil citizens have online access to register their businesses, vote, medical prescriptions, insurance claims, banking besides hundred of government services. In the Middle East, UAE especially its commercial capital Dubai is fast progressing to become a total digital economy. In Africa, countries like Kenya and Ghana are far advanced towards digitalising. With almost every country leaping towards 100 percent digitalisation goal, we can see the next decade almost a cashless and online society. Digital economy eliminates fraud, bribe and corruption, and it is burglary-safe unlike cash.

Block Chain and Crypto-currency

Cryptography is the study of secure communications techniques that fallows only the sender and intended recipient of a message to view its contents. These transactions are monitored under the technology called Block-chain platform. Here when such a transaction is digitally recorded, it is called a block, and when multiples of such blocks are recorded, which is known as Block-chain, where each block is connected to one transaction partners. This system can accommodate any number of such accounts and can exchange and transfer as required, but without being accessible to anyone else than the seller and buyer and is being called as 'distributed ledger'. Not recognized by any governments or central banks, it is traded all over the world, controlled through quantum maths and virtual exchange. Here, data is encrypted using a secret key, and then both the encoded message and secret key are sent to the recipient for decryption. It is a network built on trust and transparency, but a huge challenge to sovereign currencies.

The idea of digital currency- crypto-currency dates back to 2008 by Stochi Nakamoto in Japan. In two decades the number of crypto-currency in the world got increased to more than six thousand. This form of currency does not come under any government regulation like Federal Reserve or any ministry of finance, as a result it has no security reserve or regulatory guarantee. It is a computer-generated and stored currency with high volatile virtual value, operated on quantum maths and block-chain technology. The important accelerators of Crypto-currency and Block-chain services are Data Mining, Big Data and AI. If government currencies are mostly stable and rated, crypto-currency lacks trust with extreme ups and downs hence very speculative and hedged. All its transactions and mining are governed and controlled by cryptography. When Tesla Motors officially announced not to recognize Crypto-currency, its market price fell by 35 percent. In October 2021 when Apple's CEO Tim Cook confirmed buying into, all crypto-currencies surged, but his company ruled out any recognition of such digital currency. It is gaining market in countries like Lebanon, Zimbabwe, Venezuela and Columbia whose currencies are so weak and deeply depreciated. Off late financial service institutions like JP Morgan, Visa and Goldman Sachs started recognizing crypto-currency. Considering the fact that the total value of all the coins and banknotes in the world is roughly $7.6trillion,

Bitcoin the first crypto-currency form in the market in 2009, now commanding a market share of 43 percent of the total $2.3 trillion market value of crypto by 2021, which is 30 percent of the world's currency market. Interestingly, the total volume of 'above the surface' gold in the world is 187,200 tons commanding a value of $.7.7 trillion. In comparison, the total market cap for all the world's stocks is estimated to be $.73tril. Of late, there is an overwhelming campaign for its regulation.

Interestingly, 15 Indian banks including ICICI Bank, Axis Bank, Bajaj

Allianz, SBI, Kotak Mahindra Bank have reportedly planned to adopt block-chain technology to start a new trade finance system. Reports say the new system will verify data using invoices on goods and services tax (GST) and e-way bills which will quicken transactions and also eliminate risk of frauds. Recently, financial market regulator Securities and Exchange Board of India (SEBI) gave a nod to Invesco Mutual Fund's Invesco CoinShares Global Block-chain ETF Fund of Fund (FoF). This fund is India's first mutual fund scheme to be opened in December, 2021, that invests in global companies in the block-chain ecosystem. With a surge in activity and demand, now the country is seriously considering regulating Crypto with an entry stage GST and to list as an asset like Gold ETF, Shares and Bonds. Its union budget-FY 2022-23 declared a 30 percent tax on income from digital assets like Crypto.

Crypto-currency will destroy the corruption at all levels, as every transaction is transparent as it is encrypted and stored. As a result, political leaders and bureaucrats are reluctant to recognize and regulate it. So far crypto is in its infant stage, and it is beyond anyone's guess about what impact it will create in future currency markets?

Bitcoin is a crypto-currency financial service which accounted for 28 percent of the Block-chain transactions for eight years until 2020. IBM is the largest company in the world embracing block-chain and established a division called Enterprise Block-chain Solutions and Services. With over $200 million invested in research and development, the tech giant is leading the way for companies to integrate ledgers and the IBM cloud into their systems. It is a computer controlled registry that records all transactions and contracts. This segment will also become an alternative to the conventional banking system we had seen. Block-chain based contracts make the role of lawyers and accountants in drafting agreements irrelevant as such contracts will be replaced by AI, Data Mining, Automation and Big Data solutions for creating documents. As a result, Crypto-currency will become the next parallel to digital banking. Once currencies were equal to the number of countries, which as of today already exceeded by far. All these changes will make the future of government currencies and banking system so vulnerable and uncertain. The major Block-chain operators are, Ethereum, Salesforce Platform, Amazon Quantum Ledger Database (QLDB), Kaleido Block-chain Business Cloud, Azure Block-chain Workbench, IBM Block-chain Platform, Corda and Hyperledger.

The central banks are seriously concerned about the danger that crypto could pose, like payment transactions for drugs, violation of forex, commission of arms deal, corruption and black money transfers etc, outside its control and records.

G-Pay has universalized the instant cash payment at no cost. Banks are already online for all their services from transaction, deposit and lending. As more people, especially the younger generation prefer to use apps, banking jobs are likely to get more and more robotised and with increasing rate of automation future banking will go without any banks or bankers. G-Pay is scaled universally with no profit and once it starts making profit on a much larger scale, Facebook and Amazon are waiting to enter with similar payment apps which one can guess the reach rate of technology taking away the entire payment transactions. This is reducing the space engaged by banks and currencies. When banking or internet connectivity are paid services, this disruption that Google, Apple and Amazon could create is that such services will become free as Google search, Gmail, Apple store and Amazon Pay.

We are now creating more information content in a single day than we created in decades or even centuries of the pre-digital era, hence the time required to get from 0.1 percent to 1 percent on an accelerated curve, is equal to the time required to get from 1 percent to 100 percent. The convergence of AI, Cloud, ML, IoT, Sensors and Big data are behind the success of these five largest global technology firms which raised the livelihood of rising billions.

If we had just 500Mil internet connected devices in 2005, which went up to 8Bil in 2015 is expected to explode to 50bil in 2025 and one trillion in next ten years. In this process, anything and everything stand a threat of disruption and extinction of million jobs. In this explosion, if any company designed for success in twentieth century doomed to failure in its following century, and the present revolutionary companies will shorten this failure cycle to decades.

11 Big Problems are Big Opportunities!

Industrial revolution unfolded nearly over a century; personal computers spanned for four decades, while smart phones made a global scale penetration in half that time. It has become a common tool especially for those neglected segment of people. Wrist watches are synonymous to Switzerland, when its army needed a means of coordinating among soldiers in the rugged terrains of Alps. As the watchmakers were all located around Geneva, so most of the factories followed them. Later Japan became the world leader, but with the birth of Swatch with wide celebrity marketing, Swiss watches regained what they lost.

Japan conquered the word in Cars, Electronics, Xerox, Printers, Calculators, cameras, Radios, Stereos, TV, VCR, and most other breakthroughs which originally took place in US or Europe. But it is so surprising that the digital technology equipments like PCs and Smart phones were not successful in Japan unlike in China and Korea.

Technology is very meaningless, unless it can reduce costs. Then by reduction in costs, it can easily reach out the poor, by which it opens a Blue Ocean space. Car was once a rich man's toy and it was a real big problem for others to afford. When Henry Ford wanted his workers to own his car, he innovated by eliminating all those avoidable parts, replacing the old ones with lighter and less expensive ones, and above all by introducing assembly line into manufacturing. Every change we saw afterwards is a further improvement until the car industry changed to renewable energy. Here a big problem that only rich can buy cars, was a golden business opportunity for Ford and he disrupted that rule through relentless innovation in technology.

Mobile connectivity is another good example where from a talking devise, it absorbed internet, Android, data storage, Google, Facebook, What's-App, Playstore, games, cinemas and AI, without being asked for, but at a continuous reduction in costs. Today with the device, we get everything else almost free. Here connectivity was a big problem with its high cost until three decades ago, which turned to be a golden business opportunity for Motorola, Nokia, Apple, Samsung and Huawei which opened up large number of employments in R&D, assembling, logistics, retail and service. Today with more than 4Bil (half the global population) users, it is being used by those cannot even read and write. This has become the root device behind all the exponential innovations that facilitate E-commerce, Food delivery, car lift, banking and government services.

Airline or hotel booking were a real problem for corporate as it delays the confirmation, besides a dictated price. Online reservation and payment eased this problem in a matter of ten minutes, sitting at home or office.

A Binding Responsibility on India

India being the largest GDP, population and economic growth among the SAARC (South Asia) countries, it has the responsibility to change the future of the region. The region secured independence from colonial rule almost seven decades and its biggest problems are like, Poverty, Hunger, Healthcare, Education, Emission, Infra, Water and Power, besides religious extremism and bilateral trade, which remain still unsolved. When India takes the leadership to addressing these problems, its business opportunities will benefit more the initiating country, with every other country sharing the benefits. The following pages explore how these big problems could be turned to the region's biggest innovation opportunities.

Largest Indian Corporate

US has a well tracked list of companies since the WW2, whereas in India the research is not that in detail. In the previous chapter, we examined a comparison of five largest US companies in 2006 and 2018. Below list shows those largest five Indian companies in 2000 and 2020, which had remained stagnated with industrial, engineering and software sectors, which explains how we are lagging in technology innovations?

Top five Companies in India-2020-21.	**In 2000**
Reliance Industries Ltd.	Reliance Industries Ltd

Tata Consultancy Services Ltd.	State Bank of India
HDFC Bank Ltd.	ONGC
Infosys Ltd.	ICICI Bank
Hindustan Unilever Ltd.	Indian Oil

Talent Exodus

Totally disconnected from the last century, technology dominates our business and life in this twenty-first century. Those founders and CEOs of these companies are the glittering celebrities in our modern world. They had eclipsed the old-world magnates of Oil, Steel, Automobiles, Chemicals, Banking and Investment sectors like John Rockefeller, Paul Getty, Andrew Carnegie, Henry Ford, Agnelli, Toyoda, Du-Pont, Barings, Morgan and Warren Buffet.

If many of the largest number of CEOs in US are from India- a country of world's 18 percent population, why we are so lagging in producing so many successful CEOs in its home turf? On the other side, Chinese do not have to migrate to US to rise to the top, as opportunities are plenty in their country. If so many Indian CEOs work for so many large technology companies founded by Americans like Microsoft, Google, Facebook, Apple and IBM, China has much more technology giants like Tencent, Huawei, Xiomi, Alibaba, Foxconn, Didi, Baidu, Byte-dance and Tiktok, but hardly such an ecosystem in India, where we educate and train engineers to become the CEOs in US.

India is rich in her resources, but lag in government vision and policies. This biggest problem is her biggest opportunity, which is the challenge for private entrepreneurs.

Unfortunately, no start-ups or companies started since 2000 appear in India's top five list for 2020-21, which alarms the pathetic situation of our innovation index. If we look this as a big problem, then big problems are biggest business opportunities when India is still the largest GDP and leader in digital technology sector in South Asia and Middle East region. For decades, Industrial sector in India did not produce any billionaire than its promoters or families. Whereas on the other side, a technology company like Infosys, co-founded by seven engineers in 1981 made all of them multi-millionaires. Technology companies follow not only wealth creation but also its distribution in a fair manner.

How Physics, Maths, Electronic and Comp. Science make the foundation for Innovation?

In Material science companies like GE, DuPont, 3M, Dow Chemicals, Intel and BASF, innovation is a part of daily life. Most of their innovations were driven by physics in the form of material science, electronics and maths. Some are pioneers in developing new materials from plastics, titanium, graphite, ceramics, silicon and derivatives of glass, alloys and chromes which are scientific substitutes to heavy metals like Iron and steel, copper, cadmium, brass, etc which are expensive and heavier. Their products are extensively used as superior substitutes in aircraft, automobile, home appliances, computer and cell phones, defence equipments, semiconductors, electro-optics, electro-magnetic, electronic chips, solar panels, sound and heat insulation, etc. These companies have given extensive support to defence contractors like Raytheon, Lockheed-Martin, Thales, Dassault and General Dynamics besides Boeing, Airbus and NASA Missions. This shows the might of physics, maths, computer science and electronics to drive innovations with or without necessarily resulting new business start-ups.

STEM – (Science, Technology, Engineering and Maths) Disciplines

By around 2025, the new exponential technologies are expected to change what the global job market will demand. It will create about 85Mil high-skilled and another 90Mil semi-skilled jobs, while destroying 135Mil low-skilled, aged and high salaried jobs in disproportionate to their performance. No doubt these top of the range high-skilled jobs are so integral to these new technologies. Both these segments make India the biggest beneficiary with its largest pool of English educated engineers and science graduates, complemented with a satisfactory level of social and adaptable skills.

Material Science is one of the most important and integral subject to STEM education. The newly developed composites have great potential to replace the conventional components within most finished systems. Today Carbon Fibre composites are widely used as replacement to metal and plastics which helped in reduction of weight, size and costs with accelerated performance with diverse application into, aeroplanes, locomotives, automobiles, spacecrafts, weapons, machines and human parts. When these advanced materials are used adopting new manufacturing technologies like 3-D printing and additive production methods, it eliminates waste and emission with an accelerated speed, precision and cost benefit.

On the other side, STEM graduates account for 26% of the degrees in India, in comparison of 42% of the degrees in China where in contrast these two countries are expected to add over two-thirds of the entire global increase in STEM graduates by 2030. This demands for an immediate shift in seat allotments in our universities which replaces a large number of seats in Humanities and regional languages with STEM syllabuses. If so, we need to examine the advantage of learning of Mogul history, how British won Plassey war, pre-historic poetry of Malayalam and Tamil and great Greek renaissance etc, as its scope of jobs is limited to teaching and research. This situation demands a substantial increase of seats for STEM subjects in proportion to filling the future job projections.

Educated youths with high emotional maturity and resilience in their twenties make great asset to any organization, hence India's education model has to seriously consider about both these skills deeply integrated, when the entire world is looking for skilled talents from the country. It is worth noting that Sanskrit literacy provides an ideal foundation for both these attributes in the course of school education. It will not only determine the rise and might of the country, but also complement to enhanced global productivity and achievement

If STEM focus makes us believe that technopreneurs have to be exceptionally good at maths, science or finance, it is surprising that none of those successful start-up countries have a good score in these subjects, where most of the best known innovators had a childhood clash in their maths and science classrooms.

As education demands more critical thinking than memorization of syllabus knowledge, and an imposing need of discussions and workshops than long lecturing, India has to reform its existing model if it has to conquer and be a leader in the job market during next two decades.

How powerful was Sanskrit in ancient India's innovations?

We shall revisit Page-3 of this book which explains a number of discoveries and inventions that ancient India contributed to the world, where the influence of Sanskrit had a significant support. Sanskrit explores most of the scientific learning; physics-atom, neutron, heat, gravitation and density, maths, materials, trigonometry, calculus, algebra, astrology - future prediction worked out on planetary status, astronomy and study of solar system, planets and universe, creating tools and weapons for defence, farming and metal craft and woodcrafts.

Ancient theories lacked an empirical base but they were brilliant and imaginative explanations of the physical structure of the world and to a large measure agreed with the discoveries of modern Physics. Said A.L.Basham, an Australian Indologist. Sanskrit was a medium for every stage of humanity from stone-age to metal-age, from agricultural to industrial civilisations. As Forbes magazine reported in June 1987 that Sanskrit is the most suitable language for software encrypting. Sanskrit was the medium of Vedic Maths which discovered Zero, dot (decimal), calculation, Pythagoras theory (Buddhayana), Algebra, Trigonometry and Calculus, quadratic equations, numbers as highest as 10 to the power of 53, most accurate time taken by earth to orbit the Sun.

During the glorious period of Sanskrit, India had incubated our ancient wisdom, discoveries and inventions. It is most a serious matter to debate how Sanskrit can return to its lost glory with a future vision to driving disruptions and innovations in the present digital revolution.

India in the fast phase in Innovation Start-ups

Bangalore is home for Indian technology sector way back since 1980s, with two software companies entered the business of BPO extending human-intensive software and IT supports to major Global banking & Financial, Insurance and Corporate. That was the time, India was home for more than 400,000 engineering graduates a year, educated in English which created the world's largest pool of technical skills and talents. As a result, the city once known as the knowledge centre of India, began to be known as India's Silicon Valley, attracting large number of migration from all around the country. In fiscal year 2020, the total revenue generated by export from the IT-BPM industry was nearly 150 billion U.S. dollars. In that year. This sector was growing due to strong global demand accelerated by its local expertise. When IT share was $79 Bil, BPM $33 Bil, the remaining part of $34 came from Software & Engg services. This contributes as the single largest export earning sector for the country.

With the abundance of talents and technical skills in the city attracted almost 40-50 percent of Fortune 500 companies, who opened their offshore establishments, especially their R&D and Engineering campuses. The amazing success as well as the recognition of Bangalore prompted other state governments to establish the infrastructure, and attracted investments and jobs. Bangalore was followed by Chennai, Hyderabad and Pune, Gurgaon in the NCR, with satellite tier-2 cities like Coimbatore, Thiruvananthapuram and Kochi in down South. As on March 2021, the country's total jobs in this sector exceeds 4.5Mil.

It is always a reality that when the software & IT sector matures, it begins to seed new technology ventures what we call innovation start-ups. If this started two decades back in Silicon Valley, fifteen years in China, Israel got into prominence around the same time first with military innovations followed by business start-ups. For India the weather for start-ups matured around ten years back, and today it has become such a high priority sector for the government. Recently Prime Minister officially released his vision that if Software & IT were driving the economy during the last here decades, Innovation Start-ups are to drive the country's GDP in the next two decades.

Over the last ten years, starting from Bangalore, Mumbai and New Delhi, today the country ranks third start-up ecosystem after US and China, followed by Israel with a total number of Unicorns at ninety with forty five of them in 2021-22 alone. If the world's largest start-up community is centred around Silicon Valley in US, Tel Aviv (Silicon Wadi) in Israel, the same around two or three cities in China, today the start-up enterprises are from not only Hyderabad and Chennai but most of the tier-2 cities which shelters 45 percent of the total start-ups and 40 percent with women founders. This trend is expected to spread towards urbanised villages in next four to five years.

NASSCOM reported that the FY 2021-22 added 2250 new start-ups, an increase of over 600 numbers than previous year. These start-ups raised $.24.1Bil the corresponding year, with 3X increase in Unicorns, backed with the confidence of about 2400 angel investors.

Freshworks is a cloud based software solution for businesses founded by Girish Mathrubhutham in 2010 in Chennai, got listed in Nashdaq in December 2021 is valued at $13Bil and traded at $23.10 per share. Zoho Corporation founded by Sridhar Vembu in Chennai, makes web based tools. The company has 5,000 employees and generates a yearly revenue of nearly $500 million and estimated market value guessed between $5 billion – $15 billion, still being a private firm. PayTM completed its record public offer last month and Nykaa also the same month with a record earnings when listed, indicating a combined $6Bil via public markets. Now the largest Unicorn Byju's education platform is entering stock market in next few months. Another ten technology firms are in the waiting. The cumulative valuation of start-up companies till date stands at $320-330 Bil. The sector provided 6.6 lakh jobs so far, besides 34.1 lakh indirect jobs. The FY2021-22 stood to be an outstanding year for India well over US, China, UK and Israel. This indicates India's recovery back to the past glory of ancient India.

Bangalore still boasts the largest number of start-ups, which received a total FDI of $2.3Bil in the current fiscal. Karnataka state is home to 13,000 of the country's 61,000 start-ups, with a 22 percent share. The state has established an ART Park-AI & Robotics Translational Park at IISc campus.

A tiny state in South, Kerala received a record funding of $250Mil during 2021, where the highest gainer was Open Finance Technologies founded by four family entrepreneurs in a remote suburb called Perinthalmanna in Malappuram district. This neo-banking start-up ranks as the first Unicorn from Kerala with a valuation of $1.10Bil is geared to attract a new investment of $100Mil from major investors like Google and GIC. Most of the start-ups in the state are SaaS based technologies. Most of these investments will support new jobs and they collectively created more than 35,000 jobs. Kerala though a traditional communist bastion, has established Digital University of Kerala to nurture start-ups. Besides two major technology parks, the state has innovation parks under private sector, ULCC in Kozhikode and Mather Village in Kochi. The lesser known Kozhikode, its UL Cyber Park boasts eighty firms employing 2000, with an export income of Rs.38 Crores in FY:2020-21. The Three Government Cyberparks in the state recorded a collective revenue of Rs.15,100 Crores during the current fiscal-2020-21, with an export revenue of Rs.27Crores. It is not only in tier-1 cities, which has moved to tier-2 and now to unknown and unheard suburbs like Kozhikode and the question is where all in next five years? Now who drives this; not necessarily the most brilliant students, but it exposes the power and numbers of our back benchers and drop outs.

Indian start-ups secured a record of $42Bil funds in 2021. Eleven Unicorns went public and got listed in BSE and NSE during FY 2021-22. If some low skill jobs in technology sector had disappeared, new start-ups created even more jobs. According to a recent report released by Dept of Promotion of Industry and Internal Trade under Gov of India, the total start-ups in the country stand at 61,000 numbers. This is an indication for every possibility to make the Prime Minister's vision a reality. On January 16 this year, he proclaimed that every 16th of January to celebrate the country's official start-up day.

As the darkest hours are just before the dawn, India will capture its past glory in a matter of four to five years since now, how ancient India contributed to the world. Now in short term, her most critical challenge is to win $5 Tril GDP by 2025, then the next phase will be accelerated by Moore's law.

The Might of Backbench and Drop-out brains

India being the largest technical talent pool in the world, is also the largest resource pool for technology laggards and drop-outs. If we know that those brilliant students enter career with best known employers, we have no idea of where the backbenchers are settled down. If we could accept the truth that the best brains may be found on the last bench of classrooms, we realise the potential of their collective brains which create the most creative thought streams for innovation and enterprise. Recognized being totally misfit to work under instructions, they are left with the single choice of own enterprise. As India has the largest pool of backbench talents than rest of the world, they make most ideal garage teams in groups of three or four together can disrupt rules to their own imaginations.

India- Abundance of Problems and Constraints

If creativity thrives best when constrained, their brains explode with brilliant ideas and imaginations. It is amazing that you can accomplish great results, if you do not care who takes the credit. We are increasingly getting into reacting than thinking, at a time when creative and innovative thinking are desperately needed. Fortunately, India has perhaps the largest number of problems than any other country in the world; also plenty of constraints. Not US, China, UK or Israel, this alone makes diverse opportunities for the future than elsewhere. Modern

India is on her return back to the ancient India's past glory of discoveries and inventions. Imagine the opportunities from problems; also the rise in creativity when constrained! The future looks more than optimistic!

Private Sector Incubation

It is so surprising to see that India's private sector IT & Software companies were not serious in creating their in-house incubation centre for start-ups despite continuously recruiting the best talents from reputed engineering campuses and placing them to programming for the last three decades. Therefore, Sensex-30 companies shall dedicate 0.5% of their Gross Profit (Income tax-Free) to employ bright graduates in Maths, Physics, Comp Science or B.Techs in Elec or Comp. Science dedicated to research and innovation side-by-side with their academics.

University syllabus, say Maths, Science, Humanities, Technology and Engineering or others, is mostly about the knowledge which existed in the past. On the other side, nurturing Start-up Innovation as a subject is not a knowledge that existed from the past, hence we require a new knowledge and imagination about the unknown and uncertain future to its successful incubation, which is more or less an extended advancement from a successful university research culture like Stanford. This culture is totally in conflict with the culture of any large corporations or government initiated missions. Innovation is the only knowledge which is not known and does not exist.

Since independence, India adopted an imposing campus tradition from the British, focusing on memorization rather than learning and enlightenment which were her tradition. If we are wrong at entry level and beginning stage, then the start-up and innovation will remain stagnated without starting. First of all, IT and Software are labour-intensive programming platforms, where AI-enabled Innovation is a different subject. India has created a number of apex and state level start-up missions which include both successful start-up founders as well as VC investors on the assumption that both are part of creating start-up incubation bodies. Very sorry to state that we have so many VC investors who jump into any such government start-up missions to become the first among many investors to know the new start-ups to fund potential businesses before others. Without past experience in Innovation and start-ups, they tend to misguide the young disruptors. For example, some of those successful business start-ups in India are not innovations but imitations of those innovations in US. Successful start-ups like Oyo Room, a copy of Airbnb and Booking.com, Ola an Indian Uber, PayTM an Indian version of e-Bay or GooglePay, Flipkart a copy of Amazon or Alibaba, and many of the delivery platforms with exception to a new idea like Byjus which originated with a passion for online tuition that scaled up to a successful unicorn. Most of these successful start-ups were not founded on the subjects of Maths and Physics, but has explored the use of electronics and computer science including AI as the medium for their technology platform. We have few visible successful start-ups, but hardly such successful innovations, except some in Defence Research. On the other side, India has a large number of science and technology universities, which produce world's largest number of science and engineering graduates in Physics, Material science, Maths, Electronics and Computer science with one of the world's lowest deployment into successful research and innovations.

At present all our innovations and start-ups are centred around technology graduates and digital platforms, where the knowledge of physics, maths and computer science are not enough employed, but realising their potential and application can trigger to greater heights of results. If the Private sector and Military start with recruiting the best brains limited to a thousand students from these branches into innovation, it can create a world record like what we see in US or Israel.

Last three decades were the opportunities for China which is today under the grip of ageing and shortage of talents. As such India is far from a substitute for China and when the world democracies gradually moving away from it, we have a very large optimistic space for the next two decades.

What made Silicon Valley so successful which others could not imitate, was its university culture which goes to the credit of Stanford, whose faculties initiated the early innovation start-ups and ingrained and continued that tradition for future. Having experimented with a large number of start-up missions at both central and state governments as well as private sector, India shall also make a new dedicated attempt of establishing a start-up village within one of the best and tested campuses of its twenty IITs and most successful university research centres. For most of those fund-starved start-ups in SV, Stanford backbenchers and drop-outs make the largest talent resource, who are willing to accept challenges but at affordable salaries.

Next, the country is losing a large number of technology students as back benchers and drop-outs, who shall be identified within the classrooms and encouraged to network to teams of three or four to explore opportunities with new ideas and projects. Every technology campus shall establish its own incubation as similar to Y-Combinator Start-up School with private sector partnership and allow a seed fund of $.15,000 to each one, which will be converted to ownership at its first funding meet, which gets topped up by VCs and Angel Investors. If two or three out of every ten start-ups strike success, the entire funding generates a massive return. Investors jump not into billion dollar companies but into billion dollar ideas, especially when the founders have the grit and ethics. It is a crucial reality of start-up investing where financiers are betting on an uncertain future which they cannot see.

A social connectivity platform like Facebook, or a search engine like Google both with external revenue from digital advertisement or an integrated internet company like Tencent is yet to be born in India.

Innovation- Future Opportunities

The demand for STEM talent is soaring with demand exceeding the supply by far, and organizations will try to relocate where such talents are available plenty. This is an opportunity where many of the overseas companies will be attracted to tier-2 cities in India. We shall not spare time, but get ready with acquisition of land, developing infrastructure, technology parks in and around cities like Surat, Pune, Coimbatore, Tiruchirapalli, Amaravathy, Kakinada-Vizag, Aurangabad, Kota, Mangalore, Varanasi-Prayagraj corridors which are well connected Education and healthcare hubs, besides highways and airports. If it was just six or seven states out of total twenty eight in the country which were driving the IT&Software sector, the same success repeated by other states can take India at least a three-fold growth level, where the expansion to tier-2 cities gives an optimistic future.

If Unilever is an example of assigning about two hundred managers from its India subsidiary to global roles as the company's 57 percent of global revenues come from emerging markets. Google has a couple of

India-born senior managers, Mastercard, Adobe, Cognizant, Microsoft, Softbank, Sun Microsystem, Berkshire-Hathaway, McKinsey, Deutsche Bank, Softbank, Richemont, HSBC, CitiCorp, etc are among others which opened their HQ positions to Indian leadership. Still about 30 percent of US companies feel that they have not exploited global opportunities enough because they have too few managers with international competencies.

South Asia has Big problems; hence the Big Opportunities

The South Asian countries have a combined population of 1.95Bil, 25% of world's total of 7.85Bil, which lies in the high-poverty region after Africa. India being the most developed country in South Asia in areas as education, healthcare, banking and GDP, it has great opportunities of Start-up Innovations in the region and being the fourth largest country in the world after US, China and Israel. The region can achieve tremendous growth only if India rises up to the challenge. At present the cross-border trade of SAARC is exploited only by one-third of its potential which means a revenue loss of $.23 Bil per year. If migration is a boost to innovations, it does not exist in the region with almost closed borders and deficit in diplomacy.

Next, if SAARC offers such problems and opportunities, CIS promises equal or more. CIS-Kazakhstan, Turkmenistan, Tajikistan, Kyrgistan and Uzbekistan are surplus in hydrocarbons, but deficit in technology talents. Next is East Europe including the former Soviet block. Though we can see technology conquering almost every private and government sector in Gulf countries, India's contribution is far less than its potential. With such a vast region with hardly any remarkable growth as US, China and Israel had achieved, we shall not stay away from if any strategic co-operation between Israel and UAE arises after the Abraham Accord. The UAE Minister for AI recently shared a conclave with the CEO of SNC-Start-up Nation Central of Israel on a future cooperation in Start-up Innovations, where the innovation brains of Israel will leverage with the Angel investors and Venture capitalists of UAE. But entrepreneurship and capital alone cannot move forward unless complemented with talent, which is the gold-mine opportunity for India to break.

The Internet connection in all the eight SAARC countries is as low as 48% in 2020 with India, Bhutan and Maldives scoring above 50 mark, India alone boasts 630 Mil. This opens a grand challenge to connect the bottom of the pyramid's 50 percent, to result an accelerated boost in each country's GDP. Internet opens up people connectivity in breadth and width resulting exchange of political freedom, human rights, citizens right and knowledge between people which ignites a desire and necessity to break the barriers of religious and dictatorial restrictions towards better education, equality and democracy. This technological growth will result in an increase in e-commerce, online government services, net-banking, transactions and a large number of services, by saving a lot of time and money available for other productive works.

India carried out the world's largest coronavirus vaccination in 2021, which was so successfully processed, identified and administered with the support of technology, by registering and intimating each individual with certificates. Such a largely populated nation has an effective management of recording and accounting each and every bank transaction to the customer's smart phone.

If people above fourteen in US, Latin America and East Asia are engaged almost 80 percent on social media like Facebook, Instagram, Twitter or WeChat, those in Europe and Middle East are 70 percent. By contrast, it is 20 percent in South Asia and Saharan Africa, and 30 percent in India. These low-penetration regions have a huge business opportunity to grow the smart phones and networking which can also become the most preferred business platforms. This can be made possible only with India's abundant resources of technology and skilled talent pool.

If internet can help quality education to the masses at more affordable costs, South Asia can achieve high literacy level which the region failed in its past seven decades. The modern farming can multiply the agricultural output at far lower costs making food affordable to millions below the poverty line. Manufacturing and services sectors with adaption of these convergent technologies, can produce more at lower costs which will open up the border trade, which is so miniscule at present days. This will increase the rate of travel, exchange of culture and arts, people relationships which will drastically reduce the divisive and conflict-ridden mentality and result peace and harmony thus saving billions spent of defence and counter-terrorism.

1. The Defence Sector

Indian Military is very much way forward in Electronic and Digital warfare; on the other side it is highly human-centric. Its technical advantages are mostly with imported technologies and equipments. Here STEM discipline innovators can drive a "Make-in-India" import substitute mission which can also surge our military exports. More the technology in warfare, the lowest of front-line soldiers required, hence it can eliminate the human casualty factor in a war.

We have a number of ordnance units, HAL and BDL, producing second generation artilleries and fighters, are new cradles for innovation, which could become tomorrow's RADS, IAI and Elbit which are forces behind the world recognized military edges of Israel.

2. Military, Defence and Space Research

ISRO is an example which is self-reliant as the most favoured institution in sending satellites for a number of foreign countries. A CDS-DRDO-ISRO R&D Jv is an ideal proposition that can play as a role-model. This combined unit can play a creative role in nurturing and incubating innovation labs as in the case of Unit-8200 and Talpiot under IDF. Most of the resourceful students and employees ever seen are those who served in the military service. Hence aligning education with military internship can enhance the human capital and innovation.

3. Healthcare sector

The SAARC region has one of the poorest healthcare infra, where a healthcare centre is either far by location or very unaffordable at their income level. Innovations in healthcare had resulted huge cost advantages and alternatives across North America, Europe and East Asia, which gives enough challenges for innovators in India. Scientific innovation in Biotechnology, Genomics, 3D Printing, Stem cells can revolutionize our healthcare sector, making it more accessible and affordable to an extent of unbelievable costs.

4. Farming and Food

Netafim turned the Israeli deserts to high-yield farm lands through irrigation technology and repeats the same success across sixty countries through their global network. Evogene, a Monsanto affiliated crop performance company uses plant genomics and biotech to boost yield with high immunity to pests and stress. Kaiima attained highest yield/per hectare basis in its agro-outputs besides high-yield dairy farms, no-cow milk farm, no-animal cultured meat farm, etc. Like our military, Indian farming is one of the most primitive and human-driven systems prone to calamities and climate changes, with heavy storage losses. Water is the most over-used, abused and underpriced among our natural resources. This segment opens a 'Blue Ocean' of Innovation opportunities.

The South Asia region especially India and Pakistan contains large areas of infertile land, which is not suitable for agriculture. About 12 percent (31Mil Ha) of India's total geography is occupied by hot arid land. Out of total 80Mil Ha land in Pakistan, about 70 percent are in the bone-dry and semi-arid range. This remained as a grave and unsolved problem for decades despite extreme food shortage and starvation, which if we can learn lessons and inspiration from Holland and especially Israel, is an equally big business and innovation opportunity. Innovations in areas like drip and sprinkler irrigation, yield-boosting biotech, hi-brid seeds and saplings, automation in farming and harvesting, alternative and non-hazardous manures, extended storage life, logistic models, transportation and farm-to-user delivery helped these countries to achieve high yields from such uncultivable lands at substantial reduction in prices. A tiny country like Holland is one of the world's largest agricultural economies with high export income from dairy, poultry, vegetable and flowers. As Shimon Peres said, agricultural is 5% farm work and 95 percent science.

Israel had a severe problem of food, as a result of Arab boycott and isolation, which had only 20 percent arable land. This imposed a necessity on the government to convert its deserts and arid lands to farming, which ignited a big innovation opportunity.

5. 3-D Printing

If a printer can precisely match a computer-determined special colour print page with two cartridges – b&w and colour, then why any physical object like auto parts, human transplants, toys and electronic spares cannot be printed as per the command given by a computer?

The Industrial revolution began with steam engine, the second revolution with mass production through assembly line as invented by Henry Ford, which later adapted to automation and robotics, and finally by 3-D Printing, where production requires no plant.

To produce a weapon during stone-age, men used a large block of rock and chiselled it down to a much smaller tool which left a lot of waste pieces of the rock as debris. This is called 'Subtractive Manufacturing-SM' where too much raw material was wasted to produce a small tool. This translated to production of things like wooden furniture, left a large quantity of wood as waste. When wood substitutes like plywood, chipboard and MDF were used in large scale with CAD design and to modular system, the waste factor was brought down to a considerably lower level..

Today technology developed far forward, which is capable of producing a product from a combination of three or more raw materials, where its consumption is determined by a computer with almost nil-waste. This is called 'Additive Manufacturing-AM' which further advanced to 3D Printing enabled by Internet, AI and Sensors.

3D printing has proven how Construction sector can achieve the speed and cost saving. Material Sciences, 3D Printing and AI can redefine our housing sector which remains as one of the biggest challenges in our region, where India alone has a shortage of 29Mil urban shelters in 2018.

Factories were changing from manufacturing to assembling almost a century ago which resulted larger output, more jobs and cost reduction. Today the $12 Tril global manufacturing sector is passing through a revolution where material science with an AI-enabled 3D Printing and automation can simplify the process with accelerated speed and cost savings in areas like material waste, defects, channel-supply, transportation and logistics with high scope for customisation that can result significant reduction in costs.

As 3-D Printing requires very small factory space, it can decentralise and localise the production closer to retailers and customers by saving huge transportation cost on raw materials and finished products. This will take away 35-40 percent of the total $12.5Tril global manufacturing.

6. Internet

50% of India population are without internet, 59% of Bangladesh and 65% of Pakistan, which alone makes an empty space for innovation opportunities. Today world's biggest problems are the biggest business opportunities. The network is almost free of cost, power is also so cheap, the price for devices and equipments are falling steep, the platforms like Google, Facebook, What's-App, Instagram, Twitter, etc are also free, but together it can drive a variety of businesses in E-commerce, Banking, Food delivery, Home Cinema, business communication, taxi-ride, Online-education, Online 3-D Shopping, etc. Convergence of AR and VR with AI transformed off-campus learning, shopping and entertainment, where sensors and satellite mapping with AI in security and defence.

More the Internet can penetrate, it drives cross-border trade, cultural exchanges, and people-to-people relation which are very low across SAARC region, to a more friendly relationship by eliminating terrorism, religious extremism, extremist ideologies, illiteracy and poverty to peace and prosperity. The post-pandemic period showed an increase of 70-80 percent in Bangladesh's online sales to $708Mil in 2020. On the other end, as the health and monetary assistance schemes were distributed online, about 51 percent of women were out of the beneficiary list and with 81 percent children lacking internet were out of home schooling, which together could risk girls to early marriage and child labour losing billions of dollars in future earnings.

People under thirty make a majority in the Muslim world, where internet and social media are most powerful connectivity which could liberate them to a borderless modern world beyond the extreme radical violence. According to Google CEO Eric Schmidt, laying down fibre optic cable for a wireless infrastructure to empower Iraqi citizens could have saved US over $800Bil spent on regime change. On the negative side, Internet is abused by Hamas, Hezbollah and Al-Qaida as a powerful recruiting tool. Similarly Facebook was used to schedule protests to dethrone Hosni Mubarak in Cairo, Twitter to coordinate and Youtube to release the audiovisuals to outside world.

On a simple measure that if a smart phone can result an increase in a common man's average income by twenty percent, its impact on a national GDP is so abundant that no other economic sectors can equal. The present Smartphone (Mobile Internet) connectivity in India is less than 60 percent, followed by Bhutan and Maldives with Pakistan averaging at 40 percent, about 900Mil are below smart phone access. If this rising billion is connected, it automatically results a 20% increase in their annual income which means an average 10 percent increase in SAARC GDP. Though the major responsibility on this remains with India, it opens a huge business opportunity for the nation as the regional hub of technology, research, education, training and providing.

7. E-Commerce

With more shutdowns and restrictions during the pandemic, SAARC countries could not embrace online sales to its potential as compared to West, which led to 64 percent decline in off-line retails including the women-led SMES facing the worst. This is a grave dent on the region's economy and lending sector, but makes an excellent innovation opportunity. Ecommerce has a potential to create more jobs than those lost in off-line businesses. When off-line shopping is restricted under shut-downs, it increased the trade online. VR converged with AI, further supported by AR and 3D view, can make a unique shopping experience from home. In addition to time saved in account of going to shops and vehicle parking, E-commerce benefits the customer with a remarkable price advantage of costs saved from middlemen brokers, warehousing, showroom and inventory besides the time saved.

8. Education

Education is moving at an accelerated speed from off-line to on-line, where the best education can be made accessible, practically at no cost. What it costs for infra, faculty and staff, transport, mid-day meals, uniforms and utilities, which are covered under government subsidies or born by students becomes a big saving for all sections with Internet and devices. Education largely a government project, the ministries are to re-set their intuition and to adapt to these new demanding rules. With illiteracy and affordability being so detrimental to the region's peace and prosperity, this sector makes one of the biggest business and innovation opportunity. As education is very ripe for disruption in South Asia and CIS region, it promises a huge business opportunity for India as a regional hub.

9. Renewable Energy

Sun is the cheapest and most available resource of energy which we do not use. Surprisingly sun is brighter over the underdeveloped and developing countries. The pace of growth in solar power is highest than other energy sources in the last two decades. With world's poorest countries are located under tropical region with highest sunlight penetration, this causes draught, scarcity of drinking water and power but it is also a big business and innovation opportunity. If three largest countries of SAARC in area and population are major concerns of carbon emission in the world, solar power and electric vehicles are very large business opportunities. Renewable energy, especially solar is working cheaper every year, which has a potential to mass availability at almost free in another decade.

10. Banking and Finance

Easy and low-cost capital is available in plenty, where technology innovation has increased the speed and eliminated the cost of processing transfers and loans. Today anyone can process money transactions from anywhere to anyone at a fraction of a minute. Changing over to technology, it minimise the risk and fraud with better regulatory compliance in transactions. This eliminated the cost of tellers and low-skilled jobs and also customer grievances in banking sector.

11. Food deliveries

India, Pakistan and Bangladesh have a combined population of 1.8Bil where the online food delivery system is limited to major cities, but has a very huge business and innovation potential once it matures and penetrates to other areas.

12. Robotics

The region still depend heavily on manual labour as compared to East Asia or West, hence it is going to be under pressure to employ advanced robots to replace low skilled jobs like retail, warehousing, restaurant, clothing, assembling and homecare. Very soon the drivers are to be replaced by driverless e-vehicles in view of global enforcement of emission-free policies where frugal innovation in robotics and automation will become necessary. This also makes a big business opportunity.

Women are the worst victims of drinking water shortage in South Asia and Africa, where they walk three to five kilometres to bring pot water on head. Drones are very suitable to transport drinking water to households in large volumes. Drones can ensure timely movement of emergency patients from remote villages and army camps to urban hospitals, and also emergency medicines, critical organ replacements and equipments to surgical rooms that can save large number of lives. During the last decades of twentieth century, Bangladesh had demonstrated how to empower the rural women supported by Grameen Microfinance. More women liberated from the households in the SAARC region have a great potential to raise the GDP at least by 15 percent. At a national perspective, if a smart phone can raise the income of these rural women liberate from households by 20 percent, it can further accelerate their business income with a multiple effect.

Drones are becoming cheaper year after year which makes a very potential business opportunity for India with its wide market in South Asia. Let it be Unmanned Aerial Vehicles for Military, or rescue operation in mountains, sea or fire, delivering goods and drinking water to remote areas, aerial spraying in farms, dropping forces in left-infested forests, hide-outs and narcotic farms, patrolling across LAC and LOC etc are the endless opportunities.

13. Service automation

With such large population in this region, there will be an imposing pressure on governments to run the public services online, like how India automated its PAN-permanent Account, passport delivery and Aadhar-National ID systems, besides online payment for most of its services. Today almost every government services and banking are turning to online. Though automation results in job losses, it creates new jobs by 2.3 times. For example, ATM machines eliminated teller jobs in banks, but as it reduced the operational costs, banks increased new branches by 40 percent which created more teller jobs than destroyed by ATMs.

14. Sensors

What is the technology that enables transport navigation, security surveillance and autonomous vehicles? It is sensors, now can be coupled to as much as 120Mil facial images. Google driverless car has a rooftop sensor with a 64-eye lasers that can scan 360 degree generating 750 MB of image data per second. According to Stanford Uni T-Sensors Summit, the number of sensors in the world is expected to grow into trillions by

2023. India and her neighbouring countries accounting for perhaps the largest number of traffic accidents and loss of lives in the world, can gain immensely with the sensor technology if in operation with autonomous cars, which can also save billions in insurance claims. By the same time as this region boasts one of the highest rate of political violence, civil offences and crimes, sensors and data can be successfully utilised to track and check such incidents. In India, Mobile phone tracking has emerged as one of the major sources of tracking and punishing criminals.

15. Electric, Autonomous, Connected Vehicles-EACV

The South Asia, especially India has huge potential for EACVs considering a high density of carbon emitting vehicles and high dependence on thermal power in the country. All major global auto manufacturers are independent of any IT, Software or Digital technology business and they outsource their requirements of chips, programs, sensors and such accelerators. Contrary to this, major Indian car makers like Tata Motors runs a number of IT and software businesses like TCS, Tata-Elxi, CMC and the recently acquired Big-Basket e-commerce, which enables Tata Motors to develop new advanced versions of not only Battery fuelled cars as well as driverless cars commanded by AI and Sensors. In the case of the second largest indigenous car maker, Mahindra & Mahindra has the synergy drawn from its Tech-Mahindra, which is the country's fourth largest software and BPO business.

Leave alone the car, the South Asia is undoubtedly the world's largest volume market for electronic two-wheelers, lithium battery and domestic charging units. As India is the world's largest market for two wheelers, adaption to electric models will make the country the world hub for innovation, assembling and exports.

The Sensor technology is not widely known due to its intangible, but limited areas of application. A BMW car has more than two thousand sensors tracking everything from tire pressure, fuel level, transmission to parking. Its traction control system reduces wheel slip. A Google car with its Light Radar–LIDAR scanning a 360 degree around with sixty-four lasers collects almost a gigabyte of data per second per car. A car is more becoming a computer on four wheels.

India has the highest number of English-educated science and technology graduates where the highest scores are recruited by technology companies. Considering the fact that back-benchers and drop-outs hit as more audacious disruptors, we still have plenty of them to raise as successful innovators with highest innovation opportunities arising from biggest regional problems we face in areas like poverty, energy, healthcare, military, education, e-commerce, farming, food and banking.

The South Asia region has powerful and resourceful countries as Iran and Pakistan but both are either politically unstable and economically vulnerable, a severe setback posing a challenge for their leadership. On the other side, most of those politically stable and developing democracies are short of resources and talents. This calls for a responsibility and leadership on India to accelerate the benefits of modern technology across millions.

16. Drones

Drones can perform many tasks from irrigation, aerial spraying, fire-fighting, rescue operation, emergency healthcare, border patrolling, surveillance and military services. It is already experimented to be a successful option that can replace human delivery of parcels and food. It can also easily reach-out to remote locations without roads and vehicles.

Capital, No More Expensive as Before

Europe, Japan and US are no more growing with its relocation to emerging economies which offer huge investment opportunities. If SWF-Sovereign Wealth Funds collectively managed $3-5Tril assets in 2013, Pension Funds landscape is at $32Tril assets under management. When developed nations saturated in growth, now these funds are exploring new investment opportunities in the developing regions. New technologies, especially Mobile internet, VR and AI transformed the business towards a high-speed cash-flow model.

Glorious Past is Opposite to Future Vision

Largely it is always those retired academics, scholars, scientists and bureaucrats or such aged celebrities with their past knowledge and experience to plan our future. They are made of eighty percent of past glory with hardly twenty percent future vision, where children or our future citizens are made of eighty percent future dreams and hardly twenty percent past knowledge. This is a major conflict when we require future vision to predict the unknown and uncertain things of future which did not exist before. When many of these scholars, academics, scientists or bureaucrats are short and deficit of sufficient literacy in mobile phone and internet, it again conflicts with assigning them to our technology and innovation strategy, where backbenchers and dropouts with a serious classroom conflict and who were problematic and less obedient to teachers and their instructions were found to be successful as disruptors and innovators. More the past knowledge and experience bring in a pessimistic approach which turn to result how things will not work than how the same can work. When most of what we think to be right get to be proven wrong, our intuitions are becoming no more relevant to foresee the reality of future. This causes a psychological block- cynicism, pessimism and fear, a culture of contemporary thinking. Ideas coupled with technology can solve most of the problems in our world and its economy.

Mostly successful innovators who challenge the future were in their pre-forties and they move on to become anchor investors and VCs once their disruptive minds become dry after fifty. At late forties, people slip into sunset in life when their brilliance settles] to a downward curve, with an inability to catch-up with new learning.

To Reset Our Childhood Model

Children at 1t standard at an age of six, with a left-over future of average six to seven decades, have more than 90 percent of their lifespan as their remaining future life. In contrast most our education policies are conceptualised and drafted by aged experts with 95 percent of glorious past and only five percent of ventilator life. Here what is important is to select experts only those who are open to new knowledge with a deep insight into future.

As children have a glorious future like we experts had a glorious past, they should be brought up through a process of 3-D vision; ie, Dream, Determination and Drive across their education. The objective is to nurture this 3-D vision alongside their campus education which should make them restless and alerted. What one embraces to his heart, no doubt it becomes certainly his! Electronics, Computer Science, Space and Aircraft technology and Automobiles are few subjects children dream to learn and participate with, hence such subjects shall be integrated to this 3-D Vision program.

"If you want to build a ship, don't start by getting men together to produce timber, by assigning tasks and distributing work, but instead teach them the longing for the wide and endless sea". Said Antoine de Saint-Exupery, a French aviator and writer, which is relevant and adaptable to our education where teachers impart the same with students.

People who were so underprivileged to get education, know the might of education. Those who had a series of failure, can enjoy the taste of success and only a penniless man can feel the happiness of money. First education looks bitter to taste; but it makes the future so sweat! Almost 96% of the people were more educated, wealthy and happy than their parents.

The lessons from new technologies:

- Information accelerates everything.
- Cost of skills and facilities are dropping hence disruptions are not as expensive.
- Smaller the better and faster to perform a 10X matrix.
- Experts tell you how things cannot be done.
- Lease assets, not own.
- Everything can be turned into data, hence measurable and knowable.

'Innovation is possible with young minds!'

The only thing what we know about future, is that we do not know much about it. As it is too uncertain and unknown, how our collective intuition, which we had hard-earned over from our past experience and knowledge can determine our future and its forces mitigate with it? Secondly the more our brains are filled with the knowledge already exists, it leaves less space to think of new knowledge about the future. Such a situation demands and dictates that scholars, academicians, bureaucrats and political leaders are to be kept outside of any start-ups and innovation missions. Such experts and intellects are too risk-averse, who are smart in advising with a number of reasons how a new idea or venture will not work. Along with ageing, people become more cautious and averse to failures where in contrast, where one attains more strength from falls and defeats, which is considered to be a driving factor for start-up entrepreneurs.

Mostly scholars, academics and bureaucrats, who make a normal choice to head state-run innovation missions are largely of a framework of too busy always, it is too difficult task and not from their past domain, and turn the future of such missions the way they are comfortable and accustomed. Such missions requires people who are attracted because it is difficult task and from an unknown domain. Those really too busy do not keep saying too busy. Really busy people or busy desks keep getting more challenging tasks and performing to the expected levels, and we require people to take up challenges knowing pretty well that it is very difficult. Such wrong people who occupy such challenging responsibilities find all possible ways of how a good idea will not work.

Most of our Innovation Missions are headed by aged technocrats, many of them largely Angel and VC investors. This is a dangerous trend and will destroy innovation. MoE has example of how our NEP-2020 got complicated with a panel of retired scientists, scholars and bureaucrats with a past glory than future vision? Also how Western Ghats Commission went in serious conflict with Gadgil recommendations? When one of India's national political parties wanted much higher youth participation and leadership, a panel of three octogenarians above the age of seventy-five were appointed to submit a report, which strongly recommended for preserving more elders in leadership positions for their experience and knowledge over youngsters. The more aged, academic and experienced people, especially from their fifties stay away from risks and rapid growth because for every new idea, they see how it cannot work than favouring a debate and experiment.

Those potential future entrepreneurs in their HSE and technical education dream looking far into the future because their future is many times longer than their past. In contrast, those who scholars and bureaucrats who head those innovation missions in their late fifties or early sixties who possess a long history of knowledge, experience and achievements tend to get largely engaged looking into their glorious past where their remaining future is a fraction of their long past. This generally poses a conflict of interest, though exceptions are there who keep growing up without biologically growing old. In short the disruptors dream too far into their future, where the mission leadership look back deep into their past, or one looks towards the north-pole, where the other to the south-pole. Hence it is important to be too sensitive in considering leadership roles, especially to those who are young in their perspectives and can nurture ideas.

Most of the governments and large companies allocated their resources based on their figures of the past, rather that the future opportunities. Take their budget, business plan, or financial forecast which is mostly following the guidelines of what we call incremental over previous year. Twenty-first century corporations do not function like a Nineteenth century military unit. If a sea level increases by three feet, the traditional thinkers whom we call experts, are inclined to add another three feet to the existing sea wall. Prof.Felix Dothan and Prof. Shaul Yatziv of the Hebrew University, proposed the Talpiot program insisting that innovation was possible only by young minds !

At least our new strategy on Start-up Innovations shall not go with experts with too hard with knowledge and experience from their glorious past. Technology moves fast forward to its future, hence experts with too much a past glory will take the mission backwards. Hence two years wasted, cannot be covered up with its running speed. Intuition is a product of our past knowledge, experience, hard-earned and time consuming. It is attained over the course of decades in career and that helped us to understand the world, which worked well and shaped most of our decisions until twentieth century. People who had risen to power and responsibility trust and rely to a great extend, in their intuition. It is out of anyone's genius sense to ask such a person to reset his intuition on a subject like future innovation, which is unknown, uncertain and risky. As a result, whatever we believed as a detailed education from our B-Schools, followed by a management and leadership career, may require a reset in their intuition if to run twenty-first century enterprises.

In India and its neighbourhood, we have the biggest problems than elsewhere in the world; when these problems are turned to become the biggest opportunities, innovation stands to be the best tool to driving these opportunities. India's internet economy is expected to double from $125billion as of April 2017 to $250 billion by 2020, majorly backed by e-commerce. India's E-commerce revenue is expected to jump from $ 39 billion in 2017 to $ 120 billion in 2020, growing at an annual rate of 51 per cent, the highest in the world. As a similar growth can be predicted if the other SAARC nations, India is already and can become the e-commerce and Internet hub of South Asia. Similar opportunities exist in other sectors like food delivery, internet banking, on-line education and government services.

If every new smart phone has a potential to increase the user's income by 20 percent, it can surge the respective nation's economy, besides livelihoods. A decade back, India successfully carried out a national mission of biometric data named Aadhar, (meaning foundation or support) to register its 1350 million citizens, the largest such government initiative in the world which offers a number of innovative solutions to socio-political problems like tracking offenders, property transactions, banking and income tax, vaccination, pension and salaries besides subsidies to farmers and the underprivileged. In February, Sri Lanka entered a contract with India to register its every citizen a UID platform like Aadhar. South Asia can follow India's achievements in UID-Unique Identification, PAN-Personal Account Number and Passports which are IT processed and controlled. A single smart phone substitutes the need for a music system, TV, newspaper, movies, search, computer, calculator, online ordering, relationship and communication.

UN 17 SDGs for 2030

UN has defined seventeen SDG-Sustainable Development Goals for 2030 of which all these goals pose great challenges to South Asia, Middle East, CIS and Africa, where the region rank a very poor score of below the global-100. Internet and AI are ideal tools which can raise the income of the underprivileged, resulting drastic reduction in poverty, hunger, illiteracy, water, shelter, sanitation, clean energy, transport and healthcare problems and providing a quality living more affordable. As a result, the region will turn to become a burgeoning middle class economy. India, already the leading force in technology and talent in this region, is the natural choice to lead these responsibilities that alone can liberate 2 billion people from miseries. Here our limit is our ambition, and the future depends in monetising these grand challenges to business opportunities.

In 2016, the present NDA government carried out a national drive to empower every poor family to open a 'Jan Dhan' –zero balance bank account linked to their mobile phone to ensure all subsidies, monthly schemes and medical benefits are directly credited to each respective account without delay and any third party misappropriation. Otherwise 50 percent public spending on basic services like healthcare, energy, family welfare, agriculture pension, drinking water and sanitation do not reach the beneficiaries because of corruption, inefficiency or diversion to other projects. Such online direct remittances get straight credited to their respective bank accounts. If innovation could immensely benefit Israel in core areas like farming, healthcare, military and banking, South Asia has similar problem areas with a huge potential of opportunities. This is an opportunity in the entire South Asia region with 1.75 Bil population, where voter ID cards can prevent fraud polling, enable tax payments and every government services online. Digitalising the stock exchange and financial markets eliminate all possibilities of in-house trading and future fixing, and digitalising the farming sector benefits directly the farmers without any role for the middle men and brokers. Today cyber technology is widely recognized to track offenders in shortest time. India had proven to the world about how to integrate one of the largest numbers of passports, the largest citizen identification mission (UID), Personal Account Network-PAN, largest voters network and electronic voting system, digitalising the Railway booking, and many more in the world's ranking.

Out of 1,350 million population in the country with fifth largest GDP, India reports just less than five percent of them to pay income tax, which shows both the large numbers below the tax level as well as the number of people who do not disclose their income. Once the government completes its mission of digital currency, it will expose everyone above the taxable income, resulting substantial expansion of tax payer's base, and also with such a significant rise in tax receipts, government could consider more relief in tax structure, leaving more dispensable public money for spending which will boost the national GDP. Today South Asia depends heavily on India for reforming these areas of governance with the help of technology, which will transform the region to more peaceful, prosperous and developed place to live in close compliance to 2030 UN 17 goals. One of the biggest setbacks in South Asia is that the cross-border trade is the lowest than elsewhere in the world, largely caused by political and diplomatic mistrusts. Eric Schmidt, the CEO of Google said, "The connected world is a new world with new problems, but new solutions are now within our reach."

12 Silicon Valley Doctrines

Silicon Valley-SV is almost half a century old. Located in southern shores of San Francisco Bay, CA, its intellectual capital is Palo Alto, the campus of Stanford. Its curator was Frederick Terman, a faculty at Stanford Technology School who motivated his faculty colleagues to establish own firms mainly into silicon chips and semiconductors. Today SV shelters the corporate campuses of HP, Google, Facebook and Apple. Tesla is also based in Palo Alto, but as its major activity had grown to produce e-vehicles, it will soon relocate its headquarters to Austin, Texas with its R&D and Innovation at SV.

The computer science education at Stanford was structured on close exchange relationship between the students and teachers, where teachers mostly follow the students. We can see a similar university culture inside Google, largely working on research for nurturing new ideas and inventing new applications, with hardly any guidance and instruction from seniors to its engineering staff. With that research culture of Stanford, Google allows its engineers to come with new ideas and strive on them, where failure is tolerated and considered as a driving force to try out next idea.

Silicon Valley-SV is one of the most imitated and copied formula the world over, and also by Boston University, a major knowledge centre in US. Singapore is known as the SV of Asia, while Bangalore in India, Tel Aviv is known to be the Silicon Wadi of Israel and Dubai has its own Silicon Oasis, which all these put together is not even one third of Silicon Valley. Their efforts to attract innovation start-ups proved that incentives and subsidies, rental concession and infrastructure alone are not the winning factors to stem innovations. One of the most inspiring factors of SV is the University culture of Stanford, a universal learning, sharing and relationship culture prevailing in Palo Alto. On the other side, most of the start-up and innovation hubs were government missions, head by bureaucrats or B-School scholars with boards occupied by VCs and angel investors with their business interests.

When governments venture into start-up missions, they remain largely imitative of SV than being innovative beyond the originally inspired example. When such mission CEOs are bureaucrats, they get busy with a large canvass of administration, payrolls and meetings; and B-School scholars are nurtured to run established companies and not off-springs firms, which end up with more of cost and activities than innovations. The SV culture nurtures collaboration as a winning factor than competition, which is so visible with Google, Amazon, Facebook, Apple, Microsoft, IBM and Tesla. Name any prominent smart and powerful personality in Silicon Valley, they are persistent, polite and persuasive, where freedom to establish relationship and share ideas is more than anything else, what innovation requires.

If Stanford University culture is the most dominant success factor behind Silicon Valley, the next successful innovation centre in the world-Silicon Wadi (Tel Aviv) is powered by defence institutions like Talpiot and IDF Unit 8200 with a purpose of making their military most innovative unit in the world, followed by all possible support to the nation's technological innovation. Both Silicon Valley as well as Silicon Wadi share a common research culture of University and daring inspiration of Military that drives research, engineering, development and technology. This culture is what missing in most other start-up missions worldwide.

Silicon Valley has a significant presence of foreign entrepreneurs. 38-50 percent of SV start-ups have foreign founders. 36 percent of SV residents are foreign born, compared to 13 percent of US national average. Today it continues to attract those most technology talents from all over the world than elsewhere.

Indian migrants are such a powerful force in US to an extent which is capable of deciding the US elections. If in 2008, Barak Obama became its first migrant president, in 2021 an India-born Kamala Harris won as Vice President. In UK, the second-line leadership choice is between both Finance and Home Secretaries, who are India-origin, besides a Pakistani-born as the Mayor of London. About more than thirty CEO positions in Fortune 500s are held by India-born Americans. The power of immigrants has risen so high to command even the parliaments and governments. The day seems not too far for an India-born President or

Prime minister to lead from White House or Pentagon, Parliament of Canada, Australia, New Zealand or UK, besides a majority of law makers in Germany, France, Ireland, Holland and Switzerland. A reverse model of colonial rule?

Migration has changed the global diplomatic alliances. Once Opec and OIC had looked at India as unfriendly country for her policy on Kashmir under strong influence of Pakistan, the massive migration of workers to Middle East and its economic effect on bilateral trade including oil resulted a tremendous shift in their policies towards India. On the other side, Indian Americans are a strong force which can influence US presidential election results, both Republicans as well as Democrats cannot ignore the community for referendum and funds. The strong lobbying of Indo-American leaders on US Government has helped bringing both countries to very close allies, as against once India was a strong force behind NAM-Non-Alignment Movement and a supporter of Soviet Block for five decades since its independence. Similarly, as migration helps to improve cultural relation, we can see a change in the global diplomacy between EU and India, both exchanged their culture with movies, food habits and dress codes, and caused by migration.

In contrast, those countries like Russia, China, Japan or Nordic countries, who are closed to migration remained without any change in its diplomacy. China has expanded its relationship with several countries in Asia, Africa and Latin America with long term debt investments but not by migration, where this leads to severe debt trap, where migration diplomacy is more sustainable with long-term collaborative.

Internet is uniting the planet by breaking all the walls of region, religion, country and ideology, hence harnessing the advantages of collaboration, trust, relation and sharing which will foster migration to wherever the economy relocates. Those countries which are short of talents thus open doors to skilled migrants from countries where they are plenty available.

Ford Motor Co, despite its large establishments of corporate office, R&D, Innovation and production in and around Detroit, decided to establish its Greenfield Labs at 3521 Hillview Avenue, bordering the PARC-Palo Alto Research Centre, a five minutes bike-ride from Stanford. This shows the polar to polar difference between automobile engineering and autonomous cars and the reason for staying far from the influence of Detroit. Most of the three hundred Ford employees are from Stanford and Apple. Ford has its in-house software called "The Verge" to domain its battery powered self-driving cars.

For Marc Fields, the charismatic CEO of Ford Motor Co such a billion-dollar investment to an uncertain and unknown future is too much a risk, when it is locking horns with Google, Apple and Tesla which follow a different model of low-cost start-ups and that can attract more brilliant talents than Ford, besides their agile and audacious culture to fail and rise up fast at nominal costs. At Palo Alto, the autonomous car is as simple as a seating sedan on wheels with sensors and software to which we dispense our destiny. Unlike Ford, most of the autonomous car companies in SV are not with an automobile history as in Detroit. Changing a business model with a new technology in legendary companies is very harder and risky, but so easy and simple in start-ups. Secondly, corporate companies fail mostly for their top-down hierarchy structure, where ivory tower managers are disconnected from reality so that wrong ideas and decisions supersede, money gets wasted and innovation gets lost.

In 2018, General Motors invested $1.1Bil into its self-driving car division, which in the next few months Softbank followed with additional infusion of $2.25Bil. Interestingly, Softbank has acquired 15 percent stake in Uber which promises an assured market for GM autonomous cars. Autonomous cars are to become 4-5 times cheaper than owning a car which can make a human-driven car so prohibitive by next decade. Google, Tesla, Ford and GM together with Silicon Valley innovations, have a potential to place America again to its lost glory in the global car market.

Twentieth century witnessed fierce wars; Ford locked horns with GM, Coke crossed swords with Pepsi, GE with Westinghouse and McDonald's with Berger King, either to establish market leadership or to push the rival out of market. In contrast, it is surprising to see that twenty-first century corporations like Google does not bother about Facebook, Apple does not matter to Microsoft, leaving SpaceX without competition, where all are sharing, collaborating and still growing on each other's technology. When Hilton poses a close competition to Marriott, Airbnb occupied a new blue ocean slot with its market value exceeding all those global five hotel groups combined. The global fleet of passenger cars are about one billion in 2018, which is to increase towards 1.7Bil by 2030, with higher numbers of electric and autonomous models.

What a small new comer SpaceX achieved in successfully sending satellites to outer space orbits in its FalconX, was a long pending project for Boeing, Arianepoace or Roscosmos. It adopted a method to reuse the damaged satellites and saving satellite-enabled internet costs by 20 to 40 percent as benefit to customers. If you are going after grand challenges, our experts are not much helpful in collaborations. Those young engineers who got us to the moon were not experts, but too young to understand or could not think of the impossible risks of the mission. Scott Cook, Chairman of Intuit, a fin-tech software said, "It remains a failure if we fail to get the learning". For Ratan Tata, "Failure is a goldmine!" It is too common and the rule of the SV culture.

"Curiosity of what does not exist, and what we cannot see opens up a new ocean of imaginations", stated Walt Disney who revolutionised the world with Donald Duck and Mickey Mouse, without which imagine what our childhood would have been? If Microsoft took 15 years to cross $1Bil revenue, Amazon achieved the same benchmark in less than five years.

Carlos Ghosn said, "B-Schools prepare people to deal with internal crisis, but I think we need to be more prepared for external crisis, especially in an increasingly volatile world where technology moving so fast for companies which built their culture, strategy and processes in the old world of global competition". McKinsey Research states that 50 percent of all efforts to transform companies fail because senior role models fail to drive change or because their inherent tendency to defend status quo.

Corporate Consulting

Legacy companies require huge resources, capital, leadership talent and facilities, besides corporate consulting to begin with any new business where on the other hand, so simple that start-ups do not require any of these resources. Speed, culture of adaption and agility are major factors that money cannot buy, which remain as a winning edge to start-ups. E-commerce is devastating the relevance and existence of malls, shopping centres, brand stores and retail shops worldwide.

Corporate consultants were part and parcel of legendary companies. As CEOs are appointed based on their industry experience, market sensitivity, turnaround skills and people management, these consultants are not that specialists in most of these core areas and unlikely to quality for a similar CEO position, who will still advise how things will not happen and magnifying the risk factors of a new venture without any direct accountability in execution. When B-School CEOs listen more to consultants and discourage own team from conflicting, Start-up CEOs listen more to their teams and encourage conflicts.

AT&T reported to have spent US$.500 Mil on consultants during 5 years till 1994, divided among McKinsey $.96Mil, Monitor (Michel Porter) $.127Mil, Anderson $.40Mil, until AT&T realized their mistake and stopped. When AT&T decided to acquire NCR to compete with IBM, Porter did not advise them against, that Computer does not add synergy to Telecom. Monitor Inc filed bankruptcy in 2012, with no funds to pay bills and salaries, which was founded by the legendary HBS professor Michael Porter.

Worst is that CEOs are even hiring consultants to define Mission and Vision statements. What is in common with Consultants is that they seldom admit mistakes for failures but blame the client's internal problems. A.T.Kearney was rolled up by Sears for being cost effective to be more profitable. Kearney advised to cut cost of the fast moving DieHard batteries which its supplier Johnston controls declined. This led to Sears sourcing this brand from other cheaper suppliers resulting inferior quality and weakening the brand.

No More The Rich and The Poor

Once the world was divided between prosperous and backward, where most global companies did not need to see beyond US and Europe to do well. Starting with Mobile and Internet, the remaining backward of 5Bil people emerged as an economic force from Asia and Africa. The global economy by next decade will be driven by these new emerging customers. This will generate more robots than workers, more currencies than nations.

Innovation University

Computer exceeded human intelligence by the fall of twentieth century, with IBM- DeepBlue Supercomputer's victory over Kasperov in the

World Chess championship, accident-free autonomous cars, and digital warfare. Despite this rapid growth in machine intelligence, we had no syllabus, teachers or schools to offer an integrated and entrepreneurial curriculum in these emerging technologies.

Ancient universities were founded on religious teachings, and it began with a Buddhist school in fifth century in India. This model was extended to Christian mission which founded Europe's best known universities. Though the basic models of faith changed, their core methodology remained unchanged. Most of these today's schools do not address to the grand challenges of future. They produced scholars but hardly thinkers, specialists in their narrow subjects than what matters to society and human lives at large. Universities of Oxford, Cambridge, Boston and Texas created great scholars, scientists and academicians of high knowledge, but not an imagination of future of how to liberate human lives from poverty, to ensure mass education, healthcare, affordable quality food.

By 2020, human sensitivity and AI combined could exceed the memory and computational ability of the human brain which could improve the way we live.

Optimistic and challenging, thought-provoking and engaging they are, Spiritual Machines are the ultimate guide on our road into the next century. When jobs are disappearing and getting replaced by machines, we have challenges of food, clothes, homes, healthcare and education. When cars get driverless, we seldom know the car, but the car knows everything about us from the first ride as every time the route is organized with our smart phone. It does not require any traffic signals, as sensors command the ride. As advanced technologies move faster than people can absorb changes, and offer both unprecedented rewards and unpredictable hazards, we have to choose between the potential rewards over its hazards.

SU

Ray Kurzweil and Peter Diamandis, perhaps the best known research analysts in exponential technologies, put forward an idea in 2008 of founding a University with a curriculum in Biotech, Computational systems, Network and Sensors, AI, Robotics, 3D-Printing, Material science and Nanotechnology, which have the potential to impact billions of people, combat grand challenges and reinvent industries. Their vision gave birth to Singularity University in CA.

SU has to spread regional by collaboration with other institutions, because regions have unique and diverse problems to solve, which opens up great challenging business opportunities.

Brain Power

Every audacious challenge is technologically as well as practically so difficult; it is also psychologically equally tough. Such attempts require an attitude-upgrade ie, a series of battle-hardened, time and defeat tested approach to big and bold. Big, Hairy and Audacious Goals-BHAG became mostly achievable when there is an alignment of the individual's values with the desired outcome of the goal. This worked wonderful results when Israel had no option but to win against all its wars against Arabs if the country has to still remain on the world map.

Individuals are always found to be successful than organizations in disrupting and innovating because organizations have the inertia not to disrupt the existing markets and revenues as well as pay-checks that leading to a large fear for failure; but not for individuals.

In contrast, the boys at start-up innovations are not greedy for money, except for meeting their essentials with a surplus for selective things, unlike those employed with established organizations. Here the road to winning is paved with many bricks of failure. A typical good entrepreneur tries to avoid risk and play safe. In contrast, starting a new company itself is a risk, especially when there is no money to support. For them it is a self-motivation arising from "autonomy, mastery and purpose" which means no more external interference allowed. A deep passion is very fundamental to mitigating repeated failure, then rise-up to optimism and success. So convinced about their ideas, so passionate of achieving its results, they are so notorious to listen deviating opinions and advices, but their passion and conviction attracts others to follow them. As fear is hell on decision making, threats begin to rise and brains starts limiting options.

Big goals are essential to achieve big results, but when these goals are aligned with values and purpose, they work far better. When this alignment exists, the result is a deep passion to one's work. This makes an individual or a small team to achieve what established organizations cannot dream of. Such small teams shoot up to become Unicorns in a very short period. As already indicated, men are very much local and linear until recently, which changed too fast with the advent of Internet and its derivative technologies. We are all designed for optimal performance, which is a built-in feature of being human.

Olympic records are always lauded as the highest achievements of humanity, until what we thought as impossible is broken by someone. These garage entrepreneurs are not restricted by what is impossible, they stretch beyond records and human limits until something we call impossible are accomplished and left for someone else to break.

In future, we do not need to travel to consult a doctor, as the best medical care will be accessible with Dr.Watson living in the cloud and best test labs are built into your mobile. Two decades back, it was a sign of luxury living to possess a video camera, stereo, CD player, watch, cell phone, etc which could total up to $.10,000, all which are today compressed into a smart phone, and its apps are available in a App store for less than what a coffee costs. This enables and empowers almost half of the humanity or the rising billion, which was sidelined and ignored for long. Two decades ago, no one could imagine a country like India would emerge to be an employment threat to developed world. West insists on their children to study maths and science if not Indian will steal away white-collar jobs.

So have a vision for the future, drag yourself towards it. We are all hardwired for challenge, a state of optimal human performance, which is possible only once coming out from your comfort zone. Once a man thinks himself an expert, today keeps off from him, because the one who knows do a job so well, does not consider himself an expert. When he does a job well, he presses himself of how he can do it better next time. Once he gets into an expert state of mind, everything becomes risky and impossible.

Fail early, Fail often and Fail Forward

The famous three principles so essential to drive innovation known as "Three Silicon Valley Doctrines" are Fail Early, "Fail more Often, and then Fail Forward". It is this relentless and unyielding mindset for failure that takes finally achieving success in innovation. Most experiments fail, real progress requires trying out so many ideas and by reducing the lag time between trials, we gain knowledge from its outcomes. This is rapid iteration. What those missing essentials to nurture innovation in large corporate are "autonomy, mastery and purpose" which is the reason why individuals or small teams are successful than established companies. These three essentials as key values, create a company built for speed. "If you are not embarrassed by the first version of your products, you've too late". Said Reid Hoffman, founder-LinkedIn.

Being an average in classroom is not a sin, but being so in life is! When brilliant students in classrooms are mostly after good jobs, it surprises to see that most of the successful future entrepreneurs were made from average students. When established companies recruited most of the brilliant graduates from their campuses, it did not matter much for new technology firms to select average ones and inducting them to their innovation culture with greater freedom of work.

Failure is a celebrated art at Amazon. Google is experimenting everything so skunk and monstrous projects from Space exploration, Life extension, AI, Autonomous cars and Robotics which no other company plays at such an elevated importance for failure. Most of the Google projects including the "Moonshots" which starts from Zero-base which has no past trials or progress data, are targeted to achieve a 10x (ten times or thousand percent) increase in performance which is unthinkable for any established company standards. The cost of anything to achieve 2x or 10x is more or less the same, whereas targeting more audacious goal can achieve still a higher result without much increase in cost. Same time, going 10x bigger goals go 10x times harder. Google allows its employees to spend 20% of their time on experimenting new ideas. But 'Moonshots' of Google or big goals, if aligned to values lead to exceptional and outstanding results. At Facebook atrium in Menlo Park-CA, one can see a billboard "Move fast, Break things!" Trust is more a culture at Facebook, which is the greatest intangible asset of a company. Men are designed for optimal performance- it is built-in feature of being human! Moon-shots are risky and adventurous, which requires young and audacious minds to embrace risk and challenges.

- When forced to compromise, ask more.
- If you cannot win, change the rules.
- When faced without a challenge, make one.
- Don't walk, if you can run.
- If you have no problem, create one.

- The faster you move, the longer you live.
- You get what you incentivize.
- If you think impossible, then it is for you.
- An expert is someone who can tell you exactly something cannot be done.
- If it were easy, it would have been done already.
- Without a target, you will miss it every time.
- If you cannot measure it, you cannot improve it.

Google has always been a company that listens to its engineers for new ideas. It allows a generous "20 percent time" to its employees to pursue passion projects. 3M followed a 15 percent time for project innovation for years. Toyota employees meet regularly to suggest process improvements and new methods. When a company has a listening culture, it opens up to a vista of changes. Animation unit Pixar of Disney Corporation engages it's most frustrated and impatient artists whenever it has to execute any movie too fast and also cheap.

The world's most precious and scarcest resource is the persistent and passionate human mind, especially in their twenties. Fewer people in a team is always, almost better in work, discussion or negotiation. Bureaucracy is an obstacle to be contested with persistence, confidence and a bulldozer when necessary.

Lawyers and Accountants

Lawyers and accountants are not allowed to decide independently, from a legal or financial perspective. Both are risk-averse and consider every new business with legal or financial implications hence they are allowed to function within a restricted framework that do not question the business decisions like expansion, innovation or acquisition. Company has a reason to acquiring a new business which with very limited scope to be successful, but mostly for its smart team that comes with it. Lawyers and accountants will spend more time on the trivial questionable issues without considering its far higher business opportunity. The risk-averse approach of lawyers and accountants that work well with corporate, but seldom go well in the internet century. So generalists are preferred than specialists in legal and accounting functions. Bill Gates is known to say, "spend 80 percent of your time on 80 percent of your revenue" and also “Power comes not from knowledge kept but from knowledge shared”.

Innovation is the next big thing! Any idea should be first a benefit to billions, which shall be different from whatever existed and to be brought into market in a short span of time. At innovation labs or garages, people are not instructed but allowed to do as they want. It is human nature and also our corporate belief to think incrementally rather than rapidly and in multiples. The doctrine of you are not thinking big enough, but we have Computing power, Internet, AI, Cloud and ML that empower to scale up small start-ups to big business in a short span of time. Thinking big empowers smart creative more freedom that removes constraints and spurts innovations. Once you think big enough, it is very hard to fail completely, with something valuable left over. Biggest discoveries were made possible with limitation of finance, talents and workplace.

Largely internet firms work on a 70:20:10 rule. This means seventy percent of resources are dedicated to core business which generates money for other activities. Twenty percent is committed to emerging products with good chance of success and remaining ten percent on new projects with a high risk of failure. Most innovative new ideas look small with corporate firms, where as it nurtures to big business with small start-ups.

Imagination beyond our Mindset

In 1990 it was hard to imagine that cell phones will become so thin and less weight with an astounding memory and apps. In 1995, we could not imagine that Internet will reach-out to more than three billion users with over sixty trillion addresses. In 1998, no one could imagine about a online marketplace for anything and everything we wanted. In 2000, it was beyond our thinking about a search engine and embedding all technologies of a PC to a tiny mobile phone. In 2005, we never dreamt of integrating the world to a relationship and networking platform. In 2010 no one thought of Cloud replacing servers. Today it remains unimaginable about car without drivers. Similarly 3-D Printing is to rewrite the speed and cost of manufacturing, VR and AR are making the online shopping more enjoyable and time saving, AI will make online payment easier and without a cashier besides setting our all medical and healthcare data available on our handset. It is also obvious that all these new technologies, apps and platforms are to be disappeared with emergence of new alternatives and the speed will become more fast beyond the human brain can imagine.

General rule of start-up

Fifty percent of Unicorn founders are over 35 years. Most of the founders did not have any direct relevant work experience in the industry they were disrupting. Sixty percent of those billion dollar companies were started by repeat entrepreneurs, many of them had at least $50 million in bank account. The right time to found a first experience start-up is while in University. Ritesh Agarwal was only 19 years, when he started OLA Rooms, a global accommodation chain today valued at $.9.6 Bil with a annual revenue of $550Mil. With Larry Page and Sergey Brin the founders of Google, Steve Jobs and Steve Wosniak of Apple, Bill Hewlette and David Packard of HP, and Binny and Sachin of Flipkart, it was believed that founding a start-up was possible unless two founders, which Mark Zuckerberg proved to be wrong with Facebook. But none of them had any role models, neither parents nor teachers and did not follow their parent's aspirations about them.

The progress with technology sprouts a number of new ideas into implementation while many of the present ones getting phased out. In Silicon Valley, the crowded coffee shops are known as 'Google Cafes" where almost 90 percent of the debates are on new ideas, start-ups and innovations.

GE Garage is a lab incubating start-ups in 3-D Printing, computer numerically controlled machines and laser cutting. Samsung runs an accelerator in SV and Tel Aviv, Disney invited eleven media-tech start-ups to join its accelerator program, where technology is driving the sharks to fall prey to minnows.

Biggest failure is not Failing!

Even if the possibility for access is fairly low, and if the objective is so audacious, it is worth doing. NASA which is famous for relentless explorations, is an example of a government organization's tolerance for failures. When failure is not an option, people end up with safe and incremental innovations, without much of radical disruptions. Google is an excellent example of experimentation, where if a product is not meeting its goals, and its resources could be better leveraged elsewhere, the product is shut down. P&G installed Failure Awards that honour employees for the biggest failure that delivered the greatest thoughtful insight. Similarly Tata Group offers an annual "Dare to Try" award which recognizes managers who took the biggest challenge and risk, which attracts more than 240 entries annually.

The best example of how one of the biggest failure gave good lesson to every other start-up company was Better Place founded by Shai Agassi, an Israeli Entrepreneur whose electric car company amassed $.930Mil in funds and collapsed due to wrong strategy and execution. The biggest beneficiary of this failure was Tesla which did not have to experiment with the failure of Better Place. This story gives the best lessons for every new start-up to capture success.

Garage Experience

When small start-ups operating from garages, it is so essential to adopt the five rules on their quest to success:

- Detox by disconnecting and unplugging from everything.
- Empathise and immerse so as to connect with the opportunity and goal.
- Boil ideas down to a creative brief, mantra.
- Agitate to drive ideation and mix solutions.
- Prototype rapidly to enable a fast user experience.
- Willingness to accept and reward failure.

In contrast, corporate culture rarely recognizes failure, which attracts internal politics and blame-games unlike technology start-ups where trust supersedes when someone fails. Five year plans are so common in private corporate culture, but a suicidal practice in technology firms. Breaking every record is a out-stretch of human abilities. If a company does not race in wrong and unknown direction, it gets an inaccurate picture of what lies ahead, even in its right direction. We can see this daring philosophy when Google entered the driverless car business and life-elongation, AWS created the largest Cloud space and SpaceX ventured into space internet. For them to establish a "Big Vision" or 10X trajectory is an essential culture which follows a course-correction as and when required. Here purpose trumps over strategy, and execution overrides planning.

Conquering Space

The exponential technologies gave us physical leverage, psychological tools which provided a mental edge, and its combination allows entrepreneurs to become true forces of disruption. It enables to scale up as never before. A passionate small team of innovators can change the lives of billions in a short time. They rely on the below mental strategies:

- Risk taking and risk mitigation
- Rapid iteration and ceaseless experimentation.
- Passion and Purpose
- Long-term thinking
- Customer-centric approach
- Probabilistic mind
- Rationally optimistic thinking
- Reliance on fundamental truths.

What is the attraction for Richard Branson, Jeff Bezos, Elon Musk and Larry Page to explore Space, where all others still feel not exploited the business potential enough on Earth? Space is not something these moonshot innovators ever touched or seen. Musk built four multibillion-dollar companies; Pay-Pal (Banking), SpaceX (aerospace & defence), Tesla (Elec cars) and SolarCities (Energy). The existing reach of humanity and economic influence was limited to earth, which today is outreaching the space. Dew Houston, founder of Dropbox agrees, "The most successful people are obsessed with solving an important problem, something that matters to them". The average age of an Unicorn founder is thirty-four, with three co-founders, all with a technical education. Ideally a team suits to the start-up than a brilliant and toxic, not its profit motive. The goal is not to live forever, but to create something lives forever.

Elon Musk

Born in Pretoria, South Africa, Musk sold a video game code for five hundred dollars when he was 12 years. He studied Physics at Wharton and moved to Stanford for his PhD which he dropped out as attracted to the exploding world of Internet. He was most passionate and purpose-driven towards his dreams. Even from his childhood, Elon Musk had a passion towards energy, transportation and space travel.

Towards last decades of eighteenth century, Chicago to NY took four weeks by horse-carriage, few decades on, trains cut this short to four days and later aeroplanes to four hours. Now Hyper-loop is targeting to just one hour which no surprise if could probably scale down to zero in a decade.

From a perspective of physics, it looks impossible to accelerate humans to 1000 km an hour in his Hyper-loops and then decelerate them to zero in such a short pace of time. It is just barriers which can overcome, but nothing like impossible.

When Musk started SpaceX and Tesla, the success hope was below fifty percent, but he thought these are very much needed to get done, no matter he lost the money. Space was always the game for two countries- US and Russia and recently China but not the cup of tea for corporate, but these technology companies are striving all-out to catch moon after a vacuum of three decades, as how curious we were during our childhood. If we exclude Tesla, US hadn't seen a new successful car company in three decades, that too government spending tens of billions to bail out those Big Three.

Tesla S was named the Car of the Year in 2013 by Motor Trent magazine, which was built on just seventeen moving parts, in contrast to hundreds of moving parts in a conventional car. Tesla has an acceleration mode, which Elon Musk calls a "Ludicrous Mode" of 0-60 mph in 2.3 seconds, fastest ever recorded by any vehicle.

Larry Page was born to Gloria, a computer science professor in Michigan and Carl Page, a master in both Computer Science and AI had an early weakness for computers. At Stanford, he was batch mate to Sergey Brin for PhD in Computer Science jointly did a research nicknamed 'BackRub' which led to become Google, but both dropped studies. Google, so heavily dependent on AI and Internet became the search engine, later acquired Youtube, started Chrome, an easy browser and Android, the Mobile Phone operating system. Today Google is into driverless car and LUNAR XPRIZE, both so unknown and uncertain for its founders. Both have a healthy disregard towards the impossible, and driven by a rational optimism. This culture drives people far beyond their comfort zones and act on tough challenges than ever before. In 2013, Google announced its longevity start-up CALICO its entry into anti-aging world which Time puts is as "Google v/s Death". If you do not think 10x, do not expect to be on your job for long. The smartest people on the planet usually work for someone else, but in technology start-ups, it is not just an employment. Google had made 350 attempts to secure investors and if Larry Page and Sergey Brin had stopped at 340 attempts, the world would have been different today.

Today, G-Pay and Walmart's Phone-Pe routes almost 85% of India's phone payment transaction. As margins are too low in this sector, they are considering venturing into other financial services like SME lending and Wealth management. What could be the next? The tools to solve yesterday's problems are not enough designed to meet the challenges of tomorrow.

With seven billion plus mobile phones in use globally, many equipped with a high resolution cameras, anything and everything can be recorded instantly. Every household with a Broadband connectivity becomes a threat for individual and family privacy of data by capturing the food habits, income, transactions, customised sizes of clothes and even shoes.

Disruption means breaking an existing and conventional way of doing things, as how online banking disrupted visiting a bank for a transaction, online coaching which disrupts a physical classroom learning experience and how a digital government service disrupted a physical queue at payment counters?

No doubt, we will experience more changes at a quicker rate than any previous generation, and this change driven by the devices in our hands will be more personal and engaging. Internet and mobile technology will be so common like water and electricity in coming decade.

Scale and Size

For years, scale and size were seen as desirable traits for an enterprise. Bigger companies could perform better because it could leverage economies of scale and negotiate from strength. Merely for this reason, B-Schools and Management Consulting firms focused on restructuring and managing such large corporate. NYSE and LSE gained so rich with trading the stock of such giant companies, which often merge and sell-off to create much larger and profitable companies. Contrary to this, a small team unleashed from all constraints, shows an ability to do big things, that grows over to greater levels when enabled with the new convergent technologies. As a result, smaller team has an advantage that it can take on much bigger challenges than a large one can. Start-ups have a higher upside potential and a lower downside, where lager companies are just the opposite. In coming years, adaptability and agility will increasingly eclipse scale and size in business.

Uber scales by helping its drivers to buy cars. Uber ordered for 2500 Google driverless cars, which will provide enormous data surge which it can turn into new businesses and services. Combined them through a smart phone, it gives an outstanding customer experience which turns to make a customer convenience and habit. On other side, Southwest changed its airlines like buses to a niche by itself, defeating competition.

Cloud computing allows greater storage of data and unlimited processing. As this is cost-per-use basis, it reduces upfront capital for own server room and staff which empowers smaller start-ups with an easy access to technology and tools, which makes memory storage almost free in practice. This is an advantage for smaller start-ups over big companies who runs their internal but expensive IT divisions. This gives less and less need for own factory, labs and even technology tools. This is a present model of how GE and Rolls- Royce began offering leasing programs for their expensive aircraft engines to airlines based on number of hours flown, thus making them affordable in long run. Steve Jobs said, "We run Apple like a start-up. We always let ideas conflict and win arguments, not hierarchies. Otherwise our best employees won't stay. Collaboration, discipline and trust are critical." Apple is a good example of how large companies take up such challenges. Its core competency is Design, and how it launches such innovative design attracts others to follow.

Apple leverages its core design competencies, but not Google or Amazon. First they start with a selective small team of change makers to begin at the edge of the organization to combine the new technology with a new design which could boldly disrupt an existing market, mostly its own. Starting with iPod that disrupted music players, then iTunes which fragmented music delivery, next iPhone and later iPad. For Apple new business starts from the edge of an existing product. In 2012, 80 percent of its revenue came from products that were less than five years old. This new revenue almost 10X metric, made it the first Trillion dollar company in the world.

Amazon is next example which started by selling printed books which was cannibalised by its own Kindle format. Now it is into its own Drone-delivery which will disrupt its existing business of human delivery. The drive is the will and vision. For years, size and scale did matter where bigger companies could perform more because they could leverage economies of scale and negotiate from strength and merge to become still more gigantic companies. If experimentation is the most critical attribute for new learning companies, it is too hard for big ones as their focus in on execution rather than innovation.

Taking spot payments from consumers and paying its suppliers 4-6 weeks later, Amazon operates with a negative working capital. In Q-4 of 2013, Amazon reported its receivables as $4.77 Bil against its payables of $15.14Bil, allowing the company to float on more than $10Bil of zero-interest capital. If the top ten global e-commerce retailers had the cash flow of Amazon, collectively they pool a whopping $150Bil in working capital.

But in recent past, it proved that smaller the team, it can take much bigger risks than a large one. Ability to scale very quickly and divert much faster to a better technology space, Google is the most admired example. Another example, Uber ordered 2500 Google cars which will provide enormous data surge which it can turn to another new service business. Uber could take advantage of every new technologies like Google Map, Bigdata, Cloud, AI, sensor and ML, all which cost nothing and combined together assembled the Uber platform used by millions. All these innovations result to spread of prosperity, progress in technology, decline in poverty, decease and violence, with an increase in freedom, happiness and knowledge. The emergence of successful start-ups like Amazon, Apple, Google, Microsoft and Facebook would not have been possible without Internet, AI, Apple i-OS and Google's Android. Interestingly nobody protected their innovations as their patent so that everyone could benefit and scale up from each other's assets and technologies.

Dropping Cost of Start-ups

Once start-ups of 1990-2000, capital investment used to be too large, where it has to own expensive servers to store data, lab and scientific tools etc, which today cloud storage is charged on use basis which cost almost a fraction, tools can be leased than owning, and extensive

Internet helps one to work from anywhere. As a result, garage firms can afford more risks, failures, speed and disruption at lowest manpower cost than bigger companies. Rare examples of innovation within large companies are GE and Rolls Royce entered into charging for their engines to the airlines on basis of dollar per flying hours than owning them.

From $.15Mil to built a software start-up in Silicon Valley during 1995, the money mostly went to server stacks, software, manpower and configure the technology. By 2005, the same had dropped to $.4Mil with drop in all these costs except marketing. Today with new capabilities like Cloud and social media at unbelievably low costs, a start-up can be as cheap as $.100,000. Today start-ups work on 100X scale, with one tenth of the capital it required a decade ago.

Internet has changed how the businesses are built and grown. The era of traditional and hierarchical market domination of dinosaur companies is coming to an end where the world belongs to a smarter, smaller and faster moving enterprise. Start-ups rise to success in a rapid pace, as its extinction too, while established companies are incremental in growth and not that quick in failure.

About 27 mil US businesses need capital, where more than fifty percent of the new ones fail within their first five years of operation without enough capital. Until ten years back, the big challenges of Automobile, Energy, Manufacturing or Medical transplants were reserved for government or big corporations, but today they are open for anyone with access to internet. Today billion dollar corporations compete against two-person start-ups and we see a friendly acquisition of such start-ups to prevent their future threats as well as to integrate new technologies to their own existing businesses. This allows not leaders to lead but leaders to emerge.

During recruitments, billion dollar companies look for where one studied, what subject specialization, experience and achievements, whereas new technology start-ups consider how brutally objective he is, what one is capable of, does he have the nerve to envision the challenges, then the daring and drive. It took two generations to build what Walmart is today, but two decades for Jeff Bezos to make Amazon a much larger one. Competition is no longer coming from MNCs, mostly from small start-up garages.

The world's biggest problems are also the world's biggest business opportunities. Identify the key issue. What problem keeps you unable to sleep at night? Problems are the modern day gold mines. More bigger the issue, the more valuable the solution. These problems once belonged to national leaders and heads of MNCs, but today almost anyone with a dream and passion has the power to bring the real change into the world.

By 2025, the annual consumption of emerging markets will exceed $.30 Tril, means a business opportunity of that size never existed before.

According to recent UN report, a one percent GDP growth results 2 percent poverty reduction. Given 4Bil people under poverty, which means that every 10 new smart phones per one hundred people, about 80Mil graduate from poverty with an increase of 20 percent in their present income. It is expected to add another 3Bil to the world's internet community, which has connected so many consumers with so many producers creating a huge collaborative economy without walls and barriers.

Bigger the Companies, Uncertain the Future

Most of the CEOs and leaders of twentieth century were largely brilliant MBAs from premium B-Schools, also those outgrown CEO turned management consultants who are educated and experienced in managing or consulting large and established companies of incremental growth models. In contrast the new generation founders are hardly MBAs and mostly of degree-dropouts in technology or science, who had gone through a severe classroom conflicts. Similarly those innovation-potential employees in established companies are mostly those rebels and in-disciplined who are either sidelined or ignored by seniors. B-School education is structured to manage established firms whereas technology education combined with imagination and future vision liberates ideas of how new unknown and non-existing technology can benefit the humanity in an uncertain future. If the defying metric in a normal management job is the ROI-Return On Investments, in Start-Ups the most valuable compensation is the ROL-Return On Learning.

Disruptions of Twentieth Century

Throughout the history, competition used to be with competitors. In cars Ford with GM or both with Toyota, in power sector Siemens with ABB or both with GE, in electronics Panasonic with Hitachi or both with Sony and in Aircraft Airbus with Boeing.

Sony pushed down Kodak in cameras which Canon and Nikon did to Sony, later the industry was pushed down by Nokia, an outsider selling more than industry's volume. Nokia was eclipsed by Smart phones.

The same Nokia which took Camera industry for a ride, was eclipsed by the onslaught of Smart Phones from Apple I-Phone and Google Android. Nokia which fought another industry, could not fight smaller competitors despite being the leader. Today Nokia gone into history after a Microsoft acquisition.

Once big names in Music like EMI and HMV lost heat to Mobile phones and i-Tunes.

BA, SIA or Lufthansa see competition within their industry, but with Video conferencing Google-meet and Zoom becoming cheaper and the way companies shrinking their travel budgets, where could be the future of airlines industry?

The price of VCR slashed and market size marginalized. Telefunken, Remington-Rand, Grundig, AEG and Thomson are history, even Vauxhaul or Austin cars. Three decades back Microsoft was hardly known. Fifteen years ago, no one believed Google will grow so big to challenge Microsoft.

Over the last two decades, the concentration of wealth is moving eastwards. Some well known banks in US and Europe disappeared and some of the best known financial institutions landed in highest ever loss in history, not because of competition, but disruptions.

Test Cricket was a long game. It reduced to One day-50 overs. When it condensed to a capsule size of 20-20, the length became 3 hours, almost a movie. During IPL, multiplexes in India ran empty with IPL competing with Cinemas. No wonder if multiplexes asked for rights to live IPL!

Many products vanished with the onslaught of outside competition. Typewriters, sewing machine, alarm clock with mechanical springs, Radio and 3-in-1 by MP3, wristwatches and cameras by Cellphones, Floppy disks by CDs and USBs, which all indicating the future of competition is not from competitors and the beast comes from nowhere, but it is somewhere around you. Future looks terrific and uncertain. Lehman Brothers, AIG, Merrill Lynch, Enron or ING failed not because of competition but for internal incompetence and ignorance of reality.

If Ford and GM severely lost US market share to Toyota and Honda, today we see all of them losing the entire industry to those small garage teams of Google, Intel and Tesla. Malls, Hypermarkets, brand stores and retail shops are getting destroyed by E-Commerce platforms like Amazon, Alibaba and Walmart. Multiplex movies are under grave threat from Hotstar, Netflix and Amazon Prime. Car ownership has become a less option than a chauffer-driven or driverless Uber or Lyft. Homes are likely to have no kitchen when Zomato and Swiggy deliver food at your doorstep. In recent Israel-Hamas conflict at Gaza, Drones and I-Domes fought and won for Israel but not soldiers. Robots are walking almost everywhere from assembling, logistics, retail, homecare and eldercare, replacing human jobs and will expand their role as car drivers. The pandemic taught us to remote-working, organize meetings by Zoom and teaching online which disrupted the huge assets of technology parks and campuses.

Small Eats Big

Disruption lives too deep into our lives today. Today's successful disruptors admit themselves that their future is obviously to be disrupted by small teams operating from garages in Palo Alto. Vision makes money and brings prosperity, but money does not make vision.

Twentieth century witnessed how vulnerable the top-down hierarchies like dictator regimes and communism and rising trend of bottom-up structures like democracy and capitalism. Despite this lesson from history, most of the corporations remained completely top-to-down hierarchies until even today. In such hierarchies, information and ideas pass on slowly from top to bottom filtered and misinterpreted at every level and so the reverse way hence the decisions get too slow than the pace of market forces and competition. This results in frontline employees perform to fixed and scripted tasks than using their intuition to react quickly to market needs. Here focus of attention is more internally than outside to the market. Such an environment, bureaucracy destroys any idea of new business creation as a measure of reducing risks and scale. It is self-explanatory that why new business ideas get destroyed within a large organization structure.

Rare examples of established companies transforming to new expansions, are Nokia a tire company ventured successfully into cell phones, Samsung a trading company also into smart phones, Intel starting with memory chips into processors and GE which transformed from Electricals to every other high-tech energy, aircraft engine, healthcare giant. Apple and IBM are two others which successfully rose from the ashes of bankruptcy to come out with Apple I-phone, I-pad and I-Mac and IBM integrated computing and cloud. Most European companies are mid-size with exception to Daimler, Siemens, Nesle or ABB, unlike US Companies which are more global giants. The reason is that the leadership and board of any company in Europe largely communicate in their country's language, hardly consider its market within its language region like DACH, Benelux, Italy or France but not the entire world. On the other side, the start-up companies, driven on these new exponential technologies spread across the world, breaking language and regional barriers.

"A good crisis is a terrible thing to waste" according to economist Paul Romer. Large companies are either slow or avoid crisis, as one structural reason is short-term quarterly performance which drives stock prices and earnings.

You come to realize that most of your assumptions were false and that your finish line is too far away than you thought, most of the start-ups die at this stage than scale-up. Our ability to communicate with anyone on the planet is better, and the ability to work with anyone on the planet together is also unbelievable. At start-up workplace, imagination works superior performance than knowledge and experience and putting young people at power and influence.

Airbnb owns no physical asset but is worth almost $.10Bil, which is much higher than Hyatt with 45000 employees across 549 properties. Uber converts private cars into taxis- has been valued at $.17Bil, much higher than any airline or public transport company, but no physical assets or workforce.

Until twentieth century, companies were concerned about their target markets, largely of North America, Europe, Far-east and Australia. For them the marginalised humanity of South Asia and Africa were not their target. Today with every business adapting to modern technology, and also those new generation technology companies are more concerned about scaling their business than profit. Scaling is possible only with the inclusion of this marginalised community which accounts for more than half of the global population. Today technology has become easily accessible for the poor than those mid-market engineering and electrical goods. As a result, this poor segment gets connected, listened, employed, earning, better fed, educated and healthy that ignores and leaves nobody behind.

None of us can predict future, but can approach it wisely and diligently. This goes in contrast with our conventional wisdom, intuition, leadership thought and assumptions. It makes more difficult to grant what went right in the past. Venture into any idea with a safe exit door, and avoid taking decisions that are irreversible and costly to reverse. Every day is a new opportunity and build on yesterday's success and leave failures behind and start over again. Pessimist sees difficulty in every opportunity, while optimist sees opportunity in every difficulty and every problem gives an opportunity for action.

The world what we had seen until now, will not be the same in next ten years and most unlikely to reverse. It will challenge our conventional thinking and the wisdom we recognized in the past. The winning factors of the future will be a relentless focus on the opportunity and scarcity and deficit in resources as incentives.

Peter Diamandis, co-founder of Singularity Uni says, "competition for many of the US Fortune 500 companies is no longer coming from China or India, but from two guys in a garage with a start-up leveraging these exponentially growing technologies". According to him, the day before something is truly a breakthrough, it is a crazy idea. The lifespan of a S&P 500 company has decreased from sixty seven years in 1920 to fifteen years today and almost 40 percent of them are unlikely see the dawn of coming decade. New technologies cause great companies to fall! Any company designed for success in the 20th century is doomed to fail in the 21st century.

Future of Healthcare no longer remains with Merck, Pfizer, GSK or Novartis, but with Google, Apple and Amazon. So the future of metals does not rest with Rio-Tinto or BHP, but with 3-d Printing- Systems IDDD or Stratasys 2SSYS who will use new materials replacing metals. Also legendary Ford or VW lost the future of motor cars already to Google, Tesla or Mobiliye. This is the proof for whatever you were best in the past, does not guarantee any future existence.

Imagine a senior vacancy in US or UK, will have at least ten aspirants from ten different countries, as physical presence is becoming irrelevant for most of such jobs. On the other hand when a product is bought, we know who is its manufacturer and where it is produced, but not the graphic designer or web architect is from Africa or Latin America.

Our Grand Challenges

Google announced Project-Loon, a mission to provide internet to every person on planet, with connectivity. Elon Musk has another mission aiming a literacy boom with arithmetic, both the basic of education. A study on the earth's carrying capacity- a measure of how many people can live here sustainably is 2Bil. Addressing to this study, China's one-child policy reduced its population by 300 Mil over 3 decades. Experts will advise governments to reduce people, but disruptors will strive to grow resources what they consume. Today, a combination of Internet with Micro-finance can touch and transform our poorest people to an emerging economic force. Our grand and greatest challenge is to provide water, nutritious food, affordable housing, education, medical care and clean energy and transportation to world's 9 Bil people.

Creative minds stem Innovation, where India has too untapped and excess of it, but has to be liberated from its traditional job-dream orientation, then the future is just in front of us. With technology accelerating so fast forward, touching and transforming every field of business and human lives, makes our past knowledge and experience very irrelevant for our future.

13 Equality, Trust and Collaboration

The Converters of 21st Century

If Coca-Cola, McDonalds and Marlboro were the evangelists who universalised the model of American Capitalism around the world during twentieth century, today the only difference is that these new accelerating technology firms like Apple, Microsoft, Amazon, Google and Facebook are the evangelists of democracy across the world through a common language, relationship, networking, universality, trust and equality beyond region, religion, caste, gender and skin. This progress will either weaken or fragile all those existing regimes of autocracy, monarchy, religion, dynasty, military and ideology to a most preferred choice of democracy and compassionate capitalist democracy towards or not later than the middle of twenty first century turning the world to a most peaceful and happy living than ever before in the past.

Internet is universal without borders, which empowers citizens of oppressed states to express the flaws in human rights, freedom and equality to the outer world, including UN and ICJ and such exposures will force those governments to recognize the civil rights by scaling down state-sponsored oppressions to a greater extent. Such examples will refrain other semi-autocratic states from oppression of freedom rights by force. The extensive possibilities that modern technologies foster to empower relationship, trust and collaboration, promise a very optimistic future of humanity. There is nothing more devastating for a country than with a majority of its citizens disintegrated against the state. As a result, citizens are becoming more powerful than a state controlling its citizens.

History taught us that dictator regimes never had any respect for human lives. They caused most of the wars, slavery, exodus, genocide and human sufferings in our world, which in comparison under democratic leadership did not happen. Hitler, Mussolini to post WW-2 Russia and some of the former Soviet Union, China, North Korea, Libya, Syria, Iraq, Rumania, Cuba, Belarus or Cambodia were just opposite to other democratic leadership in our world. One major difference is that the dictators were not exposed to the civilised world outside their countries or partners and went too far with military suppression to remain in power. Their worst enemy is the surge in social media and internet which expose them to the world and expose the outer world to their citizens. These dictators hardly travel to democratic countries, hence seldom learn and adapt to changing civilisations. They are mostly educated and speak only in their local dialects hence, become distanced to our present civilized world. Their laws restrict their citizens from Internet to prevent their exposure to the external world. It is either the faith or ideology which dictates their law and governance, than the welfare and progress of people.

Collaboration between two democratic countries will share ideas and discoveries to foster multiple benefits for each other. In the history, two democracies hardly fought any war each other, but in most wars one side or both sides were either dictatorship, autocratic, dynastic or ideologist. If we intertwine the complementing attributes of technology and democracy, the future of humanity will be more peaceful, prosperous and sustainable.

Internet in Conflict with Dictatorship

Dictatorship suppress opinion and freedom, hence a great possibility of violence outbreak. Democracy and compassionate capitalism foster freedom and tolerance and free the society from violence and anarchy. There has been a decline in violence with the progress of democracy and capitalism than other military, monarchy and ideologist models of government. Authoritarian governments will find it more difficult to control their new generation of connected citizens while democratic states will be forced to recognize more voices of human rights, equality and freedom of speech. This favours citizens as more powerful than governments and companies. Ten most violent countries in the world as on 2014- Syria, Afghanistan, South Sudan, Iraq, Somalia, Sudan, Central African Republic, Democratic Republic of Congo, Pakistan and North Korea were all among the least democratic or capitalist, where as those ten most peaceful countries-Ireland, Denmark, Austria, New Zealand,

Switzerland, Finland, Canada, Japan, Belgium and Norway, were core democratic or capitalist. Those dictatorship and semi-dictatorship countries do not favour their citizens to become closely connected, and they find it difficult to hide truth by destroying documents, masking corruption and nepotism because full details of such fraud activities are recoverable, having been stored in the cloud.

It is surprising that if broadcasting channels in English and the languages in the democratic world disclose more truths about the Islamic jihad terrorist outfits than those in Arabic language. With the extensive spread of internet, voice translation, streaming gestural interfaces and holographic programs to a virtual network in future, will bring the language barrier to an end. Saudi Arabia, Kuwait and several Islamic states had allowed women to participate elections, driving cars and employment in due respect to human rights and gender equality, which are indications towards democracy in future. On the other side, Internet poses a severe threat of small minor issues get escalated to big online activities, while corruption and bribery are to be on decline, as no one knows if any such transactions could be monitored by sensor-cameras or could be captured and posted viral by a smart phone at any time.

The collapse and dissolution of Soviet Union liberated fourteen new republics with a population of 51 percent, where ten of these new countries embraced democracy by discarding the old ideology. When EU and NATO clubs are considering entry for these former Soviet states, Turkey being the only Muslim majority state in Europe is not yet a member of EU, for its conflict with Club's Copenhagen norms and human rights violations. If the Russian leadership was so ruthless to open an all-out war against Ukraine, they defended but NATO and EU was guided by their democratic values and restrained from escalating the crisis fearing a World War-3 that could destroy thousands of civilian lives and their homes. The political leadership of countries take sides during war, where recently we see that internet and social media bring all people to a general consensus against any war. Rogue leadership decide the war, where ordinary people are the worst victims of such decisions.

UN and Democracy

UN has 193 sovereign states with five non-member observer states like Holy See (Vatican), Palestine, Taiwan, Kosovo and Western Sahara.

If 57 percent of the countries in the world are democratic, 13 percent are autocratic and rest 28 percent are mix of both. If in the recent past we have more autocratic countries transformed largely to democratic or some to mixed category, eradication of hunger and poverty, better literacy, and earnings push more states towards democracy. Though governments remain with autocracy or ideology, people are becoming more averse to dictatorship and gradually embracing democracy where we cannot ignore a strong influence of internet.

Those platforms like Facebook, Twitter and YouTube which were extremely popular everywhere in the world, were blocked by the Chinese government. On Chinese internet, one cannot find information about politically sensitive topics like Tiananmen Square agitation, embarrassing coverage of Chinese leadership, freedom protests in Hong Kong, Tibetan rights movement and its spiritual leader H.H. Dalai Lama and contents on human rights violations especially of Uighur Muslims. For reporting the family fortune of then Vice President Xi Jinping in June 2012, Bloomberg News was blocked in both Chinese and English versions. On the other hand, about three hundred thousand online programmers were hired by officials to post praises about their bosses, Party and government. The best approach to improving quality of life across the world is to drive connectivity and its technological opportunities. Connectivity is the solution to raise economic prosperity, social equality, self-determination, human rights and education and transfer power to the hands of people which they will take further forward. If state and business foster a culture of accountability, transparency and choice, it is not the same in a country like China where the government and private sector are intertwined.

Censorship

Other cases of Internet censorship are in Turkey, which has its own internet called BTK after blocking YouTube for two years for releasing videos maligning its founder Mustafa Kemal Ataturk. Sunni Muslim block including Saudi, Algeria and Mauritania launched "Sunni Web", Iran has own sites named Mehr and Halal, Great Firewall by China, Koryalink by North Korea, were all in place of neutral internet. Recep Tayyip Erdogan the president of Turkey termed its social media platforms as 'worst enemy to state'. Huawei admitted that its expertise in information censorship was mastered in China. These are enough examples to prove how dictatorship countries are protecting their present models of government against any possibility of slipping towards people's democracy which is unlikely to continue for long. We had seen Arab Spring, a mass movement against dictatorship and nepotism and another pro-democratic agitation we saw recently in Hong Kong, which would have not been so widespread without internet. A constant stream of information on Twitter caused the fall of dictator regimes and civil unrest in Egypt, Libya, Iraq and Tunisia. Disconnection of internet is the first step followed by governments to limit and control the intensity of agitations and violence, which shows the role of internet in reaching out to masses. We have more examples of dictator regimes changing to quasi-democracy or democracy, where hardly any change from democracy to dictatorship.

Dictators listen to admirers and praises, whereas in Democracy, the government and leaders stand open criticism and public scrutiny hence higher a sense of accountability. Dictators hardly socialise and negotiate with open world hence they illustrate a primitive and savage-like personality. Those rogue leaders cling to power mostly for a lifetime with internal oppressions. Perhaps the most admired as captain of Pak Cricket, Imran Khan lost it as the country's president. Future technology is aligned with respect to humanity, human rights and benefit towards democracy, where our technologies ignite equality. Today if we see most of the rogue dictators becoming more scared of using the state forces to suppress human rights and equality, it is their fear for the Internet which will expose such incidents to the outer world. The entire world viewed the violation of human rights, exodus of refugees and crimes during the reigning of ISIS in Syria and Iraq, next when Taliban took over Afghanistan in 2021, besides in the recent Russian invasion of Ukraine. It is the internet and social media the strongest force standing against any assault on human lives and rights.

The technologies which are fast transforming our world, act as a global platform in networking, sharing and relationship, by spreading the values of freedom, human rights and better livelihood across the world. With more connectivity among masses, poor people tend to get equal data connections and facilities like the rich, and also listened and attended with equal rights, which creating an equality sense between the poor and rich except in wealth and lifestyle. If state is more powerful than citizens in a dictatorship rule, the new technologies empower the citizens to be more important where state is forced to listen to them. Neither dictator sovereign states like Cuba or China could hold long after they masked the internet initially. In contrast every state today uses the platform for all their transactions and communications, and driving hard to digitalising all the government activities. As a result, governments and institutions find it too hard to mask the flaws in governance, corruption, and nepotism. Corruption has become too risky at all levels with the wide deployment of mobile cameras and sensors. When Russia recently opened war on Ukraine, US, UK and EU slapped severe sanctions on the aggressor besides freezing the assets of its president, foreign minister and wealthy citizens.

In protest to Russia on its invasion of Ukraine, Google officially announced sanction on the aggressor, perhaps for the first time by a private enterprise which could dent the Russian economy much more than by a country like Poland, Austria or Argentina. When the war destroyed the internet services in Ukraine, Starlinx offered satellite internet and Apple suspended its products from Russia. In future, rogue nations are to be cautious about not only any sanctions from UN and other world powers, but also how technology companies are capable to pose such severe impacts than many of the developing nations, where twentieth century corporations acted neutral and were not bothered. No doubt if there was an internal resurgence among public in Russia against the war, the barbaric invasion of Russia was widely exposed by the Internet and social media throughout the world so that the global solidarity for Ukraine and its president rose up despite a steep fall for the aggressor. In any conflict, so far diplomacy was recognized as the most powerful weapon, which now Internet shares an equally powerful tool. If at all China, a country known for invading border lands, stay away from invading Taiwan, it is mainly for their fear for being exposed by Internet. Future looks to be more peaceful, with exception for few rogue dictators already in their sunset curve. New technology entrepreneurs respect and recognize human lives, their rights, equality and welfare and confront against all forces of suppression, brutality and destruction.

Dynamics of Relationship, Collaboration and Trust

People were comfortable in building relationship and networking within a country or region like Chicago to NY or London-Frankfurt to

Zurich, but today the relationship had expanded so universal ie from Tel Aviv to Abu Dhabi, Karachi to Mumbai or Guangzhu to Seoul or Taipei breaking political and religious barriers. This will further foster to a free democracy in next two decades. If a relationship network on Facebook or a messaging connectivity on What's-App of thousands of people between a hostile Armenia and Azerbaijan, or South and North Korea, its further expansion could make the hostility irrelevant and foster closer friendship and cultural relationship. Google Search allows people living in a country of suppressive government to experience the freedom and human rights enjoyed by those people under democracy. Remote working breaks all bureaucratic barriers like visa restriction, diplomatic boycott with working from anywhere, where money transfer regulations can be eased with virtual and block-chain channels. So the next four to five decades will witness a rapid mass movement in every country under a system of monarchy, military or ideology, towards democratic welfare states. With so many people connected across so many continents, the future will contain the most outspoken, active and globalised civil society, breaking barriers of religion, ideology, country, race and colour, also empowering human rights and equality which are the pillars of democracy.

Vision is how far we can look into the reality of distant future, where the nature shaped our vision horizons to about six months forward. Once we know our limits, we tend to break it and go beyond that limit. We are living in the most peaceful time of human history, also the healthiest with a reverse inflation than never before. When we read this script, there are so many small teams of inventors who is in their relentless and passionate challenges to create a new world, which will destroy so many established businesses, transform the lives of billions which only governments and large companies could do in the past, prove that most our past assumptions were wrong which can replace every other model of government with democracy and collaboration.

As pessimists see a problem in every opportunity, the optimists see an opportunity in every problem. India has so much of problems and responsibilities that anywhere else in the world, and future India will rise again to the top of the world, not alone with technology but with more of optimism and relentless attempts. As one of the world's largest skilled talent pool, the future can be shaped better with a rising optimism among our youth with an increased emotional maturity, resilience and collaborative skills at their twenties.

Non-aggressive and not a first-time user of weapons, India never invaded any country in the last 10,000 years. When we were stronger, we were deeply compassionate to others, when we were weak, we were never a burden for others. A country with a record of fighting for peace in every global platform, most responsible country at UN Peace Keeping Force which collaborates both the inspirational essence of democracy and modern technology. If these technologies drive democratic values, the world's largest democracy with still the biggest pool of technology talents have the true potential to change the future of the humanity.

14 Inspiration and Appreciation

When John F Kennedy wanted to send a man to land in the moon, he did not know how to do it. Recently when Narendra Modi envisioned that India's GDP will be driven by Start-up Innovation in next two decades, possibly anyone would have doubted if he ever knew how to do it. So with MoS-EIT said that India will conquer the world in next two decades. These aspirations ignited my senses to authenticate with a book on start-up entrepreneurship, which I also did not know how to write.

Taking lesson from how US achieved its moon-landing mission, considering every possibility of PM's aspiration of India achieving the GDP growth from Start-ups and MoS-EIT ambition of conquering the world to become a reality, why I should not proceed with my responsibility of beginning with this tool? We are living in a crazy age of people doing what they do not now and blindness of people who can see.

Today technology dictates how we should live and every other aspect of our work, leisure, travel, shopping, mobility, eating, entertainment, healthcare, etc. It has become so essential like air, water, shelter, food and clothes and we cannot imagine a future life without. Past does not make any more interesting to us because it is the future where we are going to live.

For the last seven years, I used to submit relevant ideas to MoE and NCERT in view of reforming education with values and character, also to AICTE, DRDO and CDS to induct a Brain Unit to our military. My first two submissions were printed book format **"Living The Values"**- a Value-narrative to Grass-root Leadership and **"The State of Israel"**- a start-up nation to a scale-up nation, which were recognized by NCERT and CDS. This helped me to win attention from institutions in exceptional cases when I required support.

What makes this book so different is that it is scripted by someone who had not seen any engineering college, did not learn science or maths beyond his tenth class. If this makes a positive impact among its target readership in our technology campuses, we can do and win anything we dream and everything what we do not know, but as long as a deep passion and the nerve. Learn as if we live forever; live as if you will die tomorrow.

Now when I finished this book **"INNOVISION"** AICTE helped me to reach out to a publisher so well-connected with technical institutions and technology subjects, without which this project would have turned to ashes with me.

-Chelat Bhuvanachandran

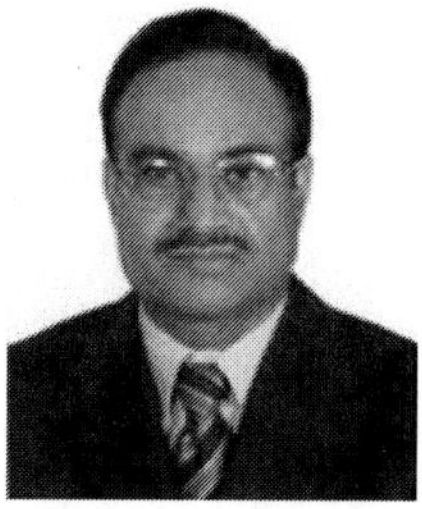

The day our PM announced his vision that 'Start-up and Innovation will drive India's GDP in the next two decades', I was becoming restless as if it imposed an unassigned responsibility on me of how to make it happen? While walking, eating and breathing, the subject pushed me beyond extensive imaginations in the distant skies. This book evolves around a theme of 'Start-up Entrepreneurship'.

First it looks impossible, next difficult, but most important is to start around the theme. Imagination if combined with passion and a nerve can stretch one beyond his limits, was a lesson from my life and work. We are so familiar with what the perspective of an expert on a subject, but we hardly have any similar thought of someone who has no credentials of an expert. This book originates from this second thought stream.

To know deep into some successful innovators and founders, I practically lived into a Henry Ford and Steve Jobs, to sensitively diagnose them though my imagination. It was a tremendous, real-life experience of living with their behaviour and brains. Once we required a ten or more years of research about companies and history before authenticating a book, which today makes easy and simple with internet and search that disrupts once the exclusive rights of traditional scholars and researchers.

Next is to editing and setting all these details to an India-context format- combining all these ideas, technology and imagination to result new opportunities in solution of those problems in the region. Once this problem to opportunity cycle is brought to progress, it accelerates the region's GDP, by raising the lives of millions.

Never in the past, a rise in GDP had such a direct and immediate impact on the poor, but today with the acceleration of technologies it will be more sustainable in the future. If countries made walls of separation, new entrepreneurs build bridges of relationship and trust. As a result, our world will become less violent and corrupted; with our problems solved with opportunities making our planet more happy and liveable.

Chelat Bhuvanachandran *chelatbchandran@hotmail.com*

Retired as Genl Manager& Signatory-ME

Ein Unternehmen der
AFG
Arbonia-Forster-Holding AG

Amriswilerstrasse 50, 9320 Arbon, Switzerland